NORTHFIELD BRANCH
847-446-5990

YOU'LL DO

YOU'LL DO

A History of
Marrying for Reasons
Other Than Love

MARCIA A. ZUG

STEERFORTH PRESS
LEBANON, NEW HAMPSHIRE

Image Credits:

Page 24: University of Michigan. The Weld-Grimke Manuscript Collection.

Page 68: Venereal Disease Visual History Archive. Courtesy of Erin Wuebker.

Page 71: The National Portrait Gallery, London, England. Licensed under CC By- NC 4.0.

Page 117 (top): The New York Public Library.

Page 137: Smithsonian American Art Museum, The Ray Austrian Collection, gift of Beatrice L. Austrian, Caryl A. Austrian, and James A. Austrian.

For information about permission to reproduce selections from this book, write to:
Steerforth Press L.L.C., 31 Hanover Street, Suite 1
Lebanon, New Hampshire 03766

Cataloging-in-Publication Data is available from the Library of Congress

ISBN 978-1-58642-374-2

Printed in the United States of America

Contents

To my parents, Joan and Chuck,
who married for love;

To my daughters, Willa and Lucy,
who I hope will marry for love;

And to my husband, Geordie,
who is sure to get grief for this book.

Introduction

First comes love. Then comes marriage.
Then comes the baby in the baby carriage.

— AMERICAN SCHOOLYARD RHYME

If you ask Americans why they married, almost everyone will say "love." Love is the only publicly acceptable reason to marry, but it is far from the only one. Despite romantic notions about love and marriage, marriage is fundamentally a legal institution. It is a way to confer valuable rights and benefits, and sometimes it is the only way to receive these rewards. A vast misconception about modern marriage is, as the nursery rhyme states, that love comes first. This isn't always true. Sometimes love comes later. Sometimes it doesn't come at all, and legally, love is irrelevant.

You'll Do was inspired by the marriage of my great-aunt Rosie, a brave woman who didn't marry for love. In the late 1930s, Rosie was working in a garment factory on Manhattan's Lower East Side. Like most of the workers, Rosie was Jewish. Her best friend in the factory was also Jewish, and both understood the dangers posed by the rise of fascism in Europe. Rosie and her friend were safe, but her friend's brother, Sol, was not. Sol lived in Poland and, as the Nazis rose to power, Sol's family began to fear for his life. They desperately sought to bring him to America, but the US's draconian immigration restrictions severely limited the immigration of "undesirable" groups, such as Jews. Sol was stuck. America would never grant his immigration application, with one exception — marriage. The only way to get Sol out of

Poland, and save his life, was to marry him. So that's what Rosie did. In late 1937, as Nazi Germany was preparing for war, Rosie left the safety of America to marry a man she had never met and save his life. Sol entered the United States in September 1938. He moved in with Rosie; they had a daughter and fell in love. Rosie and Sol's story has a happy ending, yet it's a tale that haunts me. If Rosie hadn't married Sol, he almost certainly would have died in a Nazi concentration camp. Marriage saved his life, but only because a racist US immigration law denied him entry in the first place. *You'll Do* is full of similar stories. Stories that show how generations of American men and women have used marriage as a loophole to circumvent unfair or discriminatory laws. Unfortunately, not all these marriage stories are as admirable as Rosie's. *You'll Do* reveals how the rights and benefits that attach to marriage can also perpetuate harms. My family has a second, darker marriage story that falls into this category.

Many years ago, one of my relatives lived with his wife and daughter. The daughter was mentally disabled (it may have been a birth injury), and after her birth, the couple was unable to have more children. This caused them great sorrow, and when their daughter was grown, they paid a man to marry her and provide them with a grandchild. The marriage took place nearly a century ago, and the daughter's capacity to consent does not appear to have been an issue. The two were legally married, and shortly thereafter, the daughter fell pregnant. Then, having fulfilled the terms of the bargain, the husband disappeared. Nine months later, the daughter gave birth to a healthy baby.

This second story is about marrying for money, but it is also about marrying for parenthood and for criminal and legal protections. Marriage provided the husband with money while also protecting him from criminal prosecution for rape; there really isn't any other way to describe it. In addition, marriage gave the grandparents their longed-for second child and protected the child from the legal "taint" of bastardy.

The specifics of my family's stories are unique. However, their instrumental use of marriage is not. I have a neighbor who married to lower his university tuition, two friends who married for tax breaks, and a colleague who married for a green card. These four are just the ones who have told me about their non-love reasons for marrying. Presumably, I know many others. Chances are, you do as well. Perhaps a non-love reason even motivated your own marriage.

Historically, marrying for love was considered a gamble. A popular story from a 1791 issue of the *Virginia Gazette and Alexandria Advertiser* illustrates this pessimistic view. The story describes a beleaguered clergyman who was enduring a "curtain-lecture" (meaning a scolding) from his wife when they were interrupted by a young couple requesting a marriage ceremony. According to the article, "The poor Priest, actuated at that moment to his own feelings and particular experience," mistakenly began "repeating the burial Service." The "astonished Bridegroom" then pointed out the error, to which the clergyman replied, "I am obliged to marry you — but, believe me, my friend, you had better be buried."[1] Between 1791 and 1823, this "anecdote" was printed more than sixty times.

Marrying for love was risky, and for centuries, many Americans believed marrying for the legal, social, and economic benefits attached to marriage was a safer bet. Blatantly transactional marriages were permissible and even admired.[2] In 1821, the *Louisiana Gazette* printed a story of a young man who hedged his marital bets by auctioning himself off in a lottery. Described as "of a good figure and disposition," the man offered six hundred tickets for $50 each to single women interested in marriage. The winner was then "entitled to himself and the 30,000 dollars." The paper described the scheme as "ingenious" and expressed confidence that "matches formed this way" would "prov[e] as happy as those made in the usual manner."[3]

Eventually, acceptance of transactional marriage had largely disappeared. By the late nineteenth century, the non-love match was viewed as threatening. The 1888 Supreme Court case *Maynard v. Hill* exemplified this change. In *Maynard*, the court described marriage as "an institution, in the maintenance of which in its purity the public is deeply interested, for it is the foundation of the family and of society, without which there could be neither civilization nor progress." Today, a century and a half later, such sentiments remain widespread. However, whether the *Maynard* court's fears were justified is a more complicated question.

Economists have long claimed that everything is already commodified, that such commodification is good, and that attempts to prevent the sale of certain goods and services are bad. Conversely, anti-commodificationists argue that viewing everything in market terms is detrimental and that such treatment coarsens and corrupts our world.[4] Both views are likely correct. Feminist scholar Margaret Radin has dubbed this the double-bind problem and suggests that the best way to counteract it is to identify the underlying causes.[5]

You'll Do examines the marriage double bind. It shows how the instrumental use of marriage can be beneficial, helping to combat racial, gender, and class discrimination, and how this calculated use of marriage can also further such oppression. Additionally, the book challenges the assumption that non-love marriages are problematic because love is the purpose of marriage. Since America's founding, marriage has primarily been a rights distribution mechanism. This remains the principal purpose of marriage, but that doesn't mean it should be. Marriage is an imprecise and unfair method for determining the allocation of rights and benefits. Decoupling these rewards from marriage would alleviate this unfairness. It would also, truly, make love the purpose of marriage. It might also make marriage obsolete.

You'll Do is divided into six chapters. Chapter 1 focuses on the best-known marital bargain — marrying for money. It traces the long history of "gold-digging" marriages and shows that marrying for money, especially by women, was expected and encouraged. Chapter 2 examines marrying for government benefits and highlights the government's extensive role in encouraging instrumental marriages. Chapter 3 explores the connection between marriage and status. It shows that married Americans have historically occupied a higher and more powerful status than the unmarried and that this connection continues to motivate modern marital decisions. Chapter 4 details the long-standing, but less well-known, criminal benefits that attach to marriage. Chapter 5 discusses the connection between marriage and parental rights, and chapter 6 returns to the issue of marrying for money, but with a focus on the present day.

You'll Do covers the most common non-love reasons people marry, with one significant exception — religion. In many religions, marriage is both a sacrament and a commandment. This can be a powerful non-love motivation for marriage. However, I have excluded religious marriage from *You'll Do* because the book's focus is on the connection between law and marital decision making. Religious marriages, if they comply with state marriage laws, receive the same legal benefits as all other marriages, but they are not motivated by these benefits. Spouses in religious unions would marry regardless of governmental recognition. Mormon polygamous marriages are one well-known example.

You'll Do is about the non-love reasons people marry, but even in these unions, love may be present. Marriage is complex, and people can marry for a combination of reasons. A person might decide to marry for immigration benefits, but only after also falling in love with their potential spouse; conversely, they might have loved their partner for many years, but only married when they decided to have a child. The purpose of this book is not to deny this complexity. Rather, *You'll Do* seeks to explore the consequences of a marital regime that insists love is the only acceptable reason to marry while enacting laws and policies that give Americans so many non-love reasons to wed.

chapter one

The Marital Bargain

We state and affirm unambiguously, love
cannot extend its sway over a married couple.

— QUEEN MARIE DE CHAMPAGNE[1]

In 1812, Charlotte Lucas was no longer young. She was also plain and relatively poor. She had no job prospects and was a financial burden to her family. So, when a dull and dislikable but relatively well-off suitor proposed, she said yes. It was not a love match. Charlotte candidly described him as "neither sensible nor agreeable." Still, he had a good job and a steady income, and Charlotte considered it a fair trade. She would provide wifely services, homemaking and child-rearing, in exchange for financial security. Charlotte was content with her decision, but her friend Lizzie was appalled. Lizzie believed Charlotte was degrading herself; she couldn't imagine marrying for any reason other than love.

Charlotte and Lizzie are characters from Jane Austen's famous novel *Pride and Prejudice*. The novel idealizes romantic love yet also depicts the realities of its era. When Austen wrote *Pride and Prejudice*, marrying for love was desirable but not expected. The novel's opening line is explicitly about marrying for money: "It is a truth universally acknowledged that a gentleman in possession of a large fortune must be in search of a wife." While this sentence was intended to be humorous, it was also true. Nineteenth-century women were looking for

Jane Austen.

wealthy husbands. As historian Amanda Vickery writes, in Georgian England "the length of a man's rent-roll remained the ultimate aphrodisiac." Austen recognized this reality, even as she lamented it. In a famous letter to her niece regarding marriage, Austen wrote that there is "nothing worse than marrying without affection." She also noted, "Single women have a dreadful propensity for being poor."

In early America, marriage was women's primary and preferred financial option. In an exchange known as the marital bargain, women traded domestic services for economic support. This practice of marrying for money was accepted both because women lacked other financial options and because such marriages posed no threat to male wealth. Under the law of coverture, a seventeenth-century English doctrine governing marriage and adopted by the American colonies, a husband and wife were treated as a single person — the husband.[2] Once married, wives had no legal claim to their husbands' money. They could not, practically speaking, marry for money. The most a woman could hope for when marrying a rich man was that he'd be willing to share. In contrast, men could absolutely marry for money. Upon marriage, husbands received immediate and total control over their wives' wealth. Consequently, despite their ability to pursue other economic opportunities, colonial men had a strong incentive to marry wealthy women.

Male Gold Diggers

Early American men's interest in marrying for money is apparent in various anti-gold-digging laws passed to thwart male fortune hunters. Age-of-consent restrictions were one of the clearest examples. These laws were intended to prevent mercenary males from targeting younger women based on the, likely correct, belief that teenage girls were particularly vulnerable to the charms of fortune hunters. In 1632, the Virginia Colony enacted the first age-of-consent law and prohibited children under the age of twenty-one from marrying without parental consent. The original law was gender-neutral, but when the law was amended in 1670, the legislature explained that its specific purpose was to prevent a child from being "ruynated in *her* fortunes."[3] In 1696, the law was further revised to include monetary fines and jail time. It also included a provision decreeing that "any girl between the ages of twelve and sixteen who married without parental or guardian permission forfeited her inheritance to her next of kin." Similar provisions were adopted in North and South Carolina.[4]

Colonial incest laws, and specifically the permissibility of
cousin marriages, were also prompted by a desire to deter male
fortune hunters.[5] American women had the right to inherit but
relinquished control over their inheritance upon marriage. As
a result, a woman's inheritance could be lost to a gold-digging
husband. Cousin marriage addressed this problem by increasing women's intrafamily marriage prospects and ensuring that
family wealth remained in the family.[6] Anti-gold-digging
measures like age-of-consent and incest laws sought to deter
fortune hunters, but their effectiveness was limited by the failure of state legislatures to acknowledge that the biggest incentive for male fortune hunting was married women's inability to
own or control property.[7] Eventually, married women's property
acts were proposed to address these gold-digging incentives and
provide a more effective solution.

In 1839, Mississippi passed the first married women's property
act. According to the act's supporters, the purpose of the law
was to protect women from mercenary or profligate husbands.
As a Vicksburg, Mississippi, newspaper editorial explained, "The
property of ladies should be guarded against the squandering
habits of a drunken and gambling husband. The ladies are virtuous and prudent creatures — they never gamble, they never
drink, and there is no good reason why the strong arm of legislation should not be extended to the protection of the property
they bring into the marriage bargain."[8] Similar sentiments were
put forth by Mississippi state senator T. B. J. Hadley, the sponsor
of the Mississippi married women's property act. Hadley wrote:

> [S]hall we, in this proud Republic, refuse to secure
> to [women] the certain possession of property to
> which they have as just a claim? Is there a wish of
> such gross injustice in the mind of any man that
> he would behold from woman the shield of protec-

tion which this bill proposes? Does man delight in woman's happiness? Then give them the plighted faith of our legislation, that they shall possess and enjoy the means of their own pleasure. I would sir, secure to them the product of their own labor — I would secure to them the possession of the property given them by fond parents or relatives. Secure this, sir — tis all I ask.[9]

After the Mississippi act passed,[10] other states began considering similar acts. They sought to give wives control over their money and protect them from mercenary or financially improvident husbands.[11] In 1843, the *Tennessee Observer* argued in favor of a Tennessee married women's property act, noting, "The last few years have shown so much devastation of married women's property by the misfortunes of their husbands, that some new modification of the law seems the dictate of justice as well as prudence."[12] That same year, the *Georgia Journal* expressed support for a Georgia act, writing that there was no good reason "why property bequeathed to a daughter should go to pay debts of which she knew nothing, had no agency in creating, and the payment of which, with her means, would reduce her and her children to beggary. This has been done in hundreds of instances, and should no longer be tolerated by the laws of the land."[13]

One of the clearest discussions of these acts as an anti-gold-digging measure occurred during the 1868 South Carolina Constitutional Convention when the delegates were considering whether to include married women's property rights as part of the state's proposed constitution. South Carolina lawmaker J. H. Allen argued in favor of the provision, stating:

I appeal to you who have lived here all your lives, and seen women suffering from the hands of fortune hunters; the plausible villains who, after securing the property of their wives, have squandered it in gambling and drinking, a class of men who are still going about the country boasting that they intend to marry a plantation, and take the woman as an incumbrance.

Fellow lawmaker Benjamin Randolph, made similar arguments in support of the provision. He noted, "It is a common thing for men to talk about marrying rich wives, and to marry them for no other purpose than to squander their property."[14] These pleas were successful, and the South Carolina Constitution was enacted with a provision guaranteeing married women the right to own and convey property separate from their husbands' property.[15]

Married women's property acts drastically reduced the incentives for male gold digging.[16] Men could still marry wealthy women, and potentially share their fortune, but marriage no longer guaranteed husbands a legal right to their wives' wealth.[17] In fact, once women controlled their money, it could be extremely difficult for husbands to convince them to part with it. The famous gold-digging marriage of Harriet Douglas and Henry Cruger provided one such cautionary tale.

In the early nineteenth century, Harriet Douglas was a wealthy New York heiress known for her red hair, her fiery temper, and her love of European high society. Author Sir Water Scott nicknamed Douglas the "lion-huntress of the social jungle" because of her obsession with Europe's rich and famous.[18] For years Douglas traveled around the world, enjoying her freedom and swearing she would never marry. Then, in 1833, at the age of forty-three, she changed her mind and accepted the proposal of her most dogged suitor, Henry Cruger, a handsome southern lawyer ten years her junior.[19]

A nineteenth-century political cartoon on conditions under coverture.

Cruger had worked hard for this marriage. For more than a decade, he had followed Douglas across the globe, plying her with love letters and making repeated and ardent declarations of devotion. When she finally accepted his proposal, Cruger believed his hard work had finally paid off; he would soon be a rich man. Then, Douglas presented her conditions. She would not relinquish her name (in fact she insisted he take her name), she would choose where they lived (upstate New York, which Cruger hated), and, most important, she would not cede control of her fortune.[20] To ensure this last condition, Douglas instructed her lawyers to draft legal documents circumventing the traditional rules of coverture and ensuring she retained control of her money after marriage. Initially, Cruger refused to sign the papers, but he relented when he recognized Douglas was adamant. Cruger wanted Douglas's money, but he was confident he'd be able to change her mind after marriage. He was correct, but the battle was long and painful.

At first, Cruger played the doting husband. He naively believed that by agreeing to Douglas's requests and signing the property documents, Douglas would be so grateful that she would immediately relinquish her fortune. She did not. When that plan failed, Cruger's next strategy was to sow discord between Douglas and her brothers. He hoped this would increase her loyalty to him, but she chose her brothers. Then, after these first attempts were unsuccessful, Cruger tried pouting and complaining about his financial dependency. During one such tantrum, Cruger refused to drink wine, saying he did "not own it," and refused to go riding because he did "not own any carriage."[21] When Douglas was unaffected by these antics, Cruger moved out, swearing he would not return until Douglas turned over her fortune; he caved when she refused.

Cruger's next idea was to use Douglas's friends against her, and this tactic was partially successful. After significant pressure from her friends, Douglas agreed to give Cruger a substantial yearly allowance, yet Cruger still wasn't satisfied. He continued to harass Douglas for her money and eventually, when she couldn't stand it anymore, she left him. Cruger was elated. This was the development he had been waiting for. He immediately embraced the role of the wronged husband and began writing letters to Douglas's family and church expressing his hurt and outrage at her disobedience and refusal to live with him. Eventually, the enormous disapproval of her friends, family, and church led Douglas to relinquish more than half her income to Cruger. After eight long years, Cruger had won — sort of. Shortly after agreeing to Cruger's demands, Douglas changed her mind. Another eight years passed before a court ruled her promise to share her fortune was enforceable.

HENDERSON HOUSE   JORDANVILLE, N.Y.

The mansion in upstate New York where Harriet Douglas and Henry Cruger lived, and which Cruger hated.

After Cruger's legal victory, the editor of the *New York Legal Observer* congratulated him for having "passed through this fiery ordeal unscathed, vindicated and triumphant."[22] However, whether Cruger had emerged unharmed is debatable. It had taken him sixteen years to get Douglas's money (not including the decade he spent courting her), and along the way, his reputation had been ruined. Years later, composer George Templeton Strong unflatteringly described Cruger as a man who "lived for . . . twenty years on [money] extorted by process of law from a wife he hated and whom he had married for her money."

Cruger's good friend, author James Fenimore Cooper — the two had met during a European tour and became lifelong friends — was so disturbed by the difficulties Cruger endured that he wrote an entire novel depicting the horrors of the Douglas-Cruger marriage.[23] The novel, *The Ways of the Hour*, was published two years after New York enacted its married women's property act and was intended as a warning about the "dangers" of female financial control. Cruger's difficulties were then further compounded by the fact that Douglas spent the rest of her life trashing Cruger's reputation. She is reported to have seated her frequent visitors on sofas made from the hacked-apart halves of her former marital bed while serenading them with the song "For love of gold he has left me."[24]

Female Gold Diggers

By giving wives control over their fortunes, married women's property acts largely eliminated the legal incentives for male gold digging (few men wanted to be the next Henry Cruger), but these laws had little effect on whether women married for money. The average American woman didn't have a large inheritance or her own income; thus, marriage remained her primary means of securing financial support. In 1854, a satirical English pamphlet titled "Legal Condition of Unmarried Women or Spinster" highlighted women's lack of financial opportunities, noting that "Queen" was pretty much the only desirable job available to women. American women didn't even have that option.[25]

In the nineteenth century, most female employment was low-paid misery, even for women in the middle class. For these women, governess was one of the only jobs available, and contemporary descriptions portray it as hellish. Author Mary Wollstonecraft likened becoming a governess to "going into the Bastille," and Jane Austen's description is even grimmer. Austen wrote that to become a governess means to "retire from all the pleasures of life, of rational intercourse, equal society, peace and hope, to penance and mortification forever." It is little wonder that women routinely married to avoid this fate. Charlotte Brontë's novel *Shirley* includes such a marriage. In *Shirley*, Mrs.

The Governess, Emily Mary Osborn, 1828–1925.

Pryor, a woman who abandoned her daughter as a small child, admits she "ought never to have married," but explains she did so because she "had been so miserable as a governess."[26]

Nineteenth-century women lacked viable economic alternatives to marriage. Consequently, many agreed to exchange domestic services for financial support. This marital bargain was not a "sale," but there were uncomfortable similarities. Until the mid-nineteenth century, England even permitted couples to end their relationships through a type of informal divorce known as wife selling. This practice allowed a married couple to publicly sever financial ties to each other and begin a new relationship, but it also treated the wife, at least symbolically, as a commodity. To effect the "sale," a husband would place a halter around his wife's neck and bring her to the cattle market on market day.

A "wife sale."

He would then offer her to the "highest bidder" — the man she would have married had legal divorce been possible.[27]

"Wife sales" were performances, yet the marital bargain unquestionably encouraged men, and the courts, to view wives in economic terms. Such treatment is apparent in judicial decisions like the 1886 Pennsylvania case *Gring v. Lerch*. In 1882, Charles Gring proposed to Clara Lerch and she accepted, but shortly thereafter, she informed Gring that she had an unusually "thickened hymen" and would need surgery before she could engage in intercourse.[28] Lerch promised to schedule the surgery, but three months later, she still hadn't remedied her "physical defect." Gring broke off the engagement, and Lerch sued him for breach of promise to marry. Gring's defense was that Lerch's failure to remedy her "physical defect" meant she was unable to fulfill the "sexual duties of a wife"; therefore, he was "legally justified in ending the engagement."

In ruling for Gring, the court characterized marriage as an economic exchange in which a husband trades financial support for sexual intimacy. Lerch could not provide sex, hence Gring shouldn't have to "buy" her. In explaining its decision, the court likened Lerch to a defective cow and Gring to the man about to buy that cow. According to the court, "A man does not contract to marry a woman for the mere pleasure of paying for her board and washing. He expects and is entitled to something in return, and if the woman with whome he contracts be incapable by reason of a natural impediment of giving him the comfort and satisfaction to which as a married man he would be entitled, then there is a failure of the moving consideration of such contract . . ."[29]

Gring showed how the marital bargain could come disturbingly close to treating wives as property. Still, in general, the language of economic exchange was beneficial to women. Discussing marriage in market terms acknowledged the reality of women's economic position and allowed courts to address women's relationship harms as monetary harms. Breach of promise cases, common-law marriage claims, and alimony suits were all based on this economic conception of marriage.

In breach of promise cases, courts held that engagements, like sale contracts, could not be broken without an economic penalty and applied the economic principles of caveat emptor (buyer beware / purchase at your own risk) to engagements. This economic conception of marriage meant most jilted fiancées were entitled to significant monetary compensation. It also meant these damages would increase when the failed engagement was to a wealthier man, as the courts recognized, in such cases, the financial loss was greater.[30]

Women's common-law marriage claims similarly benefited from the law's economic view of marriage. Common-law marriages are marriages created through mutual consent, without a religious or legal ceremony. This informality can make their existence difficult to prove, but nineteenth-century courts solved this evidentiary problem by looking to the marital bargain. They held that when women provided wifely services — childcare, housework, companionship, and so on

— they were "wives" and entitled to the financial benefits of marriage.[31]

Alimony was the most obvious benefit of the economic conception of marriage. This was money paid to a wife (only wives could receive alimony) upon divorce or separation. It was based on the marital bargain's support obligation but applied to separated wives. Although these women were no longer providing their husbands with domestic services, courts held that the support obligation continued.[32] By marrying, a woman gained the right to financial support for life.

The allure of lifetime support is apparent in many nineteenth-century matrimonial advertisements. Francesca Beauman, a historian of such ads, describes them as "blatant in this regard." According to Beauman, female advertisers would indicate their desire for a moneyed partner with terms like "in easy pecuniary circumstances," "industrious," "good trade and permanent income," "cultivated gentleman," and "good home." Some of these advertisers were simply gold diggers, but many matrimonial ads reveal the writer's economic desperation. In one heartbreaking ad, "an American lady, 20 years of age" sought a husband because she was "anxious for a home of her own so she can give her little girl a good education." Notably, men were receptive to such requests. In fact, many male-authored matrimonial ads specifically emphasized the advertiser's willingness to provide economic support in exchange for marriage. In one typical ad, a thirty-two-year-old backwoodsman with a prosperous farm sought "a good girl, not over 25 years of age." In return for marriage with such a lady, the man offered to "pay all expenses, receive her thankfully, and use her well . . ."[33]

For nineteenth-century women, marrying for money was a reasonable economic decision, but this did not make it an even exchange. The potential unfairness of the marital bargain is poignantly illustrated in the following 1876 letter written to the editor of a suffragette magazine explaining why the author could not attend the US centennial. She writes:

> Married in pioneer times a poor man, and by our joint efforts have made us a home worth several thousand dollars; have borne nine children, and took the whole care of them. Five are men grown, four of them voters. The first twenty years I did all my housework sewing, washing and mending, except a few weeks at the advent of the babies. For the last sixteen years have had help part time but have had from two to four grandchildren to care for the last three years, one of them a baby. And now I want to go to the Centennial and cannot command a sixpence for all my labor. Husband owns and controls everything and says we have nothing to spend for such foolishness. Have no more power than a child. Now if my labor has been of any value in dollars and cents, I want those dollars and cents to do as I please with. I feel like advising every woman not to do another day's labor unless she can be the owner of the value of it. All the property I possess in my own right is this pen and holder, a present from my brother in California.
>
> Signed,
> PEN HOLDER[34]

Pen Holder's predicament was not unique. Whether wives benefited from the marital bargain depended primarily on the kindness and generosity of their husbands. Pen Holder's letter exemplifies the degrading nature of this economic dependence, and it was against this backdrop that a new solution to women's financial dependence was proposed — love.

Marrying for Love

Love became an important aspect of Western marriage during the sixteenth-century Protestant Reformation, but it did not become a *reason* to marry until much later. Even Martin Luther, whose loving marriage was held out as the ideal to be emulated, believed that "marrying for love was unsound." Instead, the marital decision was expected to be based on more practical considerations — like money. Then, in the mid-nineteenth century, these views began to change. Increasingly, women were advised to reject the economic conception of marriage and marry for love. Love, they were told, would help them to avoid the inequality of the marital bargain.

One early example of such advice appears in the popular anonymously authored novel *Belinda; or An Advertisement for a Husband*. The novel, published in Massachusetts in 1799, begins with the heroine, Belinda Blacket, pursuing the marital bargain. In a letter to her friend Louisa Lenox, Belinda writes that she is impatient to find a husband and has decided to place a matrimonial ad in the newspaper. She will offer her beauty and domestic skills in exchange for financial support. "Beauty," writes Belinda, "like any other mercantile commodity, is become an article of traffic in our daily prints; advertisements indiscriminately announce the bargain and sale of a lady's person, or a bale of silk; and direct the readers, whither they are to repair to treat for the affection of a lady with as little reserve as if she had been a hogshead of sugar, or any other common article of commerce." Belinda makes this statement approvingly, but Louisa is horrified. As the novel progresses, Belinda also adopts this view and eventually acknowledges that "the project I was engaged in was a ridiculous one." The novel ends with Belinda falling in love with a poor chaplain named Mr. Proby, who, in an Austen-like twist, becomes wealthy when he wins a long-contested inheritance battle shortly before their wedding.

In *Belinda*, the criticism of marrying for money is clear, yet gentle. By the mid-nineteenth century, the anxiety surrounding the marital bargain had increased significantly. In 1842, a British article widely circulated in the United States expressed dismay that couples were treating marriage as a "mercantile transaction" and lamented that "before long, the state of the hymenal market will be chronicled in newspapers, in common with the other commercial affairs of the day."[35] In 1860, an article in *Vanity Fair* magazine expressed even greater dismay:

> Good people, buy your wives and husbands at the livery establishments as you would horses, dogs, etc. No more courting, flirting, bother, disappointment and wounded feelings. Step up to the office, examine the stock, take your pick, pay your money and drive to the parson. Hurrah for progress![36]

Novels from this period also reflect a growing animosity toward the marital bargain. Anthony Trollope's popular Phineas novels, published in the 1860s, in particular sought to terrify women into rejecting the marital bargain. In these novels, the heroine, Lady Laura, spurns love in order to marry a powerful and influential man. She is then subjected to horrific abuse and, finally, exile. The novel ends with an image of Laura as "worn out, withered, an old woman before her time." The warning to those who married for money was clear. Nevertheless, it wasn't fear that convinced most women to embrace the changing conception of marriage, it was hope.

A husband's love offered the possibility of equality in an inherently unequal relationship. As historian Elizabeth Abbott explains, "Romantic love was seen as the lifeline to a decent life,

Theodore Weld and Angelina Grimke.

a guarantee that in a patriarchal society, an otherwise vulnerable wife would be respectfully treated by her loving husband."[37] The wedding of famed women's rights advocate and abolitionist Angelina Grimke to Theodore Weld exemplified this possibility. During their wedding vows, Weld acknowledged the unequal and unfair power the laws of the United States gave a husband over the person and property of his wife. He then promised he would never exercise this legal authority and instead swore the only influence he had over Grimke would come from love.[38]

Women were increasingly expected to marry for love, but this created a problem for the millions of women who still depended on marriage for economic security. These women could not make love their primary criteria in choosing a husband. The

"Get thee behind me, (Mrs.) Satan!"

Free Love movement arose in response to this tension. The term *Free Love* referred to an absence of legal ties, not promiscuity. The movement was based on the belief that marriage corrupted love.[39] Free Lovers sought to promote love by eliminating legal marriage and the gender inequality that forced women to marry for reasons other than love. Victoria Woodhull, the first woman to run for president, ran on the Free Love platform. She advocated for commitments based on love rather than economic or legal concerns. In her famous 1871 speech in New York City, Woodhull declared:

> I have an inalienable, constitutional and natural right to love whom I may, to love as long or as short a

period as I can; to change that love every day if I
please, and with that right neither you nor any law
you can frame have any right to interfere. And I have
the further right to demand a free and unrestricted
exercise of that right, and it is your duty not only to
accord it, but as a community, to see I am protected
in it.[40]

Ultimately, the Free Love movement was unsuccessful, but its
argument — that money corrupted love — was influential. Once
love became the accepted purpose of marriage, rights based on
the economic conception of marriage needed to change. As a
result, relationship-based claims, such as breach of promise to
marry, were transformed from economic harms into emotional
harms. They were even relabeled "heart-balm" actions to indicate
they were a remedy for a broken heart rather than a financial
loss.[41] This change allowed such claims to continue, but it also
made them much less effective. Courts that had previously been
comfortable ordering compensation for the economic effects of
a failed relationship now expressed indignation at paying for a
broken heart. Male defendants quickly took advantage of this
change in judicial attitudes.

Breach of promise defendants began to argue that economic
compensation corrupted the purity of marriage. In one such
action, an attorney named George Lawyer won his case by
arguing that "the maintenance of actions for the breach of the
marriage contract so belittles and degrades the relation itself that
the public is coming to look upon it as a matter of business alone
. . . The divine purpose is destroyed. The sacred institution has
acquired a cash equivalent, and all its relations are cheapened
and vulgarized."[42] Once love became the only acceptable basis
for marriage, breach of promise defendants could portray themselves as the true victims and paint their accusers as heartless

James Dobie, *A Breach of Promise* (June 1885).

manipulators who sought to trap them in a loveless marriage. The effectiveness of such tactics is illustrated in cases like the 1874 Illinois decision *Donnerschlog v. Behrens.*

In *Donnerschlog*, Amelia Donnerschlog sued her former fiancé, Augustus Behrens, for breach of promise. Behrens didn't deny the engagement or his decision to end it. Instead, he claimed he was justified because Donnerschlog had wanted her mother to live with them after marriage. According to Behrens, this would have ruined his marital happiness because the mother was a "lordly and unpleasant" woman who "insisted on feeding me too much cabbage, a vegetable, I alway[s] dislike."

Traditionally, an annoying mother-in-law was no defense to a breach of marriage claim. However, as marriage was reoriented around love and personal fulfillment, such ridiculous excuses became valid. Men like Behrens could portray themselves as the real victims, and courts were frequently sympathetic to such arguments. In *Donnerschlog*, Judge Robert Banyon also saw himself as the victim of an overbearing mother-in-law who had destroyed his marital happiness, and he had no difficulty dismissing Donnerschlog's suit. In fact, he congratulated Behrens for jilting her! After Behrens stated he would rather pay a fine than marry Donnerschlog, Banyon delivered the following judgment:

> Allow me to shake hands with you. I envy your firmness. There was a period in the life of this court . . . when it was in circumstances similar to yours. If it had had the moral courage which you possess, it would have saved about twenty-five years of misery and unhappiness. The alternative presented to this court was whether it would marry a young lady and her mother, or whether it would pay $125 in gold. The court was poor at the time. It was earning an unsatisfactory living at the restaurant business. It yielded. It took the young woman and mother-in-law and kept the $125. For a quarter of a century this court has regretted its hasty action. It is glad to meet a man who cherishes happiness more than he does money.[43]

Then, in the coup de grâce, Banyon fined Donnerschlog $10 "for trying to bring a man into slavery to a mother-in-law."

Amelia Donnerschlog should have won her case. Behrens proposed and she accepted. More important, she made major sacrifices to marry him. The couple met in Germany and became engaged. Behrens then emigrated to America, and Donnerschlog waited for him while he established himself in Chicago. When he finally sent for her, she, and her presumably widowed and dependent mother, traveled halfway across the world to join him. However, after arriving in a strange country, far from friends and family, Behrens instructed her to "leave her old mother out in the cold." Understandably, Donnerschlog refused but, instead of recognizing the harm caused by Behrens's behavior, including the significant economic harm, the court sympathized with him and punished her.[44]

Reorienting marriage around love hurt women's breach of promise actions. It also had a similarly detrimental effect on their common-law marriage claims. Once trapping a man into a loveless marriage was viewed as potentially worse than tricking a woman into providing domestic services (including sex) outside of marriage, common-law marriage claims became harder to prove. To win a common-law marriage claim, women increasingly needed to show that love, rather than domestic exchange, was the basis of the relationship. This created a problem. Unlike domestic services, affection could be faked. As a result, courts began treating common-law marriage claimants with suspicion.

In most common-law marriage cases, the courts' suspicions were unjustified. In fact, the women suspected of fraud were often the ones being exploited. *In re Baldwin's Estate* is one such example. The case was brought by a young woman named Lillian Ashley, who claimed to be the common-law wife of California millionaire Elias Baldwin. The court believed Ashley was lying and rejected her claim. However, it is far more likely that Baldwin was the liar.

Ashley met Baldwin in 1896 when she was twenty-three and he was sixty-five. Ashley knew Baldwin was rich, and there is little doubt that was his primary appeal. Still, it was Baldwin who deceived Ashley. According to her legal filings, Baldwin told Ashley he was divorced, was in love with her, and wanted to marry. Then, when she accepted his proposal, he convinced her to "marry" in secret by claiming his divorce was still recent and he wished to avoid the scandal of a quick remarriage. Ashley agreed to this request and, after their secret marriage, lived with him as his "wife." When she discovered he had lied about his divorce she left him, but it was too late; Ashley was pregnant. She then asked Baldwin for support, and he refused.

Elias "Lucky" Baldwin.

There are many reasons to believe Ashley's version of events. For starters, Ashley was willing to risk her reputation and void her subsequent marriage to pursue her common-law marriage claim.[45] After leaving California, Ashley had returned east, remarried, and become a respected member of the Boston community. Her suit threatened that hard-won respectability. Nevertheless, that is not the only reason to believe Ashley's version of events. More revealing is the fact that Baldwin had a reputation for doing exactly the kinds of things Ashley accused him of doing.

Years earlier, before returning east, Ashley had sued Baldwin for seduction, and an article in the *Indianapolis Journal* noted that she was far from the first. According to the newspaper, "Baldwin has so many times been the object of similar suits that, as he says, he no longer worries about a little thing like that." Baldwin's defense to Ashley's seduction suit was that his reputation as a liar was so well known that no woman "would trust him." During the seduction trial, this nonchalant attitude so enraged Ashley's sister that she shot Baldwin in the head. Amazingly, he survived this assassination attempt, earning him the nickname "Lucky Baldwin." This moniker then replaced his previous nickname, "the gay deceiver," a reference to his penchant for lying to the women he was interested in pursuing.[46] Tellingly, Ashley wasn't even the first pregnant girl he'd abandoned. As a young man, Baldwin had impregnated his cousin, and when she sued him for support, he had her committed to an insane asylum.[47] None of these details are included in the court decision dismissing Ashley's common-law marriage claim. Instead, Ashley is portrayed as a liar, and the opinion concludes with the hope that her failed suit would be "the last of a most malodorous brood."[48]

Both *Donnerschlog* and *Baldwin's Estate* show how the rise of the love match could harm women's economic claims. Nevertheless, in the early nineteenth century, most courts still viewed marriage as an economic marital bargain, despite finding it increasingly distasteful. The 1915 Iowa Supreme Court decision *Main v. Main* is typical of such treatment. *Main* concerned a request for alimony brought by Mrs. Main against her husband, John Main. Mrs. Main was a gold digger or, as Mr. Main's counsel called her, an "adventuress." One of Mr. Main's witnesses testified that Mrs. Main had admitted, "If there wasn't some money back of old John Main I wouldn't marry him." This testimony was unflattering, but the court also considered it irrelevant.

The Main marriage was a classic example of the marital bargain. Mrs. Main had married for money, and Mr. Main knew it. When the couple met, Mr. Main was sixty-two years old, twice divorced, and wealthy. He was also unattractive and a womanizer. The same witness who disparaged Mrs. Main also described the sixty-two-year-old Main as looking seventy. Nevertheless, he was an ardent pursuer of women. The court unflatteringly referred to him as a man who "sought the graces of other women with a fervor not altogether Platonic." Notably, his amorous pursuits had already gotten him sued at least once. When he met Mrs. Main, he was in the midst of defending a breach of promise lawsuit from an earlier love interest.[49] Still, this previous romantic mishap did not stop him from eagerly pursuing the forty-two-year-old Mrs. Main.

The court described the Main marriage as a fair exchange: "Both knew from the start exactly what they wanted. She wanted a husband with money — or money with a husband. He wanted a wife to adorn his house." And it said the evidence presented at trial

> may show a lack of affection and lay bare the sordid motive which prompts marriages of the kind we have here to deal with, but it is otherwise irrelevant to the issue. The desire for a home and the comforts of wealth has been the controlling influence of many marriages, especially of those who have passed the bloom of youth, and it is not at all inconsistent with a faithful observance of all the duties and proprieties of the married state.

The court then granted Mrs. Main alimony and concluded its opinion by noting that women had the same right to marry for non-love reasons as men did. "Strategy and management in securing an eligible matrimonial partner is not the exclusive privilege of the man, and the game law of the state provides no closed season against the kind of 'trapping' of which appellant complains."

The *Main* court recognized that the marital bargain benefited both men and women. However, women's rights advocates increasingly rejected this conclusion. They feared that the harms of the marital bargain, with its emphasis on female dependency and domestic roles, outweighed the benefits. Although these advocates recognized that many women were still financially dependent on marriage, they believed this dependency would soon disappear. In the early 1900s, a handful of states had already granted women the vote, the national suffrage movement was gaining momentum, and women's job opportunities were increasing steadily. Consequently, these advocates believed the need for marital support would soon be replaced with economic opportunities and financial equality. Unfortunately, the rapid equality they envisioned did not materialize.

Throughout the 1920s, marriage remained most women's primary form of economic support — but now the small equality gains women had achieved were used against them. The New Jersey annulment action *Woodward v. Heichelbach* highlights the disconnect between women's purported equality and their continuing financial vulnerability. The case began in 1922, when Rhoda Woodward married Emile Heichelbach, believing he was a rich man. Heichelbach had encouraged this belief. During their courtship, he told Woodward he owned two cars, possessed a large bank account, and had a prestigious, well-paying job. He even showed her a bank book with $2,000 in savings. Sadly, it was all a lie. The bank book was borrowed, and the cars, the job, and the money were all fabrications. Heichelbach was broke. Two days after the wedding, Woodward discovered the truth, and she was furious.

Woodward had worked before her marriage, but it was almost certainly low-paid wage work. In the 1920s, few single women earned enough to support a family and even fewer were able to retain employment once married. Consequently, marrying a poor man could literally be ruinous. The *Heichelbach* court ignored this reality. Instead, it described Woodward as a "mature business woman," and implied she didn't need a husband for support. It then snarkily declared that since Woodward "certainly did not marry for love," she should have done a better job of investigating Heichelbach's finances. According to the court, it was not its responsibility to assist those "who make stupid contracts." The court also downplayed the significance of Heichelbach's financial deception. Instead of recognizing the potential life-altering effects of his lies, the court dismissed them as typical of any man intent on "the winning of a bride." The court wrote, "Under such circumstances a man always puts his best foot forward to impress the woman of his choice with his desirability as a mate." Heichelbach's lies were just "painting the lily."

Cases like *Heichelbach* showed that gender equality arguments could be turned against vulnerable women. Nevertheless, many women's rights advocates continued to argue that the best way to achieve gender equality was to reject any privileges or disabilities of their sex.[50] As a result, condemning relationship-based protections, especially heart-balm actions, became an increasingly important part of the women's rights movement. A 1935 editorial in the *Christian Science Monitor* exemplified such reasoning. It stated, "Women now have the legal right to collect their own wages, enter into business contracts, own property in their own name and in general to provide for themselves independently of men. One way they can prove their equality is by not asking for the kind of protection breach-of-promise laws are meant to give." The same year, the National Women's Party also attacked gender-based privileges and claimed heart-balm suits "should be laughed out of court."[51]

In 1935, Professor Harriet Daggett, one of the first female law professors in the US, described breach of promise as something that "at one time may have been a necessary . . . [but] now seems at times almost a travesty."[52] *Chicago Tribune* columnist Antoinette Donnelly echoed these sentiments when she declared breach of promise "simply does not belong in an era in which women work alongside men as competitors,"[53] and

From the *Honolulu Advertiser*, Sunday, April 14, 1935.

feminist author Dorothy Dunbar Bromley described a breach of promise action as putting "a contract to marry on the same footing as a bargain for a horse or a bale of hay."[54] However, it was Indiana state representative Roberta Nicholson, the only female representative in the Indiana legislature, who became the biggest proponent of anti-heart-balm legislation.

Nicholson claimed breach of promise suits must be eliminated because they were "based on a theory that is dead as a dodo, since the equality of the sexes has become an actuality."[55] Despite such statements, it is inconceivable that Nicholson actually believed gender equality had been achieved. As one of the few female politicians of the period, she had firsthand experience with gender discrimination. In fact, years later she described her male colleagues' reactions to her proposed bill as "wasn't it cute of her. She's got a bill. She's going to introduce it just like a man. Isn't that darling?"[56] Still, despite such experiences, Nicholson appears to have fully embraced the women's rights argument that gender-based rights were more harmful than helpful. When presenting her bill to eliminate breach of promise actions she stated, "Women do not demand rights . . . they earn them, and they ask no such privileges as these which are abolished in this bill."[57]

By proclaiming sex equality a fait accompli, early-twentieth-century feminists like Nicholson denied the continuing disparities between men and women, including the fact that most women still needed to rely on marriage for financial support. One result of this tactic was that the traditional economic protections of marriage — alimony,[58] breach of promise,[59] or common-law marriage[60] — were increasingly viewed as unnecessary and the women who sought these benefits were attacked as "parasites," "harlots," and "bandits." These negative perceptions were then further fueled by intense and sensationalized media coverage.

During the 1930s, the frequency of heart-balm actions declined significantly, but the media coverage of these suits exploded.[61] Between 1916 and 1920, the *Chicago Daily Tribune* published only thirty-nine stories referencing "alienation of affections" (a heart-balm suit based on the "stealing" of a spouse's love). Between 1921 and 1925, this number increased to 56; between 1926 and 1930, it rose to 102; and between 1931 and 1935, the paper published 230 stories, a nearly sixfold increase in coverage.[62] Many of the most publicized heart-balm cases involved celebrities.

One famous alienation of affections claim involved the movie star Douglas Fairbanks, husband of actress Joan Crawford. In 1933, Fairbanks was sued by Jorgen Dietz for allegedly having an affair with Dietz's wife. The allegations were unsupported and untrue. In fact, they were deliberately manufactured by Fairbanks's movie studio to quell homosexuality rumors. Nevertheless, the public was unaware of these machinations, and when Fairbanks agreed to pay the Dietzes $50,000, it seemed like Fairbanks was being exploited.[63]

From the *Independent Record* (Helena, Montana), Sunday, October 18, 1931.

Cases such as Fairbanks's fostered the inaccurate perception that the financial abuse of men was a serious problem.[64] This led to the elimination of most heart-balm laws but also, increasingly, common-law marriage. The 1932 New York common-law marriage case *In re Estate of Erlanger* highlighted the changing acceptance of laws that had once supported and encouraged the marital bargain.

Charlotte Fixel-Erlanger was a beautiful former Broadway actress who claimed to be the common-law wife of Abraham Erlanger, a wealthy, much older Broadway producer. The couple had lived together for decades but had never formally married. When Erlanger died, Fixel-Erlanger sought recognition as his wife and the beneficiary of his estate. Her claim was based on the marital bargain. She was a wife, she argued, because she performed wifely services. She had lived with Erlanger, traveled with him, and cared for him. In return, she had received, and depended on, Erlanger's financial support. One of her lawyer's earliest arguments was that "every department store in New York has charge accounts in the name Mrs. Erlanger." Spending

Erlanger's money — she regularly ordered his food, clothes, and housewares — was presented as evidence of marriage. As Fixel-Erlanger's lawyers explained in their briefs, "Wives do select suits for their husbands, but mistresses do not. Such conduct bespeaks the attention and life of a housewife, and not the life of a wanton."[65]

Very different arguments were made by the lawyers for Erlanger's estate. They suggested that the financial benefits Fixel-Erlanger received from her relationship with Erlanger made her more like a prostitute than a wife. Throughout the trial, the estate's arguments focused on Fixel-Erlanger's alleged mercenary motives and her presumed lack of affection for Erlanger. One witness testified to an incident in which Fixel-Erlanger nagged Erlanger to purchase a diamond-and-gold wristwatch for her and then confided to the witness, "I got to get it while the getting is good." A different witness testified that Fixel-Erlanger didn't love Erlanger and just wanted "what she could get out of him," adding, "she would buy an automobile as you would buy cigarettes." Other witnesses made even more damning accusations. One described Fixel-Erlanger as "a very bad woman . . . a dangerous woman" and warned, "If anything happens to me, and don't forget this, whatever she says about me is what she has manufactured."[66] Another claimed Fixel-Erlanger had wanted Erlanger dead so badly she had even planned her funeral outfit, "a white coat . . . trimmed with white fox fur and her emeralds."[67] Together, these witnesses painted Fixel-Erlanger as a heartless gold digger who did not love Erlanger and thus could not be his wife.

Ultimately, the court ignored the attacks on Fixel-Erlanger's character and ruled in her favor, but the court knew its decision was controversial.[68] Tellingly, the court's 500-page opinion included specifics "of every encounter, every document, every conversation, every purchase, every dinner, every disagreement,

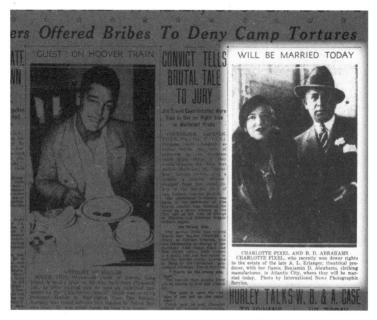

From the *Courier-News* (Bridgewater, New Jersey), 1932.

and every excursion." As law professor Ariela Dubler explains, the judge recognized "his decision would be a controversial one." In fact, the public was outraged. Most Americans believed Fixel-Erlanger had never loved Erlanger and didn't deserve to inherit his wealth. When she remarried shortly after her legal victory, this perception was seemingly confirmed. It is likely no coincidence that within months of the *Erlanger* decision, New York joined the growing list of states outlawing common-law marriage.[69]

Erlanger was decided during the midst of the Great Depression. Money was scarce, and an extra mouth to feed could cause real financial hardship. Most single women lived at home, and with few economic opportunities, many were burdens on their families. Consequently, despite the widespread criticism of gold digging, marrying for money remained an important survival tool for many women and their families. Occasionally, this reality was acknowledged.[70]

Joan Blondell and Guy Kibbee in *Gold Diggers of 1933*.

In the shooting script for the movie *Gold Diggers of 1933*, there is a scene in which a beautiful young woman is embraced by a much older man after having just accepted his marriage proposal. Moments later, she receives a call that she has been hired as a chorus girl. The woman hangs up the phone, smiles, breaks free of the embrace, slaps the man, and leaves. The implication is that the woman only agreed to marriage because she had no other financial options. As soon as she is offered a well-paying job, she loses all interest in marrying for money. Economic anxiety, not greed, was the key thing keeping her in the relationship and making her feign affection for a man she detested.

Throughout the 1930s, women lacked meaningful economic alternatives to marriage, but this changed dramatically when America entered World War II. For the first time, significant numbers of American women were eligible for well-paying

A Department of Defense photo of women shipfitters working on board the USS *Nereus* at the US Navy Yard in Mare Island, circa 1943.

jobs and could support themselves. Suddenly, women didn't need to marry for money. American men should have been thrilled. Tellingly, they were not. Women's potential economic independence made men fearful. Without a financial need for marriage, many worried that women might no longer choose to marry. Returning American soldiers repeatedly cited this fear as the reason they wed foreign brides. As one such soldier explained, "I don't know whether I am going to have a job when I get back. I don't know how things will be with me. Maybe I couldn't make an American girl happy with what I have to offer her."[71] Another simply said, "American women demand so much more."[72]

For centuries, female economic dependence had enhanced men's marriage prospects and made even poor providers appear relatively attractive. Without this economic incentive, many men worried their marital prospects were no longer as promising.

The gender equality of the war years was short-lived, however. When World War II ended, the need to employ returning soldiers forced most women to abandon their wartime careers. They returned to the home and the marital bargain. As a result, women's need to marry for money did not end in the 1940s. Nor did it end in the twentieth century. Even today, continuing gender inequality means marrying for money remains many women's best financial option. However, money is far from the only non-love reason Americans marry. Before returning to a contemporary examination of gold digging, the following chapters will explore other equally important, but less well-known, motivations that have long convinced Americans to marry for reasons other than love.

chapter two

The Government Loves a Gold Digger

Politics doesn't make strange bedfellows — marriage does.

— GROUCHO MARX

In 1835, when Esther Sumner was twenty-one, she married Noah Damon, a seventy-five-year-old Revolutionary War veteran. It was not a love match. Esther married Noah because she believed he was wealthy; she quickly learned he was broke. In fact, he needed her to support him. For one year, Esther and Noah lived on her small teacher's salary. Then Esther tired of this arrangement and sent Noah to live with his grown children. The couple never lived together again, and the marriage appeared to be a financial disaster. However, when Noah died, Esther became eligible for a widow's pension. She received this pension until her death at age ninety-three.[1] Her once worthless marriage had entitled her to decades of government support.

LAST WIDOW OF REVOLUTION.

Mrs Esther Sumner Damon, Cousin of Charles Sumner, Died Yesterday at Plymouth Union, Vt.

MRS ESTHER SUMNER DAMON.

In 1836, one year after the Damons married, Congress passed the Widows' Pension Act and began paying pensions to the wives of military veterans. Initially, the act applied only to women who married prior to their husbands' military service, but over time it expanded to include those who married later. This change meant women could now marry for pensions, and many quickly recognized the financial advantages of such marriages. If a young woman wed an older veteran, marriage could mean a lifetime of government support. Alberta Martin, one of the last Confederate widows, was motivated by such economic incentives.

In 1927, when Alberta was twenty-one, she married William Jasper Martin, an eighty-one-year-old Civil War veteran. A 2003 *Baltimore Sun* article on the Martin marriage described it as blatantly mercenary, writing, "he was lonely, she was needy" and his "$50-a-month military pension [was] a princely sum in those days for a woman who staked her whole life by poverty." The article further emphasized the transactional nature of Alberta's marriage, and her presumed lack of affection for William, by noting that less than eight weeks after William's death she married his grandson. According to the article's author, this scandalous second marriage "set so many tongues wagging in town that the local Baptist preacher had to study the Scriptures before deciding she hadn't committed a sin."[2]

The marriage of Helen Viola Jackson, the last official Civil War widow, was even more explicitly transactional. In 1936, when Jackson was seventeen, she married ninety-three-year-old Civil War veteran James Bolin. Jackson met Bolin when her father sent her over to help with Bolin's chores. Bolin lacked the money to pay but offered to marry Jackson instead. Recognizing the economic benefits of such a marriage, she agreed. "He said that he would leave me his Union pension. It was during the [Great] Depression and times were hard. He said that it might be my only way of leaving the farm."[3]

Critics of the Widows' Pension Act recognized that the law could encourage mercenary marriages. In 1843, during the debates on the act's reauthorization, Massachusetts senator Rufus King

William Jasper Martin (left), a Civil War veteran who married a woman sixty years younger than himself, and his widow, Alberta Martin (above).

urged his fellow lawmakers to reject the act because it could benefit gold diggers. He asked his fellow lawmakers: "What merit [i]s there in these women marrying officers and soldiers of the Revolution after the war, that they should be entitled to pensions? Go to the Pension Office, and you will find that most of these widows who had married those old revolutionary officers, soon after their deaths provided themselves with young husbands."[4]

King's concerns were valid yet were largely dismissed. Widows' pensions were popular, and the women who received them, even the gold diggers, were widely viewed as deserving. These women had provided marital services to their veteran husbands; thus, under the terms of the marital bargain, they were entitled to compensation.[5] Senator Perry Smith of Connecticut employed such reasoning when he voiced his support for the act's reauthorization, "not on the ground of a gratuity, but because the females of that day were all more or less compelled to make sacrifices and had besides rendered material services." In 1850, Representative

Illustration by Keppler and Schwarzmann, 1898.

Abraham Venable of North Carolina echoed these sentiments when he explained that the purpose of a widow's pension was "to give to the widow something, some compensation for the years of anxiety and care spent over her husband who fell under the effects of . . . wounds received in the service."[6]

The pension act was characterized as a continuation of the husband's support duty, and this allowed it to avoid Congress's normally strong condemnation of public charity.[7] It also helped lawmakers dismiss the concerns of critics like Senator King.[8] In the nineteenth century, women were expected to marry for support; widows' pensions were treated as just another form of marital support.[9]

In 1864, the Civil War pension statute extended pensions to the widows of "colored soldiers." It also adopted a generous and easily provable definition of marriage. The act stated that in cases where the "husband" of a newly freed woman was killed during the Civil War, the widow and her children were allowed to receive a pension for the soldier without proof of legal marriage. The alleged wife was simply required to show the couple "had habitually recognized each other as man and wife, and lived together as such."[10] In 1873, pensions were also extended to widows of "Indian soldiers and sailors" who had cohabited for at least two years and recognized "each other as man and wife."[11]

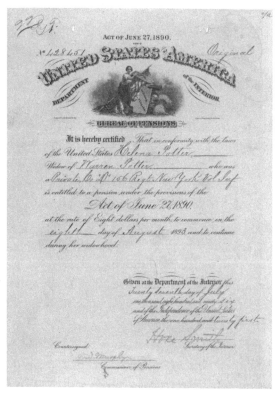

Authorization of a pension petition, August 1893.

By the 1890s, widows' pensions were supporting hundreds of thousands of women and children and accounted for nearly half the federal budget.[12] These funds provided valuable support to needy women, but they were not without drawbacks. Widows' pensions conditioned government support on marriage and, in doing so, ignored the needs of other impoverished women. Single women were ineligible for government support; they were simply instructed to marry.[13] This was not the only problem with conditioning government benefits on marriage. Linking benefits to marriage could create dangerous and even deadly incentives. The Oregon Donation Land Act of 1850 exposed this potential peril.

The Oregon Donation Land Act

Initially, marital status was irrelevant to Oregon land claims. Both single and married male settlers were permitted to claim 640-acre plots. Then, the Donation Land Act went into effect, and land eligibility changed. Suddenly, single men were entitled to only half the amount available to married men.[14] Men living in Oregon prior to December 1, 1850, were entitled to 320 acres if they were single, or 640 acres if they were married. Similarly, for settlers arriving after December 1, 1850, a male claimant could receive 160 acres of land if he was single, or 320 acres if he was married.[15] In both instances, the second parcel of land would be in the wife's name, but since the husband typically controlled his wife's land parcel, marriage effectively doubled his acreage.

The Donation Land Act's preference for married settlers reflected the well-established view that marriage facilitated homesteading. In 1838, when Iowa was the western frontier, a correspondent for the *Dubuque Iowa News* joked, "So anxious are our settlers for wives that they never ask a single lady her age.

All they require is *teeth.*" The 1846 *Emigrant's Guide to Iowa* made a similar, albeit less humorous, observation, noting, "Married persons are generally more comfortable, and succeed better, in a frontier country, than single men; for a wife and family, so far from being a burden to a western farmer, may always prove a source of pecuniary advantage in the domestic economy of his household."[16]

Wives made homesteading easier. They also made frontier communities more stable. Census figures indicate that single men were more transient than married men. For example, the 1850 census records from Wapello County, Iowa, showed that 91 percent of single men had left since the previous census, while only 73 percent of those with families had departed. Similarly, an 1860 census from Roseburg, Oregon, revealed that only one-third of single men stayed more than five years, while approximately two-thirds of married men remained. Given such significant differences, many western politicians eagerly sought to incentivize female immigration. In 1850, Samuel R. Thurston, the Oregon Territory's congressional delegate, was so eager for female settlers that he asked Congress to provide them with immigration incentives. He wrote:

> Emigrating to Oregon from the States, places the female beyond the reach of her kindred and former friends; and it is certainly no more than right to place some little means of protection in her own hands. But the object is to produce a population, and this provision is an encouragement of the women to peril the dangers and hardships of the journey.[17]

In response to Thurston's request, Congress passed the Donation Land Act and guaranteed female homesteaders a parcel of land in their own name and as a separate estate. This

Samuel R. Thurston.

was the first time the government had permitted married women to own government land, and it was a significant immigration incentive.[18] However, it was an even stronger incentive for those already living in the Oregon Territory to marry.[19] In the July 29, 1851, issue of the *Oregon Spectator*, the paper's editors noted the marital benefit of the act and encouraged Oregon's singles to wed before the December 1 deadline:

> The first day of December 1851 is near at hand. Your days of grace soon expire, and the 320 acres lost beyond redemption, unless you are up and stirring. The ladies, it seems to us, should wear their most winning smiles, and encourage the timid young man to nerve himself up to the sticking point, and boldly declare his desire to possess another half [section].

The article implies that the primary impediment to marriage was male nerves. However, the true problem was numbers.

White women were scarce in Oregon, and demand far exceeded supply.[20] In 1849, women accounted for fewer than 20 percent of travelers on the Oregon Trail, and in 1850, when the Donation Land Act was passed, male settlers outnumbered female settlers by a ratio of 2.5 to 1. In some counties, the ratio was almost 4 to 1.[21] There were simply not enough women to marry. As a result, many land-hungry men turned to teenagers and even children.[22]

Oregon settler Jennie Stevenson Miller described the marital frenzy of her childhood, stating: "I had my first offer of marriage when I was 13, and from then till I was 24 I had numerous proposals."[23] Miller resisted these offers because, as she explained, "I had a pretty strong suspicion that many of the men who wanted to marry me wanted the extra land they could get if they were married." Still, countless other girls accepted, or were forced to accept, these proposals. Abigail Scott Duniway, editor of Oregon's first women's rights newspaper, wrote about the child marriages the Land Donation Act had incentivized and highlighted the abuse inherent in these relationships. According to Duniway, "When a man of forty, thirty or even twenty-five marries a child of fourteen . . . the result is subjugation on one hand and despotism upon the other."[24] Oregon settler Elvina Apperson Fellows was the victim of such abuse. She had married as a young teen, and her husband beat her regularly. Years later, she recounted: "[He] used to beat me until I thought I couldn't stand it." She also noted she had little recourse to stop the abuse. "What could a girl of 14 do, to protect herself from a man of 44?" Some older husbands even considered the ability to abuse an added benefit of child marriage. Oregon homesteader George Bennett once remarked to a neighbor that his wife, Lureana, "gave herself to him when she was but a child," and as a result, he "had had her under his thumb ever since — he could use her just as he pleased."[25]

The law of coverture already left wives vulnerable to abuse and exploitation. Laws incentivizing men to marry women they didn't love, and maybe didn't even like, further increased this risk. Intermarriages between white men and Indian women provide some of the most tragic examples.

White Men Preying on Native Women

By the mid-nineteenth century, Indian tribes had been deprived of millions of acres of ancestral lands. However, many still retained significant, and often desirable, landholdings. When these lands were not for sale, marriage became an effective means for non-Native men to gain ownership. The 1848 case *Wells v. Thompson* set the precedent for such land grabs.

In 1821, Mary Wells, a Creek woman, married a white man named William Wells. Initially, the couple lived within the boundaries of Creek Nation.[26] In 1828, the Wells family left Creek territory and moved to Alabama. Shortly thereafter, William abandoned Mary for another woman, and Mary and her children returned to her father's home in Creek Nation. Four years later, the tribe signed the 1832 Treaty of Cusseta. Under this treaty, Creek Nation relinquished rights to all land east of the Mississippi. In return, the head of each family received a land allotment. Mary received one of these parcels, but after her death, William claimed the land as his own.

The Wells children contested William's claim. They argued that according to Creek custom, Mary had divorced William by returning to her father's home. Thus, because Mary and William were divorced before she received her allotment, William had no right to the land. The Alabama Supreme Court rejected this argument. It held that because the separation did not occur on Indian land, the marriage could not be dissolved by Creek custom and that William remained head of the family and was entitled to the allotted lands.

Wells demonstrated that marriage to an Indian woman could provide white men with rights to Indian lands. Then, the 1854 Mississippi case *Turner v. Fish* confirmed this benefit of marriage. In *Fish*, a white man named Freeman J. Smith claimed a treaty right to Choctaw land. Under the Treaty of Dancing Rabbit, an allotment of Choctaw land was given to the head of each Choctaw family. Smith argued that because he was married to a Choctaw woman and living within the Choctaw Nation, he was the head of a Choctaw family. The Mississippi Supreme Court agreed. The court acknowledged that "the treaty has reference to the head of a family living under the dominion of the Choctaw nation" but noted that "the treaty does not say that a white man may not according to the usages and customs of that nation, be the head of the family." Therefore, the court found that Smith was "head" of a Choctaw family. In reaching this decision, the court dismissed Choctaw matrilineal custom recognizing women as heads of family and declared it could "only take judicial notice of the law . . . It can take no judicial notice of local custom." As a result, Smith gained control of his wife's tribal allotment. He then immediately sold the land and pocketed the profits. His wife and children received nothing.[27]

Marriage could be an effective means of gaining Indian lands, and many white men took advantage of this strategy.[28] By 1874, the problem of marrying for Indian land had become so problematic in Cherokee territory that the Cherokee Nation passed a statute declaring that, in light of the "rapidly growing value of Cherokee lands . . . [the] rights and privileges herein conferred through intermarriage shall not extend to a right of soil or interest in the vested funds of this Nation."[29] The problem of marrying for Indian land was also vividly illustrated by the rapid amendment of the 1887 Dawes Act, which had inadvertently incentivized such marriages.

The purpose of the Dawes Act was to break up Indian land-holdings in the West and open these lands to white settlement. The act divested Native American tribes of nearly ninety million acres, or approximately two-thirds of their lands.[30] Nevertheless, even after allotment, a significant portion of lands remained reserved for tribes and tribal citizens. These were valuable lands, and to prevent tribal members from being threatened or swindled out of these remaining parcels, the act included a twenty-five-year ban on their sale.[31] This provision ensured that non-Indians could not buy allotted Indian lands — but it did nothing to prevent them from marrying for these lands. Within a year, Congress recognized it had made a grave mistake. It then passed a second statute clarifying that white men who married Indian women could not, by virtue of the marriage, acquire "any right to any tribal property, privilege, or interest whatever to which any member of such tribe is entitled."[32]

After the Dawes Act was amended, white men could no longer marry for tribal lands. However, marriage still gave them access to the reservations and their resources, and this could be almost as valuable.[33] White men suspected of marrying Native women for access to tribal resources were dubbed squaw men. This was a pejorative term, and such husbands were generally seen as disreputable and even dangerous.[34] In the August 16, 1889, Commissioner of Indian Affairs Report, Thomas Priestley of the Yakima Agency wrote, "The white men who marry Indian women for purposes of getting a home on an Indian reservation are not of the better class."[35] In the August 11, 1890, report, Hal J. Cole of the Colville Agency noted that such men are "of the lower class . . . Nine out of every ten are addicted to whisky drinking or else they have some other pernicious habit and their presence on the reservation does the Indians harm instead

Indian agent V. T. McGillycuddy.

of good."[36] And in the September 18, 1890, report, Webster L. Stabler of the Yakima Agency described "the squaw-men . . . [as] a constant menace to the welfare of the Indians."[37]

Indian agents tended to focus the on the problems caused by white husbands' drinking and gambling, but it was resource grabbing that was often the biggest threat to the welfare of the tribe. In the late nineteenth century, intermarriage had enabled white men to dominate the cattle ranching industry on the Pine Ridge Reservation of South Dakota. Although the reservation and its grazing lands were intended to be off limits to white ranchers, marriage provided a lucrative exception.[38] In 1880, Indian agent V. T. McGillycuddy lamented the advantages these white ranchers gained from intermarriage, writing, "The squaw-men assume that by marriage they have all the rights of full-blooded Indians, and they endeavor to exercise these rights not only in possession of cattle themselves, but also in ranging and pasturing upon Indian reservations large herds belonging to other white men."[39] As McGillycuddy noted, once white ranchers had access to reservation resources, their connections and understanding of the American ranching industry gave them an unparalleled advantage over their Indian competitors.

In 1893, a *Harper's Magazine* article about the Native nations of Oklahoma specifically highlighted the financial benefits white husbands gained from intermarriage. The article noted that in Cherokee Nation, "a Cherokee squaw man . . . is said to hold more land than is held by all the full-bloods of the tribe." It also reported that "a score of Chickasaw citizens, in whom combined there is hardly enough blood to make a full-blood Indian, control nearly ninety percent of the arable lands of that nation."[40] By 1908, the practice of marrying Indian women for their land was so common in Oklahoma that, when the *Taylor-Trotwood Magazine* published an article extolling the virtues of the new state, it openly advised the arriving male settlers to

Beaver Dick Leigh, 1872, with his first wife, Jenny, a Shoshone of Washakie's band, and their children. The marriage of Leigh and Jenny appears to have been a love match. After she died, Leigh named Jenny Lake, one of the most beautiful lakes in the Tetons, in her honor.

A delegation from the council of the Osage Indian tribe of Oklahoma travels to Washington, DC, to take up the question of leasing oil lands in the Osage reservation.

marry Indian wives. According to the article's author, an Indian wife "is a thing of beauty and a joy forever, and she and each of her sisters has a great big farm."[41]

Some white husbands undoubtedly loved their native wives. Tragically, many did not.[42] The Osage murders of Oklahoma are one particularly chilling example of the dangers of linking government benefits to marriage. In 1906, Congress passed the Osage Allotment Act, dividing approximately 1.5 million acres of land among the members of the Osage Nation. It also placed the mineral interest for these lands in trust for the Osage and provided that all funds due to the tribe would be divided pro rata among the individual tribal members or their heirs. These shares were known as headrights, and when oil was discovered on Osage land, those eligible for headrights became, at least in theory, enormously wealthy.[43]

The problem was that full-blooded Osage Indians were considered "incompetent" to manage their vast oil wealth. As a result, they were assigned financial guardians.[44] These "guardians" were typically prominent white residents of Osage County, who were granted near-total control over the finances of their Osage wards. Nearly all of these men were corrupt.[45] Many trustees concocted complex transactions to swindle their Osage wards. Others just robbed them outright. There was little the Osage could do to prevent this abuse; the one exception was marriage. An Osage woman could avoid financial guardianship by marrying a white man.[46] This husband would then be permitted to take the place of the government-appointed guardian. Through marriage, an Osage woman could potentially avoid the corrupt guardians determined to steal her money. Sadly, marriage often turned out to be infinitely worse. The Kyle family was particularly unlucky in this regard.

In 1919, Ernest Burkhart married Mollie Kyle for her headrights.[47] Headrights could not be bought or sold, but they could be inherited. Therefore, at the urging of his uncle and brother, Ernest wed Mollie and helped carry out a plan to murder her and her family. Mollie's sister Ana was killed first. She was shot in the back of the head, but her death was staged to look alcohol related. Shortly after Ana's murder, Lizzie Kyle, Mollie's mother, was poisoned. Then a bomb was placed under the house of Mollie's sister Rita. Both Rita and her husband were killed. Chillingly, Mollie and Ernest's children were supposed to be in the house when the bomb exploded. They were spared by a last-minute illness. Finally, after murdering Ana, Lizzie, and Rita, Ernest began poisoning Mollie. She became gravely ill, but by that time the newly formed FBI was investigating the Kyle family murders and uncovered the plan to kill Mollie. As a result, she survived.

Mollie Kyle and her sisters.

Ernest Hale, his brother, and his uncle were all convicted of murder. However, the Kyle murders were not isolated acts. Many white men were willing to marry and murder Osage women for headrights. In fact, Hale wasn't even the first husband to murder a Kyle sister.[48] Before Ernest married Mollie, a white man named Bill Smith had married a fourth sister, Minnie Kyle, who died of a mysterious wasting disease shortly after their marriage. Then, after Minnie's death, Bill married her sister Rita and presumably would have murdered her, too, except Ernest killed her (and Bill) first.[49]

Despite the tragic outcome, it is understandable why Mollie and her sisters chose white husbands: Intermarriage gave the Kyle sisters a chance to circumvent the racist laws denying them access to valuable government benefits. As the twentieth century progressed, this use of marriage became increasingly common. Thousands of immigrants used marriage to circumvent the racist, sexist, and xenophobic laws enacted to exclude them. This became a common non-love reason for couples to marry, but such marriages could also lead to abuse and exploitation.

Immigration's Marriage Loophole

Initially, neither citizenship law nor immigration regulations had any relationship to marriage. In the 1830 case *Shanks v. Dupont*, the Supreme Court held that "marriage with an alien . . . produces no dissolution of the native allegiance of the wife."[50] *Shanks* concerned the citizenship of Ann Shanks, a US citizen who had married a British officer and then fled with him to Britain during the Revolutionary War. Years later, her heirs sought to reclaim the land she had possessed before the war, and the ownership issue turned on Shanks's citizenship. If Shanks was an American citizen, then she had abandoned and forfeited her property when she fled to Britain. However, if she was a British citizen, then the land had been captured and, under the peace treaty between the US and Britain, must be returned. After considering the issue, the court held that Shanks was a British subject because she moved to Britain and voluntarily "chose to live under British protection," but not because of her marriage. In the words of Justice Story, "The incapacities of femes covert . . . apply to their civil rights, and are for their protection and interest. But they do not reach their political rights, nor prevent their acquiring or losing a national character."[51]

Twenty-five years later, in 1855, Congress rejected the *Shanks* court's reasoning and passed a statute automatically naturalizing the wife of a US citizen.[52] The new law clarified that women's citizenship, like most of their other legal rights, was affected by marriage and that foreign wives would share the citizenship of their American husband. As Representative Francis Cutting of New York explained when arguing in favor of the act, married women "possess no political rights . . . [therefore], where you confer on her the political character of her husband, it is a relief to the husband, it aids him in the instilling of proper principles in his children and cannot interfere with any possible right of a political character."[53]

In some ways, the new martial citizenship law was very broad. For example, it included wives who had never even set foot in the US. In other ways, it was extremely limited. The law only applied to women who could "lawfully be naturalized under existing laws," which meant it only applied to white wives. After the Civil War, some of the racial bars on naturalization were removed. In 1870, persons "of African descent or nativity" were permitted to naturalize.[54] Then, in 1888, American Indian wives of white men also became eligible for naturalization.[55] However, neither of these amendments applied to Asian immigrants. They remained ineligible for naturalization. As a result, marriage could not confer citizenship on Asian wives. Nevertheless, as America's anti-Asian immigration restrictions expanded in the late nineteenth century, marriage became an important strategy for avoiding these exclusionary laws.[56]

Asian Exclusion Acts

The first Asian exclusion law was the 1875 Page Act, which prohibited the entry of involuntary "Oriental" labor, prostitutes, and others coming for "lewd and immoral purposes." The Page Act was followed by the 1882 Chinese Exclusion Act, which barred Chinese laborers from entering the US. Shortly thereafter, immigration officials interpreted the act as also preventing the wives of Chinese laborers from entering the country.[57] In 1884, Too Cheong, a Chinese laborer living in the United States, challenged the act as a violation of his marital rights.

Too Cheong had traveled to China and married a woman named Ah Moy. The couple then returned to the United States, but after the passage of the exclusion act. Upon arrival, Ah Moy

THE ONLY ONE BARRED OUT.
ENLIGHTENED AMERICAN STATESMAN.—" We must draw the line *somewhere*, you know."

Exclusion act, 1882. *The Only One Barred Out.*

was imprisoned and ordered deported. Too Cheong then challenged this deportation order. He argued that Ah Moy's exclusion violated the terms of the 1880 treaty with China, which
stated that "Chinese laborers who are now in the United States,
shall be allowed to go and come of their own free will and accord,
and shall be accorded all the rights, privileges, immunities, and
exemptions which accorded to the citizens and subjects of the
most favor." According to Too Cheong, this provision guaranteed him the right to his wife's company and companionship.
The court disagreed.

The *Ah Moy* court conceded that a wife's companionship was
one of the essential rights of marriage but held that the exclusion act had limited this right. As the court explained, a wife
assumed the immigration status of her husband and therefore,
because Too Cheong was a Chinese laborer, Ah Moy was also a
Chinese laborer.[58] The court held that marriage did not create an

THROWING DOWN THE LADDER BY WHICH THEY ROSE.

Throwing Down the Ladder by Which They Rose by Thomas
Nast, July 23, 1870.

exception to the exclusion act. As a result, Too Cheong lost, but
other Chinese husbands were more successful.

In 1899, the US Supreme Court decided *U.S. v. Gue.* Gue Lim
was the wife of a Chinese merchant named Fook Kee. In 1887,
the couple traveled from China to Tacoma, Washington, and
initially both Gue and Fook were granted entry based on Fook's
status as a Chinese merchant. Five months later, the collector of
customs changed his mind and charged Gue Lim with unlawful entry. She was imprisoned and ordered deported. Fook Kee
then sued for her release. Like Too Cheong, Fook argued that as
Gue's husband, he had the right to her care and companionship
and that as the wife of a Chinese merchant, Gue's entry was not
barred by the exclusion argument.

In its brief to the US Supreme Court, the government
conceded that marriage gave Gue Lim the right to enter the

THE CHINESE QUESTION AGAIN.

The Chinese Question Again. Chinese Exclusion in New
Jersey: Immigration Law in the Past and Present.

US as a wife of an admissible immigrant. It wrote, "The United
States at the outset disclaims any intention to contend against
the fundamental and natural right of the valid wife and legitimate minor children of Chinese merchants, not being laborers, to come and remain in this country." The problem, claimed
the government, was not that wives of Chinese merchants were
ineligible for entry, but that Gue had failed to file the correct
paperwork prior to arrival. This was a weak and disingenuous
argument (the supposedly required forms were not even obtain-
able outside the United States), and the court quickly rejected it.

Consequently, *Gue* confirmed that merchant wives could "enter by reason of the right of the husband and without the certificate mentioned in the Act of 1884." In 1902, in *Tsoi Sim v. U.S.*, the court confirmed the marital immigration exception also applied to the wives of second-generation Chinese Americans. Tsoi Sim was a Chinese woman who had entered the United States a few months before the passage of the exclusion act. Twenty years later, on April 20, 1901, she was arrested for being a female laborer of Chinese descent. At the time of her arrest, Tsoi was married to Yee Yuk, a US citizen by birth. Therefore, Tsoi Sim argued, she should be treated as the wife of a native-born citizen and not as an inadmissible laborer. Tsoi's arguments focused on the sanctity of the marital relation and on "the right of the citizen husband to have and enjoy the society and company of whomsoever he may lawfully marry." Tsoi's attorneys described this right as one of the most fundamental rights of citizenship and argued that if Tsoi Sim was deported, "the founders of our great Republic [will have] fought and bled in vain, and our boasted 'liberty of the citizen' is but an idle dream"[59] The court agreed. It held that marriage had changed Tsoi's status "from that of a Chinese laborer to that of wife of a native-born citizen." It then confirmed that as a wife, Tsoi had the right "to live with her husband; enjoy his society; receive his support and maintenance and all the comforts and privileges of the marriage relations."

Gue Lim and *Tsoi Sim* showed that marriage could be used to circumvent Chinese immigration restrictions. Marriage was an even more successful means of avoiding restrictions on Japanese immigration. In 1907, Japan and the US signed the Gentleman's Agreement. This agreement banned nearly all Japanese immigration to the United States but made an exception for the wives of Japanese men already residing in the US. Although these men could not leave the United States to find wives, they could marry

Picture brides wait to meet their new husbands.

by proxy and then send for their wives to join them. The arriving women were known as picture brides, because their American husbands had only seen their photographs. Between 1908 and 1920, more than ten thousand Japanese women used this exception to enter the United States.[60]

Barring "Immoral Women"

The Chinese Exclusion Act and the Gentleman's Agreement affected only Asian immigrants, but other "undesirable" immigrants were also targeted by America's growing immigration restrictions. In 1882, Congress enacted legislation to bar "lunatic[s]," "idiot[s]," and "any person unable to take care of himself or herself without becoming a public charge" from entry into the United States.[61] Shortly thereafter, it amended the phrase "without becoming a public charge" to "likely to become a public charge." Between 1895 and 1915, this provision was responsible for approximately two-thirds of all immigration exclusions.[62]

The "likely public charge" provision was gender-neutral, but it was particularly problematic for single women, especially those who belonged to certain ethnic groups, such as Jewish women.[63] The difficulties facing single, female immigrants were then further compounded by the 1907 Immigration Act, which prohibited the entry of prostitutes and other women entering for "immoral purposes." After the enactment of this provision, single women attempting to immigrate alone ran a high risk of being accused of prostitution or other immorality. The experience of Martha Ash, a young New Zealander, is illustrative. In 1918, Ash left New Zealand to join her fiancé in America. Upon arrival, some of Ash's fellow passengers claimed she had behaved improperly with one of the officers. As a result, she was deemed a woman entering for "immoral purposes" and denied entry. Ash vehemently denied the accusations, but her word was insufficient to overcome the charges. In the end, it was only her fiancé's continued willingness to marry her that prevented Ash's deportation.

America's xenophobic immigration restrictions were designed to keep out a broad category of "undesirable" immigrants, and this goal was furthered by the racist pseudoscience of the early-twentieth-century eugenics movement. Eugenicists advocated for stronger immigration restrictions by claiming that traits such as criminality and immorality were hereditary and more likely to exist in certain immigrant populations. They also warned that "undesirable" immigrants were reproducing at a faster rate than America's white middle and upper classes and without restrictions would soon outnumber them. In 1906, President Theodore Roosevelt echoed these eugenic fears when he famously described declining white birth rates as "race suicide" and a problem "infinitely more important than any other question in this country."

US anti-venereal-disease poster from World War I, 1918.

As America entered World War I, these fears continued to intensify. During the war, military propaganda portrayed foreign women as either dangerous spies or diseased harlots. Congress then compounded these fears when it expanded the enemy alien statute to permit the arrest and confinement of foreign-born wives suspected of aiding the enemy.[64] Consequently, when American soldiers started bringing home foreign brides, many Americans worried these were the sort of dangerous or debauched women they had been taught to fear. Social workers helping to process war brides also fueled these perceptions.[65] Maude Cleveland, head of the war brides division of the Red Cross, was appalled that many of the women readily admitted to marrying for immigration benefits, and she implored the

American public to "wake up" and recognize that foreign brides were "preying upon the American army."[66]

Americans like Cleveland condemned women who had married for immigration benefits while ignoring the compelling circumstances that often motivated their marital decisions. Europe had been decimated by World War I, and many war brides had suffered terribly. Some were widows with young children, others were survivors of disease and starvation, and nearly all had seen the places they lived and people they loved destroyed by conflict. Immigration offered these women the opportunity to rebuild their lives, but as single immigrants, many would have been denied entry as too poor, too sick, or too "immoral." For these women, marriage was their only immigration option, and as immigration restrictions continued increasing after the war, more and more women made this marital choice.

In 1917, Congress enacted a literacy requirement and barred entry to immigrants who could not read. Then, in 1921, it passed the Emergency Quota Act, which established numerical limits on the number of immigrants who could enter the US and specifically limited immigration from certain "undesirable" countries — primarily Eastern and Southern Europe. Both restrictions made entry drastically harder for millions of potential immigrants. In 1921, a *Harper's Magazine* article recounted the immigration hearing of a thirty-seven-year-old Greek seamstress ensnared by the literacy requirement. In the article, the woman is described as "attractive and well dressed and obviously makes a good impression on the [immigration] board. But unfortunately, she is illiterate." When she is handed a book, she mutters the word "upsilon" because, as the article notes, "It is evidently the only letter she can recognize." The woman was a refugee whose family "had all been killed by the Turks," but this tragedy was irrelevant to her immigration petition. Marriage, however, would have provided an exception. As the article noted, "If she

THE AMERICANESE WALL, AS CONGRESSMAN
BURNETT WOULD BUILD IT.
Uncle Sam: You're welcome in — if you can climb it!

The American wall, as Congressman Burnett would build
it. Uncle Sam: You're welcome in — if you can read it!

had been married, and were coming to join her husband . . . the
literacy provision of the law would not have kept her out."[67]
Unfortunately, she was single, so she was deported.

For many would-be immigrants, marriage was their only
immigration option and, frequently, their only path to safety.[68]
Such motivations are poignantly apparent in the immigration
interview of a young Armenian woman also attempting to enter
the United States in 1921. The woman was a mail-order bride,
and when immigration officials asked her why she agreed to
marry a man she had never met she replied bluntly, "It is better
to marry a stranger than to be massacred."[69] Marriage was the

W. H. Auden and Erika Mann pictured in the year of their marriage by Alec Bangham, 1935.

sole way this woman, a near victim of the Armenian genocide, could find safety in America. Her story was not unique.

In the 1930s, as the Nazi threat increased throughout Europe, America and other Western countries continued to restrict immigration. As a result, marital immigration literally became a lifesaving strategy. In one famous example, the poet W. H. Auden, who was homosexual, married Erika Mann, author Thomas Mann's daughter, to help her escape the Nazis. The following year, Auden persuaded the novelist John Hampson to marry a friend of Erika's, the actress Therese Giehse, who was also under threat for her anti-Nazi activities. When a friend tried to dissuade Hampson from the marriage, he refused and replied, "Wystan [his name for Auden] says, 'What are buggers for?'"[70]

Marital immigration saved women's lives, but it could also encourage their exploitation. World War II was devasting even for those who had not faced direct persecution, and when the

American troops entering Naples, 1943.

war ended, countless men and women were eager to leave their war-torn countries. For many desperate female immigrants, marriage was their best, or only, chance to escape. Sadly, American soldiers were not above exploiting this situation.[71] Anna Della Casa, a sixteen-year-old Neapolitan teenager, was faced with this difficult choice when, at the war's conclusion, she received a marriage proposal from a thirty-five-year-old American soldier. Anna came from a family of eighteen, all of whom were struggling to survive. On October 1, 1943, when the Allied troops entered Naples, the local population had no food, water, or electricity. The Della Casas also had no home. The retreating Germans had burned down the family's home, and Anna, her parents, and her siblings were all squeezed into a married sister's small apartment. At the strong urging of her parents, Anna agreed to marry her American suitor. This ensured her parents had one less mouth to feed, and it guaranteed Anna's entry into America. However, it was not a love match. Years later, when asked why she married, Anna touched a shrapnel scar on her neck and answered, "To get me out of the nightmare of the war. I dreamed of the bombs, the bombs, the bombs."[72]

Similar desperation is apparent in the 1953 immigration fraud case *U.S. v. Lutwak*. Shortly after World War II ended, Marcel Lutwak and his mother attempted to bring their relatives, survivors of the Nazi concentration camps, into the United States. Lutwak, Bessie Osborne, and Grace Klemtner, all military veterans, agreed to take advantage of the spousal immigration benefit accorded discharged veterans. The three agreed they would "pretend" to marry Maria, Munio, and Leopold Knoll, in order to bring them to the United States.[73] Speed was particularly important for Munio, who had been starved and beaten in the camps and needed urgent medical care. The couples married in Paris and then immigrated to America, but they never lived together. Eventually, their scheme was discovered, and they were convicted of immigration fraud.[74] Years later, Lutwak was pardoned by President Nixon in a belated recognition of the justness of his marital decision.

Marrying for Government Benefits Today: Perpetuating Inequality

Nearly two hundred years after the first Widows' Pension Act was passed, the practice of attaching federal benefits to marriage continues. This link encourages couples, and especially women, to marry, but such marriages remain problematic. Marrying for government benefits is primarily a strategy of the desperate, and limiting benefits to the married excludes other needy and deserving individuals. Even more concerningly, this link between marriage and government benefits continues to perpetuate gender and racial inequality. Marital immigration remains one obvious example of this problem.

Marrying for Immigration Benefits

Today, marrying for a green card (entry into the United States) remains perfectly legal. A marital immigrant does not need to be in love. The only requirement is they intend to make a life with their American spouse. This is known as the "establish a life test." In the 1996 case *U.S. v. Tagalicud*, the Ninth Circuit Court of Appeals affirmed the legality of such marriages while also, inadvertently, highlighting the reason why they are worrying. In describing the difference between marital immigration and marital fraud, the court explained that marrying for a visa does not, by itself, constitute fraud, because the immigrant spouse could have "intended to establish a life together at the time they were married in gratitude for the visa."[75]

Historically, the circumstances that inspired the type of gratitude described by the *Tagalicud* court included genocide, persecution, and starvation, and many modern marital immigrants are responding to similar conditions. One recent, non-American, example involves Syrian women marrying to escape German refugee camps. As refugees, these women were subject to movement and travel bans that effectively imprisoned them in these camps. Desperate to escape these camps, many began asking relatives to find them German Syrian men willing to marry them so they could finally leave the camps.[76] These women might have the type of "gratitude" toward their husbands that the *Tagalicud* court was envisioning.

When marriage is the only option for victims of war, persecution, and genocide, it can increase the vulnerability of already vulnerable people. In the United States, marital immigrants are dangerously dependent on their citizen spouse. After the American citizen (or lawful permanent resident) petitions for their spouse's admission to the US, the immigrant spouse remains dependent on the citizen for this immigration benefit and needs their ongoing cooperation to gain permanent legal status. If an immigrant spouse is divorced or abandoned by their American spouse before gaining their own, independent, immigration status, they can be deported, and this dependency can increase the likelihood the immigrant spouse may be abused.[77]

The link between marriage and immigration can also lead to abuse of the citizen sponsor. Marital immigration remains one of the quickest, if not only, options for many would-be immigrants. As a result, underage, American girls are sometimes forced to marry foreign men to facilitate their immigration into the US. Naila Amin was fifteen when her family ordered her to marry a twenty-eight-year-old man and bring him into the United States. Amin blames her family for forcing her into an abusive marriage but also recognizes the marriage would not have happened absent US immigration law's marital preference. As Amin notes, "People die to come to America. I was a passport to him. They all wanted him here, and that was the way to do it."[78]

Linking marriage to immigration can incentivize abuse. However, the problem with connecting federal benefits to marriage is not limited to immigration. In fact, marriage-based monetary benefits may be even more concerning.

Marriage and Government Money

Beginning in the 1930s, the number of women eligible for marriage-based federal support increased significantly, but this change was not made for their benefit. Rather, it was to counteract women's growing employment opportunities and encourage them to remain in the home and financially dependent

Unemployed, single women protesting the job placement of married women before themselves at the Emergency Relief Administration headquarters in Boston, Massachusetts.

on their husbands.[79] By linking financial benefits to marriage, the government could argue that women didn't need formal economic equality with men, such as equal work or wages, because they would receive their economic protections through marriage. As historian Nancy Cott explains, great effort was taken to ensure "that the 'working girl' was the only approved female wage earner — someone passing through a phase of her life, for whom paid work was fleeting and not a continuing need and right, who could manage without equal work and did not merit the same say in government or union policy as the 'working man.'"[80] Female employment was envisioned as temporary support for unmarried women; marriage was how women were really expected to "earn" their money. Many New Deal programs reflected this conception of female work, but the Social Security Act of 1935 (SSA) was one of the clearest.

A monthly check to you for the rest of your life, beginning
when you are 65, 1935.

The SSA was promoted as an earned entitlement — not public
assistance. Recipients were envisioned as able-bodied, mostly
white, male workers who were insuring themselves against
future circumstances. Women were not part of this vision, as
Congress made abundantly clear when it chose the SSA over
a far more evenhanded bill also pending before Congress. This
alternative legislation, the Workers Unemployment and Social
Insurance Act, would have provided old-age, unemployment,
and health benefits for all wage workers regardless of age, race,

Why the Workers' Unemployment Insurance Bill? How
It Can Be Won, 1933.

sex, origin, or politics. Instead, Congress enacted the SSA.
This act excluded most women, as well as a large percentage of
non-white workers, through the provisions omitting part-time,
seasonal, agricultural, domestic, philanthropic, and government
employees including teachers and self-employed workers — the
jobs typically held by women and people of color.[81]

Four years after passing the SSA, Congress amended the
act to provide for women, but in their role as wives rather than
workers.[82] Under the amendments, women were eligible for
Social Security benefits based on their husbands' earnings and
would receive support when their breadwinning husband died

or retired.[83] The act also incentivized men to marry by ensuring they would receive 50 percent more Social Security income at retirement (through Social Security payments to the man's wife) than they would receive if they remained single.[84]

The SSA amendments were modeled on the traditional marital bargain. Men received a government pension for working, while women received a pension for marrying a man who worked. If a woman's husband died before her children were grown, the government would assume his role and provide cash assistance. If she was widowed later in life, she would receive a portion of her husband's Social Security benefits. Today, the implications of the government's decision to support women through marriage, not employment, remain substantial.

Nearly a hundred years after the SSA was enacted, women still have worse employment prospects than men and are significantly more likely to be poor. The average woman earns only 83 cents for every dollar earned by a man. She also earns approximately $10,000 less per year than her male counterpart and $500,000 less over the course of her working life.[85] Lower wages also mean the average female worker receives a substantially smaller Social Security check. In 2017, the average monthly Social Security benefit of a retired man was $1,503, while the average monthly benefit of a retired woman was $1,196. This inequality is known as the gender wage gap.

The SSA addresses this wage gap by permitting a low- or non-earning wife to receive Social Security benefits based off her husband's higher salary. However, this solution does nothing to remedy the underlying problem of female wage and employment discrimination. Rather, by obscuring the true extent of female employment discrimination, the SSA helps perpetuate it.[86] In 2019, 43 percent of women received Social Security benefits based on their husband's earnings.[87] In 2095, it is estimated that 25 percent of women will still rely on their husband's earnings in their Social Security benefits calculations.[88] That means, for the next seventy-five years, at least one-quarter of American women are expected to have fewer job opportunities and receive lower wages than their male peers and to rely on marriage for their long-term financial security.[89]

Marriage and Tax Benefits

By linking government support with marriage, the SSA encourages female economic dependency. The federal tax code is similar. Like the SSA, the tax code rewards couples willing to assume the traditional marital roles of male wage earner and female dependent. When a high earner marries a lower- or non-earning spouse, marriage significantly reduces their average tax rate. This can mean thousands of dollars in tax savings. In fact, the marriage tax "bonus" can be as high as 21 percent of the couple's total income. However, not all married couples receive tax benefits. Similar-earning spouses can face a marriage penalty, meaning they pay more taxes as a couple than they did as individuals.[90]

The tax code turns women's typically lower earnings into a benefit and can disincentivize female employment entirely. Because most married couples will file jointly, their income gets lumped together on their return. This can pull the higher earner's income into a lower tax rate. But this lumping together may also mean that the lower-earning spouse's income is taxed at a higher rate than it was when she was unmarried. Consequently, after marriage, and especially after the birth of children, it may no longer be financially beneficial for the lower-earning partner

*"'Single'? With this kind of income?
Oh, have I got a dependent for you!"*

Tax examiner cartoons and comics.

to work. A relatively low-earning spouse, typically the wife, may be taxed at such a high rate after marriage that the amount she receives after taxes doesn't come close to covering childcare. In such instances, wives would literally be paying to work. As a result, many women make the financially reasonable decision to quit the workforce and rely entirely on their husband's earnings.

The Marriage Cure

Both the tax code and the SSA treat marriage as a solution to female financial inequality and as a cure for female poverty. Scholars have dubbed this solution the marriage cure. For the

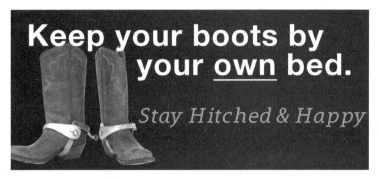

Pro-marriage billboard

past thirty years, it has been a major part of US welfare policy. In 1996, Congress passed the Personal Responsibility Work Opportunity Reconciliation Act (PRWORA).[91] The act cited declining marriage rates as the primary cause of child poverty and intergenerational poverty and authorized states to use federal and state Temporary Assistance to Needy Families (TANF) funds to encourage welfare recipients to marry.[92] Initially, these funds were used for pro-marriage expenditures such as billboards, handbooks, marital education programs, and relationship skills classes. Then, over the following decade, the money spent on pro-marriage, anti-poverty efforts increased. In 2000, the US Department of Health and Human Services authorized $10 million to be used to reward states with the greatest growth in the proportion of children living in homes headed by a married couple. In 2002 and 2003, it allocated $90 million to marriage-related research and demonstration projects, and in 2006, Congress reauthorized PRWORA and appropriated an annual $150 million in federal money (for five years) for state marriage promotion efforts.[93]

During this period, states also funded marriage promotion efforts, and some even paid poor people to marry.[94] Under Wisconsin's marriage promotion or "bridefare" program, couples

Marriage and relationship tip billboard.

on welfare received an extra $80 per month if they married, and in West Virginia, they received an extra $100.[95] Similarly, under Minnesota's program, married parents were allowed to exclude more income from their welfare benefit calculations than unmarried parents, which increased the size of their welfare payments.[96] These financial incentives convinced some couples to marry, but they were not the poverty solution Congress had envisioned. Poor husbands can't solve female poverty. As law professor Angela Onwuachi-Willig notes, "At a most basic level, if Congress wants to institute a marriage cure to poverty, it must support such efforts by creating jobs for the potential future spouses of women welfare recipients."[97] Until Congress makes these changes, encouraging poor women to marry will do more harm than good.

In her 2012 book, *The End of Men*, journalist Hannah Rosin highlights this problem when she describes a grocery store encounter with a young woman named Bethanny. Bethanny was a single mother running an in-home day care and studying to become a nurse. Rosin describes her as a woman in a precarious financial position, forced to haggle over supermarket coupons and snacks but intent on financial improvement. Bethanny is economically better off than the women in the bridefare programs, but not by much. If marriage were an obvious financial benefit, it is likely she would have married. However, her conversation with Rosin underscores the danger of encouraging low-income women like Bethanny to wed their most likely marriage prospects — similarly low-income men.

The father of Bethanny's child was a man named Calvin. Calvin was a sporadically employed house painter who rarely contributed money to Bethanny or their daughter. When Rosin asked Bethanny why she didn't marry Calvin, both she and her daughter laughed. Bethanny then pointed to her shopping cart and explained that marrying Calvin would mean "one fewer granola bar for us." Bethanny believed that without good job prospects and a stable income, marrying Calvin was financially harmful, and she was probably correct.

In modern America, individual financial security is largely based on a person's "employability." Marriage to a person with the education, skills, and experience to succeed in a competitive labor pool can be beneficial, but when one or both of the parties lack employability, like a large majority of welfare recipients, marriage is unlikely to provide security and stability. Poor women tend to have lower levels of education and work experience than richer women and, if they marry at all, are likely to marry men who are also low-wage earners. As family law professors Naomi Cahn and June Carbone have explained, "Practically, this means that while marriage is a source of strength for couples who can trade off childcare and workforce participation in ways that allow the family to marshal the resources necessary for investment in children and in adult 'employability,' it can be a threat to working class families."[98] Although the government has long assumed marriage reduces poverty, there is little support for this conclusion.

Today, one of the most comprehensive marriage promotion programs created under PRWORA, the Supporting Healthy

Marriage project, is widely regarded as a failure. The program was a rigorous multiyear, multisite program that provided marriage education to low-income married couples. It included six thousand couples, provided four to five months of classes and programs per couple, and cost more than $50 million or approximately $9,100 per couple. However, despite the generous funding and the dozens of hours of programs and services each participating couple received, the treatment and control groups had the same likelihood of divorce.[99] The program was a fiasco, and even the study's authors concluded that it would be "worthwhile [to consider] whether this amount of money could be spent in ways that bring about more substantial effects on children and families."[100] Such advice has largely gone unheeded; promoting marriage as a poverty cure remains politically popular. In 2016, then presidential candidate Jeb Bush described marriage as "the most effective anti-poverty program." In 2017, Florida senator Marco Rubio declared marriage "the greatest tool to lift children and families from poverty," and most recently, in 2021, Missouri senator Josh Hawley released his "pro family and pro work" plan, which sought to encourage marriage, and thus reduce poverty, by giving married couples double the child tax credit available to single parents.[101]

Government benefits can incentivize women, particularly poor women, to marry, but most would profit more from policies that directly address the causes of poverty — the lack of livable wages, family leave, and health care — than those promoting marriage.[102] Moreover, as history demonstrates, linking vital government benefits to marriage can encourage harmful and exploitive marriages while reducing the government's interest in finding more effective solutions to the economic, gender, and racial inequality perpetuating these problems. Finally, conditioning government benefits on marriage is also problematic, because it encourages couples to marry for reasons other than love. If love is the purpose of marriage, then attaching government benefits impedes this goal. Common sense dictates that the more benefits are combined with marriage, the more people will marry for these advantages.[103] If Americans truly believe people should marry for love, then the government should stop giving them so many non-love reasons to marry.

chapter three

The Power Couple:
Marrying for Status and Power

The only thing worse than smug married
couples: lots of smug married couples.

— BRIDGET JONES

In the novel *Bridget Jones's Diary*, the protagonist, a single, thirty-something Londoner, refers to her coupled friends as "smug marrieds." Jones uses the term to indicate the higher status that married couples enjoy, and although she rejects the idea that "marrieds" are better than "singletons" (her name for single people), she acknowledges the very real connection between marriage and status. Despite her outward disdain for the smug marrieds, Bridget Jones wants nothing more than to join their ranks.

After publication of *Bridget Jones's Diary*, the word *singleton* quickly became part of modern English vernacular. When author Helen Fielding was asked about the term's origin, she explained, "A friend made it up for a party: singletons in one hotel, marrieds in another!" She then noted that the reason she liked it so much, and included it in her novels, was that it was a positive substitute for *spinster*. Fielding described *spinster* — the long-standing term for an unmarried woman — as "horrible," because of its "connotations of spinning wheels failure." *Singleton*, she suggested, is a much more positive word and has the added benefit of "appl[ying] to both men and women."[1]

Spinsters and Bachelors in Colonial America

Fielding is far from the first to note the deep-seated connection between non-marriage and failure. For centuries, marriage has been a marker of status. Married people were treated with dignity and admiration, while the unmarried were relegated to the social bottom.[2] This disdain applied to both men and women, but the reasons were different.

In colonial America, unmarried women were seen as failures. As marriage historian Elizabeth Abbott notes, "The spinster was never to forget — nor to be forgiven for — the fact that she was not a wife."[3] Rebecca Dickinson, an unmarried woman living in Hatfield, Massachusetts, during the late eighteenth century, was frequently the target of such scorn and detailed it in her private journals. In one entry from 1787, Dickinson writes, "How often have they hissed and wagged their heads at me by reason of my solitary life." In another entry, she recounts a mortifying conversation with "[a] woman who had been exceedingly prosperous in the world [who] asked me whether I was not Sorry that I Did not marry when I was young." Dickinson was "thunderstruck" by the question. She was a skilled and financially successful dressmaker, and she angrily responded, "My affairs might be in a worse situation." Still, despite this outward bravado, the incident left her heartbroken and feeling "more than ever" like a "poor bird that was picked of all its feathers." Dickinson writes that after the encounter she "cried all the day without cessation." However, her distress was more than just a reaction to the woman's rudeness. Dickinson feared such criticisms were justified, that "to see an old maid after fifty is a Sight that would make any woman wonder." Dickinson never forgot the encounter: "It [was] one of my youthful Days Carryed into old age."[4]

The scorn faced by women like Dickinson was heartrending, but it paled in comparison with the loathing directed at single men. Free of the legal obligations of marriage, colonial communities believed bachelors would seduce single women and then abandon them and their children to become financial burdens on the public. Marriage was what transformed these potentially irresponsible men into dependable husbands and fathers, and those who refused to marry were treated as threats and undeserving of the label "man."[5]

George Washington expressed this view of the unmarried when he advised his nephew to marry so he could "quit the trifling amusements of a boy and assume the more dignified manners of a man."[6] Benjamin Franklin voiced similar sentiments when he variously described bachelors as "not yet a complete man" but only "half a man," as "one half of a pair of scissors," and as having "not nearly the value he would have in a state of union." Franklin's contempt for bachelors is also apparent in his story "The Speech of Polly Baker," in which he highlights the unfairness of charging women for having children out of wedlock but not prosecuting the fathers. In the story, Polly acknowledges that she is an unmarried mother but claims the real criminal is the bachelor who promised to marry her and then abandoned her and their child. She tells her accusers, "Take into your wise consideration, the great and growing number of bachelors in the country, many of whom, from the mean fear of the expenses of a family, have never sincerely and honorably courted a woman in their lives; and by their manner of living leave unproduced (which is little better than murder) hundreds of their posterity to the thousandth generation. Is not this a greater offense against the public good than mine?"[7]

John and Abigail Adams also viewed bachelors with deep disdain. In a 1777 letter to John, Abigail recounts a vicious attack on a merchant whom she pointedly refers to as "a bachelor." The man was accused of hoarding sugar and coffee (commodities she notes "the female part of this state is very loath to give up"), and as a result, he was attacked by an enraged female mob. According to Abigail, the women violently seized the man, "tossed him into the cart," and distributed his goods. Meanwhile, the town's men "stood amazed, silent spectators of the whole transaction." John's lighthearted response to this violence was "the women in Boston begin to think themselves able to serve their country." Neither John nor Abigail expressed any sympathy for the bachelor who had been beaten and robbed. According to Professor Mark Kann, "The remarkable thing about this exchange is that both Adamses were consistently horrified by mob actions, but responded here with humor, apparently because the 'victim' was a bachelor who stood beneath men's contempt and, importantly, beyond protection of law."[8]

In colonial America, marriage was what transformed irresponsible and potentially dangerous males into trustworthy members of society. It is also what qualified them for political rights.[9] In a 1776 letter to Virginia politician Edmund Pendelton, Thomas Jefferson notes this connection between marriage and political rights, writing, "I cannot doubt any attachment to his country in any man who has his family . . . in it . . . I am for extending the right of suffrage (or in other words the rights of a citizen) to all who [have] a permanent intention of living in the country. Take what circumstances you please as evidence of this, either having resided a certain time, or having a family or having property any or all of them."[10]

At the constitutional convention, George Mason also noted the connection between marriage and political rights when he argued that voting should not be limited to landholders. He stated:

> A freehold is the qualification in England and hence it is imagined to be the only proper one. The true idea [is] that every man having evidence of attachment to and permanent common interest with the society ought to share in its rights and privileges. Was this qualification restrained to freeholders? Does no other kind of property but land evidence a common interest in the proprietor? Does nothing besides property make a permanent attachment? Ought . . . the parent of a number of children whose fortunes are to be pursued in his own country to be viewed as suspicious characters and unworthy to be trusted with the common rights of their fellow citizens?

Alexander Hamilton took these ideas even further when he suggested that marriage and fatherhood were crucial qualifications for political leadership because such men were the least likely to abuse political power. A father, explained Hamilton, would not choose "the precarious enjoyment of rank and power" or participate in a "system which would reduce his posterity . . . to slavery and ruin." Instead, he would approach the future with caution and his children would serve as "the dearest pledges of [his] patriotism." Hamilton argued that marriage made men trustworthy, and that citizens would have the greatest confidence in a leader who was "the father of children to whom the ties of nature and habit have attached."

Marriage as Political Alliance

Marriage demonstrated suitability for political rights and power, but it could also confer power more directly. Politically strategic marriages were not uncommon in colonial America, and one of the most famous examples is that of Alexander Hamilton and Elizabeth Schuyler. Thanks to Lin-Manuel Miranda's musical *Hamilton*, the story of Hamilton marrying for political advantage is well known. In one song, Angelica Schuyler sings about this marital motivation:

> *He's after me because I'm a Schuyler sister*
> *That elevates his status*
> *I'd have to be naive to set that aside*
> *Maybe that is why I introduce him to Eliza*
> *Now that's his bride*

Marriage gave Hamilton access to the powerful Schuyler family, and this alliance helped him become one of the most politically influential men of his era. However, although the Hamilton-Schuyler marriage is one of the most famous, some of the most common political marriages of the eighteenth century were those between white fur traders and Native

Family members of Jean-Baptiste and Pelagie Faribault, circa 1850. Pictured are their son Alexander (standing at left); their grandson George (seated at left); and George's bride, Euphrasine St. Antoine (seated at center). Jean-Baptiste is seated on the far right. Father Augustin Ravoux stands between Jean-Baptiste and Euphrasine.

women.[11] As historian Catherine Denial writes, "A central skill of any successful fur trader was an eye for opportunity, especially when it came to judging which alliances would generate the most financial and political gain."[12] White fur traders were eager to marry into politically powerful Native families, while many Native women were equally interested in the political and economic benefits of having an American husband. The marriage of Jean-Baptiste Faribault, a white trader, with Elizabeth Pelagie Ainse, a Dakota woman, is illustrative of such a politically advantageous marriage.

Jean-Baptiste and Pelagie were married in 1805 when the Dakota were a powerful tribe occupying large areas of Minnesota and Wisconsin. Through marriage, Jean-Baptiste

View of Wita Tanka (Pike's Island) and Fort Snelling from Mendota. Painting by Edward Kirkbride Thomas, circa 1850.

gained access to the tribe's valuable hunting lands and a close connection to the tribe.[13] Pelagie, in turn, gained access to the territory's increasingly important white community.[14] In 1819, these connections became especially valuable when Colonel Henry Leavenworth arrived in the Minnesota territory seeking land for the construction of a new fort needed to halt Britain's westward expansion and disrupt its long dominance of the fur trade. Leavenworth quickly identified a desirable location for the intended fort. However, the land was part of the Dakota Territory, and Leavenworth needed help negotiating with the tribe. He sought the assistance from the Faribaults, who then successfully negotiated a fifteen-acre parcel of land for the desired fort. In return for this aid, the couple received a parcel of property known as Pike's Island. Then, seventeen years after the Faribaults were gifted Pike's Island, the US attempted to take it back.

The government claimed the 1837 Treaty of St. Peters, which negotiated the cession of land in Wisconsin and Minnesota, included Pike's Island. The Faribaults vehemently disagreed, and when they learned of the government's plan to steal their land, they quickly took action. They contacted their friend Samuel Stambaugh, the Indian agent out of Green Bay (who had helped negotiate the 1837 treaty), and had him advise the government that it would be wise to back off. In a letter to J. R. Poinsett, the US secretary of war, Stambaugh warned that "the Faribault family is the most powerful and influential among the Sioux Indians" and that angering them could have dire consequences. He further noted, "It is families of this description who do much good or much evil among the Indians with whom they are connected by bonds of blood; and [the] government would save much blood and treasure, if proper pains were taken to secure their friendship."[15] Poinsett got the message. Instead of taking the Faribaults' land, the government paid for it.[16] Through marriage, a frontier fur trader and his Dakota wife had become powerful enough to intimidate the US government.

The Political Influence of Wives

Pike's Island had been gifted to Pelagie in her own name, in accordance with Dakota custom and tradition.[17] As a Dakota woman, Pelagie possessed political rights separate from her husband and her marriage. Pelagie's white contemporaries rarely had such power. In early America, women's political influence was grounded in marriage. This was a significant limitation. Still, the power women wielded as wife could be substantial. In fact, many of the founders, including John Adams, believed that while men cast the votes, it was their wives who determined for what and for whom they voted. Adams even predicted it would be married women, not men, who ultimately decide whether a "Republican government is practicable in a nation or not."[18]

Portrait of a young Abigail Adams by Benjamin Blyth, painted in 1766.

John's wife, Abigail, agreed with her husband that women's political influence derived from marriage. However, she was significantly less sanguine about this fact. Abigail feared that marriage-based political rights were too precarious and that many husbands would ignore their wives' concerns and interests. In her famous letter to John regarding the rights of women, she suggested that women should be granted rights as individuals and not forced to rely on marriage:

In the new code of laws which I suppose it will be necessary for you to make, I desire you would remember the ladies and be more generous and favorable to them than your ancestors. Do not put such unlimited power into the hands of the husbands. Remember, all men would be tyrants if they could. If particular care and attention is not paid to the ladies, we are determined to foment a rebellion, and will not hold ourselves bound by any laws in which we have no voice or representation . . . That your Sex are Naturally Tyrannical is a Truth so thoroughly established as to admit of no dispute, but such of you as wish to be happy willingly give up the harsh title of Master for the more tender and endearing one of Friend. Why then, not put it out of the power of the vicious and the Lawless to use us with cruelty and indignity with impunity. Men of Sense in all Ages abhor those customs which treat us only as the vassals of your Sex. Regard us then as Beings placed by providence under your protection and in imitation of the Supreme Being make use of that power only for our happiness.[19]

Adams ignored his wife's suggestion and, in doing so, proved her point.

Marriage was a risky basis upon which to ground women's political rights. Still, the power women gained through marriage could be significant. In the 1830s, Alexis de Tocqueville traveled the United States and recorded his impressions of the American democratic experiment — including the role of women. De Tocqueville noted that American women forfeited many legal rights by choosing to marry but concluded that marriage remained to their advantage. "I do not hesitate to avow that although the women of the United States are confined within the narrow circle of domestic life, and their situation is in some respects one of extreme dependence . . . I have nowhere seen woman occupying a loftier position." De Tocqueville even suggested it was because of the limitations imposed by marriage that American women wielded such power and influence. He wrote:

> The Americans do not think that man and woman have either the duty or the right to perform the same offices, but they show an equal regard for both their respective parts; and though their lot is different, they consider both of them as beings of equal value. They do not give to the courage of woman the same form or the same direction as to that of man, but they never doubt her courage; and if they hold that man and his partner ought not always to exercise their intellect and understanding in the same manner, they at least believe the understanding of the one to be as sound as that of the other, and her intellect to be as clear. Thus, then, while they have allowed the social inferiority of woman to continue, they have done all they could to raise her morally and intellectually to the level of man; and in this respect they appear to me to have excellently understood the true principle of democratic improvement.

De Tocqueville also credited American wives as the reason for America's unexpected success. "If I were asked, now that I am drawing to the close of this work, in which I have spoken of so many important things done by the Americans, to what the singular prosperity and growing strength of that people ought mainly to be attributed, I should reply: To the superiority of their women."[20]

Marriage as a Race Changer

Marriage helped women regain some of the status and power denied due to their sex, and in the pre–Civil War period, some African Americans used marriage in a similar manner. During the colonial period, free persons of color who possessed less than a specified degree of black blood, usually a quarter or eighth, were designated "white" and entitled to legal and social privileges that came with that status. As a result, intermarriage offered black men and women a way to secure preferential racial status for their descendants. This was one reason why colonial whites viewed intermarriage as so threatening.

In 1757, the Virginia reverend Peter Fontaine wrote to his brother in Wales lamenting the practice of intermarriage, stating, "This abominable practice . . . hath polluted the blood of many amongst us." Fontaine was particularly distraught by the fact that under the law, children of mixed-race families could eventually become white. As Fontaine noted, descendants "but three generations removed from the black father or mother, may, by the indulgence of the laws of the country, intermarry with the white people, and actually do every day so marry."[21]

State anti-miscegenation laws were enacted to prevent interracial marriages and the "dangers" Fontaine noted, but these laws could be flouted. In 1819 a Scotsman named James Flint traveled to America and spent eighteen months in the town of Jeffersonville, Indiana. Shortly after arriving in Indiana, Flint wrote a letter describing how a "negro man and a white woman came before the squire of a neighbouring township, for the purpose of being married." Initially, the official refused to conduct the wedding service, citing the state's prohibition on "all sexual intercourse between white and coloured people." Then, a short time later, he changed his mind. The official "suggested, that if the woman could be qualified to swear that there was black blood in her, the law would not apply." According to Flint, "The hint was taken, and the lancet was immediately applied to the Negro's arm. The loving bride drank the blood, made the necessary oath, and his honour joined their hands, to the great satisfaction of all parties."[22]

Marriages, such as the one Flint described, were one way mixed-race individuals were conceived. Sadly, many others were created from non-consensual sexual relations. Nevertheless, the result of both scenarios was that despite interracial marriage bans, there were many mixed-race individuals in antebellum America who appeared white or at least possibly white. For these children, marriage became an important way of securing the racial privileges they were not legally entitled to possess. The case of Gideon Gibson Jr. is illustrative.

Gideon Gibson Jr.'s father, Gideon Gibson Sr., was a free black man who arrived in the South Carolina backcountry in the 1730s. At the time, South Carolina officials believed he had come to plot a slave revolt, and the governor was so fearful of Gibson Sr.'s intentions that he demanded a personal audience. Gibson Sr. complied with this request but explained to the governor that his sympathies were with white people, not black. To prove this point, Gibson noted he was a landowner, had a white wife, and even owned slaves himself. These facts reassured the governor, who then declared that the Gibsons were "not Negroes nor Slaves but Free people" and granted them hundreds of acres of land to induce them to remain in the state.[23]

Thirty years later, Gibson Sr.'s mixed-race son, Gideon Gibson Jr., was a wealthy landowner and a leader of the South Carolina "regulators" — a group that opposed the taxation and fee system imposed by colonial officials. During one regulator protest, a constable and state militia members were injured, and the Charleston authorities sent Colonel Gabriel Powell to arrest Gibson for his role in the protest. However, upon reach-

Randall L. Gibson, Confederate soldier, US senator from Louisiana, and great-grandson of Gideon Gibson Jr.

ing Gibson, Powell's men refused to arrest him. Instead, they abandoned Powell and joined the regulators. Powell was humiliated. In retaliation, he sought to have Gibson declared black and "subject him to the penalties of the negro law."[24] He was unsuccessful. Although the Gideons were descended from a black man, they had become, legally, white.

In 1783, Charleston merchant and Revolutionary War leader Henry Laurens cited the Gibson case as proof that intermarriage could remove the legal disabilities of race. Laurens wrote, "Reasoning from the colour carries no conviction. By perseverance the black may be blanched and the 'stamp of Providence' effectually effaced." Laurens did not actually consider Gibson white. In fact, he believed mixed-race individuals like Gibson, regardless of their complexion, "ought to continue a separate people." Nevertheless, he recognized that because Gibson looked white, was married to a white woman, and was treated as white, he was, for all intents and purposes, white.[25]

Similar reasoning was used in the 1835 South Carolina Court of Appeal case *State v. Cantey*, in which the court famously declared that "a slave cannot be a white man." The *Cantey* court's statement was not about skin color. Rather, it was a recognition that classification as white or black depended upon acceptance within white society.[26] An enslaved person, no matter how light their skin, was not a member of white society and must be black. Conversely, a free person accepted by white society must be white. There were several means of demonstrating white social acceptance, but as *Cantey* highlighted, marriage was one of the most effective.[27]

Cantey involved the racial status of three mixed-race men and, specifically, whether their black ancestry precluded them from testifying against a white man. The heritage of the men was not in question. It was accepted that all three descended from a mixed-race man. Nevertheless, the court held that the men were white because their ancestor had been treated as white. As the court explained, the men's "maternal grandfather . . . although of a dark complexion, had been recognized as a white man, received into society, and exercised political privileges." Therefore, his descendants were legally white. According to the court, "For a person of ambiguous appearance, evidence of reception in society and exercise of legal and political rights could overcome evidence of negro ancestry."[28] It then cited the grandfather's marriage with a white woman as conclusive evidence the man had been accepted as white.[29]

Racial determination cases post-*Cantey* further confirmed that marriage could secure a mixed-race person's designation as white. In an illustrative case from 1840, a Louisiana man named Stephen Boullemet brought a slander suit against an acquaintance for starting a rumor that he was "negro" and imperiling his impending marriage to a white woman. The case turned on whether Boullemet was, in fact, black. To refute this racial allegation, Boullemet presented evidence of acceptance by white society. He called witnesses from the white community of St. Helena, Santo Domingo, where he was raised, to testify that he was "received in good circles of society — He was received as a white man."[30] He also presented specific evidence regarding his mother's race.

During the trial, witnesses testified that after his marriage, Boullemet's father remained an accepted member of Santo Domingo's white society and that such acceptance would not have occurred if Boullemet's mother was black. As one witness explained, "If a white person was to unite to a coloured woman he was immediately considered as degraded." Boullemet argued that because his father remained part of white society after his marriage, his mother must have been white.[31] Boullemet won his case, yet it is highly unlikely his mother was white. In fact, her mixed-race status was so obvious that during the trial, Boullemet was forced to concede she might have been "Indian." Ultimately, his mother's dark complexion and ambiguous racial status didn't matter.[32] By marrying a prominent white husband, she was accepted into white society and became white.

The case of the Wharton family of Stafford County, Virginia, is particularly illustrative of how marriage could change a person's racial status. The Whartons were a formerly enslaved family who had purchased their freedom around 1830. After gaining their freedom, the family chose to remain in Virginia. However, this was forbidden under the state's 1806 removal law requiring all

formerly enslaved people freed after May 1, 1806, to leave the
commonwealth. Any person who remained in Virginia more
than one year after their enslavement ended could be put on trial
and, if found guilty, re-enslaved and sold. The 1806 law posed a
real threat to the Whartons, but in 1833, fifty-one members of
Stafford County's white community submitted a petition to the
Virginia legislature arguing that the 1806 law did not apply to
the Whartons and that they should be permitted to remain.

Unlike the mixed-race individuals in *Cantey* and *Boullemet*,
the Whartons had personally been enslaved and unquestionably
met the *Cantey* definition of black. Nevertheless, the Stafford
petition asked for a declaration that the Whartons were "white
persons" based on the family's appearance and the fact that
their most intimate social connections — their marriages —
were with white spouses.[33] Shockingly, the legislature granted
the request. Despite all evidence to the contrary, it decreed the
Whartons were "not negroes or mulattoes, but white persons,
although remotely descended from a coloured woman." The
Whartons were then permitted to stay.[34]

Intermarriage could help people of color change their racial
status, and some individuals, particularly those of mixed racial
heritage, explicitly sought out this benefit. In 1821, newspapers
in New York, Pennsylvania, and Massachusetts ran the article
"A New Chance for Fortune Hunters," which noted the many
wealthy, mixed-race Chickasaw women were explicitly looking
for white husbands. The article described many of these women
as "almost white" and explained they "*prefer white husbands*,"
because they sought to live as white wives. The article then
encouraged white men who had been "unsuccessful speculators
in the trade of matrimony" to consider these "handsome women,"
noting they were "rich in cattle, and horses, and . . . land."[35]

The mixed-race women of the Chickasaw Nation used
marriage to secure their desired racial status, and they were far

Abel Stearns and Arcadia Bandini.

from alone. In 1841, Arcadia Bandini married Abel Stearns for similar reasons. Arcadia was the daughter of one of the wealthiest landowning families in the former Mexican territory of California. The family claimed to be white but were most likely of mixed Spanish and indigenous heritage. As a result, their hold on this professed racial designation was tenuous.[36] Arcadia solved this problem by marrying Abel Stearns — a man of indisputable whiteness.

Contemporary accounts describe Stearns as exceedingly ugly. He was severely pockmarked, had long knife scar running down one cheek, and his long, horse-like face had earned him the nickname Cara de Caballo. He was also nearly thirty years older than Arcadia.[37] However, he was one of the few unquestionably white men in the California Territory. Stearns traced his ancestry back to the Massachusetts Puritans, and this pedigree made him a desirable marriage prospect. By marrying Stearns, Arcadia cemented her racial status and ensured her acceptance into white, Californian society.[38]

One of the most famous examples of marrying for racial status involves the daughters of Richard Johnson, a Kentucky

AN AFFECTING SCENE IN KENTUCKY.

Racist political cartoon depicting the Chinn daughters.

congressman and the ninth vice president of the United States (1837–1841). In the early 1800s, Richard Johnson had two daughters, Imogene and Adaline, with an enslaved woman named Julia Chinn. Johnson never freed Julia, but he freed their daughters and sought to have the girls accepted into white society.[39] This goal was highly controversial. In fact, in 1829, the objections to Johnson's relationship with Chinn, whom he publicly referred to as his wife, and his open acknowledgment of his mixed-race daughters was so significant it caused him to lose his Senate seat. Johnson's support of his mixed-race daughters was also used against him during his campaign for the vice presidency. In one particularly racist editorial, penned by partisan journalist Duff Green, Julia Chinn was described as "a jet-black, thick-lipped, odiferous negro wench," and Johnson was condemned for rearing "a family of children whom he endeavored to force upon society as equals."[40] Due to such attacks, Johnson failed to secure enough electoral votes to become vice president, and he is the only vice president in history to be voted into office by the Senate. Despite these political setbacks, Johnson's ultimate goal was achieved. Shortly before becoming vice president, and in exchange for large dowries of valuable farmland, Johnson's mixed-race daughters married well-respected white men. From that moment onward, the Chinn daughters and their descendants were officially regarded as white.[41]

Marriage helped mixed-race individuals secure the legal and social benefits they were denied due to race. In antebellum America, this use of marriage was almost exclusively confined to free persons, but once America entered the Civil War, marriage also helped enslaved individuals gain their freedom. In 1862, Congress passed the Militia Act, which encouraged African American enlistment by guaranteeing freedom to the enlisting soldier as well as "his mother, and his wife and children." In passing this act, Congress recognized that many enslaved men were hesitant to enlist because the wives and children they left behind could be subject to retaliation for the man's desertion. The Militia Act addressed this concern by ensuring enlisting men could take their families with them when they escaped and that these women and children would also be freed.[42]

The connection between marriage and African American freedom continued after the Civil War and became an important part of the debates surrounding the Civil Rights Act of 1866. During these debates, freedom was frequently discussed in relation to marital and familial rights. During one discussion, Senator Jacob Howard of Michigan asked, "What are the attributes of a freeman according to the universal understanding of the American people?" He then answered, "The right of having a family, a wife, children, home."[43] Representative John Kasson of Iowa made a similar point when he declared, "There are three great fundamental natural rights of human society, which you cannot take away without striking a vital blow at the rights of white men as well as black." He listed the rights of a husband to his wife — the marital relation — as the first of these rights.[44] Illinois congressman John Farnsworth echoed these ideas. He asked, "What vested rights [are] so high or so sacred as man's rights to himself, his wife and children, to his liberty and to the fruits of his own industry?"

After the Civil War, many freedmen and -women eagerly embraced marriage and the freedom it represented. Upon receiving the right to marry, one Virginia member of the Colored Infantry proclaimed, "I praise God for this day! I have long been praying for it. The Marriage Covenant is at the foundation of all our rights. In slavery we could not have *legalized* marriage; *now* we have it." A Mississippi chaplain made a similar connection between marriage and freedom when he noted he saw a "very decided improvement in the Social and domestic feelings of those married by the authority and protection of Law. It causes them to feel that they are beginning to be regarded and treated as human beings." Henry Bibb, the famed nineteenth-century author and abolitionist who had been born into slavery, also emphasized the connection between marriage and freedom. He wrote, "There are no class of people in the United States who so highly appreciate the legality of marriage as those persons who have been held and treated as property." To throw off the habits of slavery, Bibbs declared, "regular lawful marriage is a most important thing."[45]

Marriage symbolized black people's free status. As Wake County freedman Parker Pool stated, "Dere wuz no marriage — till after the surrender."[46] At the same time, marriage also came to represent black people's worthiness for freedom.[47] Union officers in command of black troops were some of the first to recognize this role of marriage. As historian Nancy Cott notes in her book *Public Vows*, "Supervisors of black soldiers urged the troops to be 'manly' in marital fidelity as they had been in other ways, to 'set an example for their race,' reminding them that 'the

MARRIAGE OF A COLORED SOLDIER AT VICKSBURG BY CHAPLAIN WARREN OF THE FREEDMEN'S BUREAU.

Vicksburg, Mississippi, 1866. This illustration appeared in the June 30, 1866, edition of *Harper's Weekly*. The original drawing was made by the artist Alfred R. Waud (1828–1891).

enemies of the colored race who are opposed to their progress and freedom assert that there is no virtue among them.'"

Many newly freed people acted upon such advice and eagerly married. Some even remarried. One newly freed woman explained her decision to remarry her husband of thirty-five years, stating that she was doing it because "all 'spectable folks is to be married, and we's 'spectable."[48] Unfortunately, the connection between marriage and black worth also meant that the failure to marry was increasingly viewed as a threat to racial acceptance. Recognizing this threat, many black leaders devoted significant time and resources to promoting African American marriage and ensuring it conformed with white expectations. One black preacher exemplified this practice when he admonished his congregation, stating, "Look at de white folks. D'ye eber see a white man want to marry a woman when he had a lawful wife a libing? Neber! I neber heared ob sech a thing in all my life. A white man is 'structed; he knows dat's agin de law and de gospil."[49]

As marriage became "proof" of black respectability, this induced many freedmen and -women to marry, but it also encouraged the black community to exert pressure on those who resisted. In 1867, a Freedman's Bureau official described such tactics, writing:

> The Colored people of this place are trying to make their colored bretheren [sic] pay some respect to themselves and the laws of the country . . . and stop the slave style of living to gather [sic] without being married. A colored man has been promising to marry a girl for the last year [and] has been begging with her most of the time. They have had four times set for marriage, but at each time has put her of[f] with some excuse. The colored men of this place appointed a committee to wait on him and see if they could not influence him to do better.[50]

In remarking on such coercion, law professor Angela Onwuachi-Willig notes that in the postwar period the "connection between marriage and racial acceptance was so powerful that even the 'colonized' defended the civilizing tool of marriage."[51]

Marriage and Social Status

The pressure on African American men and women to marry was intensified by the fact that African American men had few other means of acquiring status. By the mid-nineteenth century, white men were increasingly able to avoid the traditional stigma attached to non-marriage if they were wealthy. In large urban centers like New York, affluent bachelors were admired and even courted. Men's clubs and apartment houses sprang up to cater to these men. These businesses provided unmarried men with the domestic services traditionally performed by a wife but without any of the obligations of marriage. Many residents described this arrangement as paradise. One wealthy bachelor wrote, "Each member is as much at home as if he were in his own castle; the building . . . is kept with the same neatness, exactness, and comfort as a private dwelling. Every member is a master, without any of the cares or troubles of a master."[52]

Wealth could insulate men from the stigma of being unmarried, but for men without money, marriage remained an important status symbol, and this was especially true for African American males. Black men had fewer opportunities to become wealthy and were specifically encouraged, often by the US government, to look to marriage, rather than wealth, as a source of social status. The government hoped that by linking social status to black men's role as husbands and providers it could minimize its own economic responsibility for the newly freed African Americans — especially for black women and children.[53] The lecture series given by General Clinton B. Fisk, head of the Tennessee Freedmen's Bureau, exemplified such governmental efforts. Fisk told his listeners that to "be a man" meant supporting a wife and family and warned that husbands who failed in this regard would lose the love and respect of their wives. "Your wives will not love you if you do not provide bread and clothes for them," he admonished. "They cannot be happy and greet you with a kiss, when you come home, if they are hungry, ragged, and cold."[54] Poor African American men were encouraged to marry for social status, but when wealthy white women did the same, they received a very different reaction.

Until the Civil War, America's wealthy elite had been largely secure in their social superiority. This changed in the postwar period, when a generation of newly rich Americans sought to breach these class barriers.[55] The infamous social battle between

Caroline Astor (left) and Alva Vanderbilt (costumed for one of her masquerade parties).

Mrs. Caroline Astor, a scion of old-money New York, and the newly rich Alva Vanderbilt highlighted this class struggle. It also showed that marriage was how this battle could be won.

In the late nineteenth century, Caroline Astor controlled entry into New York's high society by limiting invitations to her famous balls. Attendees were almost exclusively "Old New York," meaning families whose money was acquired generations earlier by the city's original Dutch and English settlers. "New-money" families, like the Vanderbilts, were not invited to these events.[56] Alva Vanderbilt was unwilling to accept this state of affairs. She was determined to win acceptance into New York society, and she made it her mission to receive an Astor invitation.

Alva's plan began with the construction of a sumptuous mansion on Manhattan's Fifth Avenue. Then, as the home neared completion, Alva planned an extravagant housewarming party to display the new home's wonders.[57] All the prominent

Alva Vanderbilt in costume for one of her fancy dress balls; Vanderbilt Mansion on Fifth Avenue.

men and women of the city were invited, and the New York press predicted the upcoming Vanderbilt ball would be the party of the century. Finally, when anticipation was at its peak, Alva let it slip that Carrie Astor, Caroline Astor's daughter, was not invited. She explained that Mrs. Astor had not "called," meaning she had not recognized Alva socially and therefore, under the social conventions of the period, Alva "couldn't" invite Carrie. Carrie was devasted, and Caroline Astor capitulated. She sent her coachman to the Vanderbilt mansion with her calling card. Alva Vanderbilt responded with an invitation. Through impressive scheming, the Vanderbilt family gained admission into New York's high society. However, Alva didn't want grudging acceptance; she wanted to outrank families like the Astors. So, to beat Caroline Astor, she wed her daughter to a duke.

In 1891, Alva's daughter, Consuelo Vanderbilt, married the Duke of Marlborough and cemented peer marriage as the way for new-money families to bypass the social controls imposed by

Consuelo Vanderbilt on her wedding day.

families like the Astors.[58] For those with millions, peer marriages were easy to arrange. One year after the Marlborough-Vanderbilt wedding, an article in Henry Labouchere's *Truth* magazine noted that "the dream of the New York 'dollar magnates' was to marry English noblemen," and where "one side has to offer a title and the other side money, the dream is easily realized."[59] Rich Americans were wed to European nobility and completely upended the American class structure. As historian Maureen Montgomery writes in her book *Gilded Prostitution*, due to these marriages, it became increasingly common "for some member of [New York's old-moneyed class] to . . . to find some compatriot who is taboo on the other side of the water to be received with open arms in Belgravia and Mayfair."[60]

Between 1870 and 1910, American women accounted for one-tenth of all English peer marriages and one-half of all foreign alliances made by peers. However, as the practice grew, so did the criticisms. In 1902, William T. Stead, a well-known British newspaper editor (and soon-to-be victim of the *Titanic*), criticized aristocratic English husbands for "regard[ing] the American girl as a means of replenishing the exhausted exchequer, a kind of financial resource, like the Income tax." Stead admonished these husbands, but it was the women's actions that truly bothered him. He wrote, "It is not too much to say that where there is no love in the matter, it is only gilded prostitution, infinitely more culpable from the moral point of view than the ordinary vice into which women are often driven by sheer lack of bread." In 1904, the British novelist H. B. Marriott Watson issued a similar rebuke. He described the American women who married for titles as "cold of heart and cool of head" and was appalled that a woman could "allow her personal ambitions to dictate her sexual relations, rather than marrying for love."[61]

American criticisms of these marriages were equally harsh. In 1906, President Theodore Roosevelt wrote, "I thoroly [*sic*] dislike . . . these international marriages . . . which are not . . . even matches of esteem and liking, but which are based upon the sale of the girl for her money and the purchase of the man for his titles." Congress also condemned such unions and even considered passing laws to ban them.[62] Eventually, the dislike of peer marriages became so widespread that heiresses were specifically praised for not marrying aristocrats.

In 1907, the *New York World* published a piece about the marriage of Miss Mills, a Pittsburgh steel heiress, and warmly commended her for picking "a Pittsburgher though she might have had a Duke or even a Prince." In praising her apparent choice of love over money and status, the editors wrote, "She is not marrying young Mr. Phipps for the money that someday he will have. She has plenty already, and more to come than she can ever spend. And she certainly doesn't marry him for social position, because no Mills needs social position from anyone in New York . . . It is just a love match, pure and simple. There is no exchange of wealth for title, no barter of millions for a coronet."

Criticizing women who married for status rather than love was common at the turn of the twentieth century. However, such criticisms implied that most women had a meaningful choice. This was rarely true. Women were expected to marry. Despite the rhetoric about not marrying for status, women's status remained firmly linked to marriage. In her famous novel *The House of Mirth*, Edith Wharton highlights this expectation when the book's protagonist, an upper-class young woman named Lily Bart, complains to a male friend that people are starting to say she should marry. Bart expects sympathy from her friend. Instead he replies, "Well why don't you? . . . Isn't marriage your vocation? Isn't it what you are all brought up for?" As historian Pat Jalland notes, during this period an unmarried woman was still "judged by her contemporaries to be a human failure, condemned to a lonely life of futility, ridicule or humiliation."[63]

The Continuing Political Power of Wives

In the late nineteenth and early twentieth centuries, women's social status remained firmly linked to marriage. Similarly, their political power also remained tied to marriage, and it is no coincidence that opposition to women's suffrage stemmed in part from the fact that the movement sought to base women's political power on their status as individuals rather than as wives.[64] After the Civil War, when the Fourteenth Amendment was being debated in Congress, senators repeatedly dismissed female enfranchisement as unnecessary based on the view that married

women voted through their husbands. As Senator Timothy Howe of Wisconsin explained, unlike the freedmen, women could be denied the vote because "they exercise it by proxy . . . Females send their votes to the ballot box by their husbands or other male friends." Senator Ben Wade of Ohio made a similar argument. He described women's suffrage as superfluous because women were "in high fellowship with those that do govern," by which he meant they had husbands to "act as their agents." Others argued against women's suffrage because they feared giving women the right to vote would detract from their domestic responsibilities like caring for children and managing the household.

Maternalist Feminism

Women eventually received the vote, but the difficulties they encountered convinced many women's rights advocates to focus on issues that aligned with women's roles as wives and mothers. The maternalist feminism movement arose out of this idea.[65] Maternalists argued that on certain issues, especially those relating to child welfare, women were in a superior position to demand political and social reforms. Maternalists concentrated on reforms that would improve the lives of women and children, and they were often highly successful. In the early twentieth century, maternalists achieved wage increases and work hour limits for mothers and children, funded mother's pensions, passed child labor protections, expanded compulsory education, and developed juvenile court systems.[66] They also succeeded in creating the Federal Children's Bureau. Moreover, as law professors Naomi Mezey and Nina Pillard have noted, these achievements were "all the more extraordinary for coming at a time when women did not have the vote, and when the country failed to enact social welfare reforms for male industrial workers like those that were emerging in Europe."[67] Maternalism was a successful reform strategy, yet it came at a significant cost.

To achieve their goal, maternalists were willing to limit women's political power and influence to family issues. Historian Lisa D. Brush describes this as "feminism for hard times." By accepting domesticity as the primary source of women's political power, maternalists gained important victories, but they also further entrenched gender inequality and female dependency. During the 1920s and '30s, women's political successes were almost entirely based on their status as wives and mothers.[68]

Given the link between marriage and female political power, it is not surprising that, during this period, the congressional widow emerged as an important political figure.[69] In 1922, shortly after the death of California congressman John Nolan, the California Republican party approached his widow, Mae Ellen Nolan, and encouraged her to run for Nolan's congressional seat. As Nolan's wife, Mae Ellen was assumed to share her husband's political beliefs, thus she was viewed as the ideal replacement.[70] Mae Ellen accepted the nomination, and during her campaign she repeatedly emphasized that as Nolan's wife she was both uniquely qualified and morally obligated to continue his political work. In one speech she declared, "I owe it to the memory of my husband to carry on his work . . . His minimum-wage bill, child labor laws, and national education bills all need to be in the hands of someone who knew him and his plans intimately. No one knows better than I do his legislative agenda." This political strategy was successful and, in a special election held to finish her husband's term and serve the next one, Mae Ellen defeated six opponents and became the fourth woman elected to Congress.

Mae Ellen's political success was not unique. Between 1922 and 1934 eight additional widows were elected to Congress, and it became clear these women had a strong advantage over

Mae Ellen Nolan.

other female candidates. In a study of first-time House candidates elected between 1916 and 1993, 84 percent of widows who
ran for office won, while only 14 percent of other non-widowed
women were victorious. In fact, of the first one hundred women
elected to Congress, more than one-third were widows.[71] In her
1978 study on female political success, political scientist Diane
Kincaid quipped that "for women aspiring to serve in Congress,
the best husband has been a dead husband, most preferably one
serving in Congress at the time of his demise."[72]

The outsized success of congressional widows demonstrated
that well into the twentieth century female political power
remained most acceptable when it was linked to women's roles
as wives and mothers. By claiming the desire to fulfill their
husbands' legacies, rather than their own ambitions, these
women conformed to accepted gender roles. However, by the
mid-twentieth century, this connection between female political
power and marriage became increasingly problematic. In 1964,
almost two hundred years after John Adams refused his wife's
request to "remember the ladies," Congress used nearly identical
reasoning to justify its refusal to include women in the Civil

Phyllis Schlafly demonstrating against the Equal Rights Amendment in front of the White House, Washington, DC, February 4, 1977.

Rights Act. The act's opponents reiterated the centuries-old argument that women did not need this political protection because marriage gave them power and influence over their husbands.

During the debate on the women's rights amendment to the Civil Rights Act, Representative Emmanuel Cellar argued against the inclusion of women, stating:

> Mr. Chairman, I heard with a great deal of interest the statement of the gentleman from Virginia that women are in the minority. Not in my house. I can say as a result of 49 years of experience — and I celebrate my 50th wedding anniversary next year — that women, indeed, are not in the minority in my house. As a matter of fact, the reason I would suggest that we have been living in such harmony, such delightful accord for almost half a century is that I usually

have the last two words, and those words are, "Yes, dear." Of course, we all remember the famous play by George Bernard Shaw, *Man and Superman*; and man was not the superman, the other sex was.[73]

Cellar's speech was met with laughter and agreement.

Marriage provided women with a path to political power, yet it also justified their political exclusion. In the 1970s, the Equal Rights Amendment (ERA) failed in large part due to maternalist feminists, particularly Phyllis Schlafly. Schlafly claimed that the family, as "the basic unit of society . . . is the greatest single achievement in the entire history of women's rights," and that the special power women wielded within the family would be lost with the ERA. These arguments proved persuasive, and the ERA failed.

Marriage and Middle-Class Status

Marriage helped circumvent gender inequality, while simultaneously helping to perpetuate it. The use of marriage to overcome class barriers produced similarly conflicting results. In 1914, car manufacturer Henry Ford announced that he was doubling the minimum rate paid to "[all] married men living with and taking good care of their families."[74] Until this time, male factory workers had earned too little to support a family on a single wage. As a result, wage-earning families were largely excluded from the middle class.[75] Ford's working wage meant married factory workers could now achieve the middle class "ideal" of a working husband and a dependent wife.

Support for the working wage quickly expanded. In the 1930s, social reformers like Katherine Lenroot, chief the US Children's Bureau, described "a living wage for the father" as "the primary essential of child welfare."[76] Similarly, US Women's Bureau director Mary Anderson believed the problems of women's wages and working conditions "could be taken care of if the provider for the family got sufficient wages. Then married women would not be obliged to go to work."[77] Such reformers considered working mothers a threat to children's health and development, and for many families the wife's ability to leave the workforce and become a full-time caretaker was beneficial. Nevertheless, as the sole-provider model became more common, this caused problems for women who wished to remain employed.

The rise of the family wage meant women's paid work was increasingly characterized as either temporary (occurring during the expected short period between the end of school and marriage) or unnecessary. Both reasons were then used to justify paying women lower wages. Married women also faced the additional hurdle that their decision to work was considered harmful for their children. Women were expected to put their family first, and working wives, especially working mothers, were viewed as selfish and irresponsible.

Working women were also viewed as a threat to male social status. The family wage made male middle-class status available to wage-earning men, but it was dependent upon husbands fulfilling the breadwinning role. As Professors Marion Crain and Ken Matheny have noted, "The business of making a living was fundamentally a man's business and women were not welcomed because by competing for what were seen as male jobs they threatened men's breadwinner status." Male and female workers became pitted against each other. Wage-earning men, through their unions, responded to the threat of female workers in three stages. First, they supported safety laws limiting the type of work women could do. Later, they used their superior organizational power to maintain and perpetuate sex-segregated job structures. Finally, they advocated for equal pay for women in an effort to prevent employers from using female labor to undercut the male wage structure.[78] Together, these efforts kept women out of the workforce and ensured that the male breadwinner / female dependent model remained the norm throughout the mid-twentieth century.

The family wage ideology cemented gender disparities; it also helped justify racial prejudices. The family wage made it possible for a working husband to become the sole provider for his wife and children. At the same time, it perpetuated the belief that families that did not conform to the sole-provider model were deviant, lazy, and incompetent. The fact that racial and social prejudice made it harder for members of certain racial groups, particularly black men, to obtain jobs providing a family wage was ignored. Instead, the inability of black husbands to become the sole financial provider for their families was used as evidence of black inferiority.[79] The link between marriage and wage earning helped white men achieve middle-class status, but it simultaneously reduced the social status of black men and their families.

Modern Status Marriages

Under the family wage ideology, both men and women received status from the husband's occupational and financial success, but the reverse was not true. In their 1974 study, "Social Status and the Married Woman," sociologists Marcus Felson and David Knoke demonstrated that the "wife's occupational prestige on [the family's] subjective class was negligible."[80] They demonstrated that only the husband's achievements affected class identification, and today not much has changed.

In the twenty-first century, women continue to derive status from their husbands' success. People may snigger when a man marries his female secretary or when a male doctor marries his female nurse, but such relationships are clichéd rather than taboo. Marriages in which men "marry down" in education or earning power do not harm male status. In fact, these marriages are often status enhancing (for both the husband and wife) because they conform to the traditionally desirable roles of male provider and female dependent. At the same time, a wife's professional success remains largely irrelevant or even detrimental to her husband's social status.

In their 2002 study of class identification of married and employed women and men, sociologists Kazuo Yamaguchi and Yangtao Wang found that when a husband's income is smaller than his wife's, such husbands routinely discount the effect of this income on their class identification. These men would forgo elevating their income status to avoid borrowing their wife's prestige. In explaining this behavior, Yamaguchi and Wang suggested that "borrowing your wife's income status" is psychologically degrading for men because it contradicts the traditional role of the male breadwinner. Yamaguchi and Wang also noted that while higher-earning wives increasingly use their own income in identifying their own class status (a change from the studies conducted in the 1970s), "they do not downplay their spouse's contributions, probably because such a downgrading undermines the traditional role of husbands as family breadwinners."[81]

The psychological effects of male/female income disparities can be a significant factor in marital instability. In their study "When She Brings Home the Status: Wives' Status, Status Leakage and Marital Instability," Canadian professors Alyson Byrne and Julian Barling found that when wives had a higher professional status than their husbands, this often led to resentment and marital instability. Byrne and Barling coined the term *status leakage* to describe what happens when a woman feels her status is lowered on account of her husband's lower level of occupational prestige. They found such women became embarrassed by and resentful of their husbands. These results also have a racial component. The long-standing connection between breadwinner status and black male worth means that status leakage can be especially pronounced for black couples. Studies demonstrate that black women are nearly twice as concerned as white women with their potential husbands' ability to provide a good income and are much less likely to marry unemployed or financially unstable men.[82]

The lopsided gender connection between marriage and status has hindered the creation of egalitarian marriages and stigmatized the role of the supportive male spouse. Men who earn less than their wives feel less secure in these relationships and will compensate by helping less. Studies show that while a wife's economic dependency increases the amount of household labor she performs, a husband's economic dependency reduces his domestic contributions. American men view caretaking as status lowering, thus men who earn less, help less.[83] This doesn't have to be the case.

Women have long derived status from their husband's achievements. If men also believed they benefited from their wives' successes, they might be more willing to assume support-

Julia Letlow.

ive roles. As business school professor Alyson Byrne notes, this is the egalitarian future we want. "When husbands provided their spouses with tangible support — childcare, domestic work, elder support — it signals to the wives, 'I'm supported at home'. . . A dad who takes parental leave is really a great thing, as opposed to a negative thing."[84] Moreover, if men gained status from their wives' successes, the professional achievements of women might also be more widely valued. Instead, women continue to downplay their achievements and hide their ambition behind their roles as wives and mothers. In 2020, Julia Letlow used this age-old strategy when she became the most recent beneficiary of the widow's succession.

Julia ran for office shortly after her husband, Luke Letlow, the congressman-elect for Louisiana's 5th Congressional District seat, died from complications relating to Covid. Like earlier congressional widows, Julia ran as a wife seeking to honor her husband's legacy and continue his work.[85] This strategy worked, and she became the first Republican woman elected to Congress from Louisiana and the only woman among the state's current congressional delegation. In her victory speech, Julia emphasized her domestic obligation, stating, "What was born out of the terrible tragedy of losing my husband, Luke, has become my mission in his honor to carry the torch and serve the good people of Louisiana's 5th District." Julia's political ambitions were aided by her status as a politician's wife.

The recent appointment of Amy Coney Barrett to the Supreme Court provides an even more dramatic example of how marriage and motherhood are still used to make female ambition more acceptable. During the nomination process, Coney Barrett received significant praise for centering her identity as a *mother* before any other personal attribute or accomplishment. When first introducing herself to the nation as the SCOTUS nominee, it is significant that she began by listing all seven of her children. She then added, "While I am a judge, I am better known back home as a room parent, carpool driver, and birthday party planner." As the speech continued, Coney Barrett repeatedly emphasized her role as a wife and mother over all other potential qualifications. In fact, aside from a brief mention of her time clerking for Antonin Scalia, she made no reference to her professional achievements. She appeared to recognize that her nomination to the country's highest court would be most acceptable if it was presented as secondary to her domestic accomplishments.

Marginalizing the Unmarried

One of the greatest costs of linking social, political, and economic status to marriage has been the continuing marginalization of the unmarried. During the fight for same-sex marriage, LGBTQ advocates highlighted the problems with the differential treatment between the married and unmarried. Ultimately, however, the success of the same-sex marriage movement further entrenched the privileged status of marriage.

In the early same-sex marriage case *Perry v. Schwarzenegger*, the court accepted the argument that non-marital relationships "lack the social meaning associated with marriage" and that same-sex marriage bans were effectively "assigning same sex, largely homosexual couples to second class status." In *Obergefell v. Hodges*, the Supreme Court agreed with this assessment and held that only marriage could confer true acceptance of same-sex relationships. Consequently, *Obergefell* reaffirmed the social importance of marriage but simultaneously denigrated the status of the unmarried. As law professor Melissa Murray notes, "According to the [*Obergefell*] majority, life outside of marriage is not only undignified, it is a dismal affair . . . Their intimate lives lack the dignity, transcendence, and purpose that come with knowing that they are a part of a two-person union unlike any other in its importance."[86] The *Obergefell* court is far from alone in this assessment of marriage. As sociologist Andrew Cherlin writes, "Marriage remains the 'ultimate merit badge.'"[87] To be single is still a socially inferior and essentially shameful status.

Today, most forms of discrimination are no longer acceptable, yet it remains largely permissible to deny legal benefits and protections to unmarried people. Title VII of the Civil Rights Act of 1964 does not prohibit workplace discrimination against single people.[88] Similarly, the federal Fair Housing Act of 1968 does not include marital status as a protected class. As a result, the majority of states permit employers to fire single people and landlords to deny them housing. Unmarried couples or families can even be barred from living in entire neighborhoods.[89] Moreover, not only is it permissible to discriminate against the unmarried, it is common. In their research on housing discrimination, Professors Wendy L. Morris, Stacey Sinclair, and Bella M. DePaulo found that landlords repeatedly preferred married people over singles and had no qualms voicing this preference, which they viewed as legitimate and acceptable.[90]

The hundreds of financial benefits available only to the married also remind single people that they are considered less valuable than married people. Admission to a club, charity dinner, or gym is frequently discounted for the married (or at least coupled) and costs significantly less than double the single-person rate. Employers also routinely offer insurance or other employment perks that are cheaper on a per-person basis for couples than for singles. The preference for married people even extends to a belief that their lives are more valuable.

Studies of prisoners show that married prisoners receive more probation than the unmarried and are also less likely to be sentenced to death. A 1967 study of California prisoners noted that "the recommendations of probation agencies and the dispositions of the courts tend to result in the placement of married offenders on probation and the commitment of unmarried offenders to prison."[91] Similarly, a 1980 study focusing on female defendants found that married women were significantly less likely to be imprisoned than their unmarried counterparts.[92] More recently, a 2005 Department of Justice report examining death row inmates also found that these offenders, the ones given the harshest punishment, were typically unmarried.[93]

The unmarried are also less likely to receive lifesaving medical treatment. Research conducted by sociologist Satia Maroatta and public health professor Keren Ladin demonstrated that when married and unmarried patients were equally medically qualified for a transplant, the married patients were more likely to be recommended. Similarly, researcher Joan DelFattore found that single people with cancer were offered less-aggressive treatments by their oncologists than married people.[94] The inevitable conclusion researchers draw from these studies is that the lives of single people are treated as having less worth than the lives of the married.

In his book *Single: Arguments for the Uncoupled*, Michael Cobb, an English professor at the University of Toronto, describes singles as "a hated sexual minority" and argues that they have, essentially, been shamed out of existence. "We live in such a couples-obsessed society that there really are no 'singles' out there — everyone is pre- or post-coupled," says Cobb.[95] He further suggests that even supposedly "pro-single" shows like *Sex and the City* didn't really challenge the elevated status of marriage. "It showed off that you can be single and interesting and buy expensive clothing and go to great parties in New York for a little while but eventually you are going to grow up. Eventually, you're going to wisen up, put a ring on it and go forward and be coupled and move to Connecticut. We aren't going to pathologize you for playing around for a protracted amount of time, but eventually you're going to have to settle. And the marker of success, the end of the romantic story, is [marriage]."[96]

The social and cultural preference for marriage has obvious negative effects for single people, but it also harms the married. A desire to retain marriage's preferential status is one of the most cited explanations for why people remain in unhappy marriages. In an illuminating Facebook thread, journalist and former academic Anne Helen Peterson asked her followers, "What keeps feminist bourgeoise women from leaving shitty spouses?" Peterson then received hundreds of responses, many of which focused on the status benefits of marriage.[97] One respondent noted that it may be "superficial," but the "public shame" should not be "discounted" and added that the proliferation of social media has further increased the social benefits of marriage because "so much of the wins online are connected to marriage." A second woman responded to Peterson's inquiry, writing, "Oh man reading these comments has really reminded me how being in a relationship is so socially desirable many people would rather be completely and utterly miserable in one than even a tiny bit unhappy and single." A third described multiple "friends (who have the means to leave) who seem to value marriage more than their happiness." She then added, "I think it has something to do with the class privilege they occupy and a lifestyle that depends upon doing things with spouses."[98]

Many of the women who responded to Peterson's inquiry noted that the social status attached to marriage can be compounded by race. For example, one woman answered Peterson's question with the statement, "Proximity to whiteness," implying that marriage provides people of color with greater racial acceptance by the white community. Another respondent expanded on this idea, stating that "for white families there is a cultural affinity for 'the more perfect union.' The constant seeking of status, approval . . . The individual family unit is fetishized as the ultimate expression of success. So yes the proximity to whiteness as [the above respondent] points out, but I think it is immersion in whiteness, the desire to remain immersed in whiteness, to never be associated with anything else. I'm a relatively bougie white lady and I'm in a good relationship but the idea of that falling apart scares the shit out of me and I reckon part of that fear is a sense of cultural failing. That my family wouldn't 'look like it's supposed to'. . . I could make it work if I had to, but it is still terrifying and a big piece of that is because I'm white."[99]

Historically, the unmarried were pitied, reviled, and relegated to the social bottom. Today, that social ostracization continues. For many Americans, marriage remains a defining feature of a person's worth. It is therefore unsurprising that people continue to enter into and remain in loveless marriages. Zsa Zsa Gabor once quipped, "Getting divorced because you don't love a man is almost as silly as getting married because you do." As Gabor recognized, in America the social penalties for the unmarried remain high. For many men and women, avoiding this stigma is a good enough reason to marry.

chapter four

The Marriage Defense

But if they cannot contain, let them marry:
for it is better to marry than to burn.

— I CORINTHIANS 7:9

One Friday night in October 1884, William Ward and Margaret O'Rourke attended a ball in the small town of Mount Vernon, New York, forty miles north of New York City. William and Margaret were likely already acquainted. In fact, they may have known each other for some time, because when William suggested going back to his rooms, Margaret readily agreed.

William lived in Mrs. Butterfield's boardinghouse. This was a reputable business that did not condone non-marital sex, so when Mrs. Butterfield discovered Margaret in William's room the next morning, she was horrified. She informed the couple she was not running *that* kind of establishment and promptly kicked them both out. Mortified, Margaret sought refuge with her friends. She told them about her night with William and their subsequent discovery by Mrs. Butterfield. The friends then informed her father, who had William arrested. After the arrest, Margaret was questioned about her night with William. She admitted to having sex but claimed she only acquiesced after William proposed. Based on this testimony, William was charged with seduction under promise of marriage. He was then brought before a judge and given a choice. He could go to jail, or he could marry. Not surprisingly, William chose the latter. A minister was called into the courtroom, and the couple was promptly wed.

A century and a half later, it is impossible to know what really happened the night of the Mount Vernon ball. Perhaps William did propose and would have married Margaret without any legal threats. It is also possible, as Margaret's father clearly suspected, that William said what he needed to say to get Margaret into bed and that he had no intention of following through with his promise. It is even conceivable that William never said anything about marriage and Margaret fabricated the alleged proposal to save her reputation or to trap William. We can't know what truly happened between William and Margaret the night of the ball, but what is clear is that by marrying Margaret, William avoided prison.[1]

Sex and the Unmarried

For most of US history, only the married could, legally, have sex. Fornication, defined as voluntary sexual intercourse between unmarried parties, was criminalized, and this was done intentionally to encourage marriage.[2] As the influential eighteenth-century English philosopher William Paley explained, "The male part of the species will not undertake the encumbrance, expense, and restraint of married life, if they can gratify their [sexual] passions at a cheaper price; and they will undertake anything rather than not gratify them." Paley believed the only way to convince men to marry was to make the price of non-marital sex extremely high. Early American laws sanctioning monetary suits against male fornicators reflected this idea.

Initially, fornication was punished through two types of legal actions, suits for seduction and suits for breach of promise. Seduction suits were brought by an unmarried woman's father against the alleged seducer for the economic injury he suffered as a result of his daughter's unintended pregnancy. Many of these

Before the Seduction, by William Hogarth, 1731.

suits were brought by working-class fathers against higher-class men, often employers (or their sons), who had taken advantage of the young women in their care.[3] Seduction suits were a way of discouraging such behavior.

Breach of promise actions, unlike seduction suits, were brought by the woman against her former fiancé and were based on the presumed economic injury resulting from a failed engagement. As these suits recognized, marriage was essential to a woman's economic security, and a broken engagement, with its taint of impropriety (it was frequently presumed, often correctly, that many jilted women were no longer virgins), affected a woman's potential marital prospects and her future economic well-being.

By the mid-nineteenth century, the distinctions between the two causes of action had collapsed. Pregnancy began to feature in breach of promise suits as grounds for increased damages, and

The Spurned Bride by Eduard Swoboda.

a promise of marriage, which induced a woman to consent to sexual intercourse (regardless of pregnancy), became a common feature of seduction suits. The emotional suffering caused by the man's behavior also became a feature of these suits, and the rise of industrialization transformed them still further.[4]

As young women left the safety of their rural communities and moved to the cities for work, they became increasingly vulnerable to sexual exploitation and assault. Increasingly, seduction cases were brought by these young working-class women after a rape by friends or other acquaintances. Such women had not consented to sex, but because rape between dating partners was rarely punished, seduction suits were often the only way to hold these men accountable.[5] However, the remedy these women wanted was not money, it was marriage.

Martha Olatka's complaint against Michael Polokoff is typical of such cases. In 1914, Martha was a twenty-three-year-old domestic servant. In May of that year, she began dating Michael Polokoff, a twenty-four-year-old immigrant laborer. For ten

Bell Time, by Winslow Homer.

months, Polokoff took Martha out twice a week and repeatedly told her he wished to marry her. He also constantly pressured her for sex. As Martha later told the police, during their dates, Polokoff would try to pull up her clothes, touch her body, and kiss and hug her. Martha testified that she vigorously repulsed these efforts but that on the night of the "seduction," William found her alone in her cousin's house and physically overpowered her. According to Martha, "[Polokoff] came to me and he locked the door, and he put me in the bed. I started to holler, and he closed my mouth, and he said, 'Don't holler,' and he pulled up my clothes and then he had connection with me . . . I tried to stop him, but I couldn't; he said, 'Don't you worry, I am going to marry you.'" After the first assault, Polokoff raped Martha on three additional occasions, each time telling her, "I won't marry you if you won't let me."[6]

By July 1915, Martha was pregnant and desperately trying to convince Polokoff to marry her. After he repeatedly refused, she warned him, "If you don't marry me, I'll take you to court."

Polokoff didn't believe her, but one week later, Martha filed criminal charges. Polokoff was then brought to the Manhattan District Attorney's Office and threatened with imprisonment. At that point, he finally agreed to marry Martha, but begged for a little more time. According to Martha, "He came to me, and he was crying, and said I should give him a chance of one month to think it over." Martha unwisely took pity on Polokoff. Three days after agreeing to marriage, Polokoff came to Martha boasting, "I fooled the court, and I fool you; I am not afraid of the court; they did nothing." He then disappeared, along with $36 Martha had given him to pay the rent on his plumbing office. Shortly thereafter, Martha miscarried. For weeks she was too sick to take further action, but December 18, 1915, Martha had recovered enough to appear in magistrate's court and have Polokoff charged with seduction. On January 19, 1916, Polokoff was arrested.[7]

At a time when women had little legal recourse against sexual assault, forced marriage protected them, and their children, from abandonment and destitution. It was also, unquestionably, a punishment for the men. As law professor Melissa Murray has written, "Though marriage did not require the physical deprivations of incarceration, it nonetheless deprived the defendant . . . of other liberties by imposing upon him a particular set of burdens and responsibilities — fidelity, sobriety, responsibility, wage-earning — that he could not cast off lightly."[8] Consequently, by the reasoning of the times, the problem with using marriage as a punishment for rape was not that it was ineffective or undesired but that this remedy was not available to all victims.

In late-nineteenth- and early-twentieth-century America, interracial marriage was illegal in many states. As a result, marriage could not be used to punish white men who seduced

/ sexually assaulted black women. It was this disparity in the availability of the marriage remedy that convinced many civil rights leaders to oppose anti-miscegenation laws.[9] In the 1920s, civil rights leaders, like Archibald Grimke, president of the American Negro Academy, argued that the best way to stop illicit sex was to legalize interracial marriage. According to Grimke, "When it comes to a [white] man marrying a colored woman, he does not want to do it," and as long as such laws were in place he could not be compelled to "do it." As Grimke noted, anti-miscegenation laws prevented black women from being as "sacredly guarded by law and public opinion against the sexual passion and pursuit of the white man as is the white woman." NAACP president James Wheldon Johnson made a similar observation. He labeled these prohibitions the "magna charta [*sic*] of concubinage and bastardry [*sic*]."

An additional limitation of the marriage remedy was that it was only available to virgins. Nineteenth-century jurists believed that once a woman consented to non-marital sex with one man, she possessed a character for unchastity and could be assumed to have consented to sex in all other instances as well. In the 1838 case *People v. Abbot*, the New York court expressed this view of female chastity when it sanctimoniously declared, "An isolated instance of criminal connection [fornication] does not make a common prostitute . . . [I]t only makes a prostitute."[10] Only a chaste woman could accuse a man of a sexual crime. Tellingly, this assumption regarding sex and honesty did not apply to male witnesses. In the 1895 case *State v. Sibley*, which concerned the defendant's alleged rape of his twelve-year-old stepdaughter, the Missouri Supreme Court noted, "It is a matter of common knowledge that the bad character of a man for chastity does not even in the remotest degree affect his character for truth, when based upon that alone, while it does that of a woman."[11]

Widespread Bigamy

The marriage defense provided protection against criminal charges of fornication and seduction. It also, ironically, protected against charges of bigamy. In nineteenth-century America, bigamy was a crime, but if a man or woman lived with someone as their spouse, meaning the parties assumed all the traditional rights and obligations of marriage, the law would assume the couple was legally capable of marriage.[12] The justification for presuming the validity of a bigamous marriage was twofold. First, the law presumes innocence, meaning courts would assume a person claiming to be married was married. Second, even if courts suspected bigamy, they still supported these illegal "marriages" as preferable to legal divorce. The result, as Professor Lawrence Friedman has written, was that "unhappy spouses would divorce with their feet." They would physically separate, often by moving to a new city or state, and then start over with a new husband or wife. If the new, bigamous marriage looked like a valid marriage, judges would treat it as valid.[13] Most bigamy prosecutions were limited to brazen or fraudulent acts.

A typical bigamy prosecution was that of Fredrick A. Smith. In 1897, Smith was charged with bigamy after he abandoned his first wife and began "housekeeping" with another woman a short distance away. The first Mrs. Smith quickly located her husband (and her furniture) and had him arrested for bigamy.[14] The 1890 bigamy prosecution of Horace Knapp is similar. Horace Knapp was a California miner who met Annie Gale through a matrimonial advertisement. Knapp described himself as a "good fellow, with means and prospects," and Gale eagerly responded to his advertisement. The two met in person and quickly married. Shortly thereafter, Annie received an anonymous note. It read:

> Mrs. Knapp, your husband has another wife living not far from you. He has three children whom he has deserted. He married you to get whatever money you had or could acquire. She is innocent and knows nothing of him having married you. Don't bother her, poor thing; she has a hard enough time to feed her babies.[15]

After confirming the truth of the note, Gale had Knapp arrested for bigamy. However, such prosecutions were rare. Most bigamists were never prosecuted.[16]

By the mid-nineteenth century, bigamy was so widespread that many matrimonial advertisers — men seeking mail-order brides — felt they needed to specifically note if they were not open to such marriages.[17] An 1867 issue of *The Miner*, reprinted in the *Montana Post*, included such a stipulation. It read: "Wanted — a wife, by a young, temperate, industrious miner. No old maids or fast widows need apply." A "fast widow" was a married woman looking for a new husband.

Historian Beverly Schwartzberg's fascinating study of nineteenth-century widows' pensions also reveals the extraordinary prevalence of bigamy. During her research, Schwartzberg uncovered thousands of pension cases in which more than one woman (sometimes many, many more) claimed to be the widow of a single Civil War soldier. She similarly discovered it was also common for the women to have multiple husbands. The example of Amelia Van Gedler and William Bacon is illustrative.

William and Amelia married in 1865 in Southport, New York. Six months later, William deserted Amelia and "married" a woman named Cordelia. When asked "how he could marry again without getting a divorce," William told his friend, "Lots of them did . . . that." After William's desertion, Amelia also

The business card of one of the many attorneys special-
izing in pension claims, circa 1895. Civil War pensions
became so legally complicated that entire legal practices
were created just to handle these claims.

"remarried," and after her second husband died, she remarried
again.[18] Then, after her third husband died, Amelia learned that
William was also deceased so, because Amelia was now single,
she applied for a pension as William's widow.

Bigamy allowed spouses like William and Amelia to elude
America's draconian divorce prohibitions. It also protected them
against charges of fornication or adultery. Both of these benefits
were especially important for abused wives. The pension claim
of Civil War veteran William Butler shows how bigamy helped
protect abused women.

William Butler had multiple wives. He was also a violent
man. His pension claim reveals that his first wife, Marion, left
him due to "ill treatment," and although the record is silent as
to the details of Marion's abuse, the testimony of his third wife,
Nannie, indicates it was likely horrific. In her pension interview, Nannie testified that she left Butler "after he removed
every stick of furniture from the house and locked her and
her children in." She further testified that, had it not been for
neighbors, they would probably have died of exposure. Marion's
bigamous remarriage helped her avoid Nannie's fate. It gave her
the economic support to leave Butler and protected her against

criminal charges of adultery. Years later, when the pension examiner inspected Marion's claim, he decided she was eligible for Butler's pension because her bigamous second (and then third) marriage meant she was not living in "open and notorious adulterous cohabitation."[19]

Spousal Privilege

The criminal defense benefits of marriage helped alleviate some of the injustice caused by women's inequality and powerlessness. Unfortunately, the marriage defense also incentivized highly problematic and dangerous marriages. The spousal testimonial privilege, which prevents spouses from testifying against each other, is one obvious example. This privilege derives from the law of coverture, which treated the husband and wife as one person. Under coverture, a married woman had no separate legal identity from her husband. This meant, among other things, that she could not testify against him. It also meant that marrying a witness, or even a victim, could be an effective criminal defense strategy.[20]

In his 1827 treatise *Rationale of Judicial Evidence*, the famous English philosopher and jurist Jeremy Bentham railed against the marital testimonial privilege because it allowed a person to convert her home into a "den of thieves" and ensured every married individual "one safe and unquestionable and ever ready accomplice for every imaginable crime."[21] Bentham's fears were valid, but they were unpersuasive. In fact, even after the rule of coverture was replaced with the rule of love, support for the privilege did not disappear. Instead, the justification changed. Now courts upheld the privilege as necessary to marital harmony and declared that marital relations would become frayed if husbands and wives were forced to testify against the other. The continuing strength of the testimonial privilege is clearly demonstrated in the 1903 Texas murder trial of A. J. Moore.

The case began on a warm Sunday night, shortly after evening church services had concluded. One of the attendees, Matt Hunt, began to walk home with Susie Jones. Susie was A. J. Moore's girlfriend, and Moore objected. When Susie ignored him, he slapped her across the face. Hunt intervened, and he and Moore began shouting at each other. Eventually, Susie left with Hunt, while an enraged Moore followed them. Shortly after the couple reached Susie's house, Moore shot Hunt in the head. Susie was the only witness. Moore was subsequently arrested and the state expected Susie to testify. However, on the eve of trial, Susie and Moore were married. The following day, Moore argued that because Susie was now his wife, she could not be forced to testify. The court agreed. Although the Moores' marriage was only hours old, the court ruled that the prosecution could not compel Susie's testimony. According to the court, "It makes no difference at what time the relation of husband and wife begins . . . When the marriage ceremony is performed, no matter what the motive was or may be, the witness thenceforward becomes the lawful wife of the defendant, and is prohibited . . . from testifying against her husband."

Protecting Domestic Violence

Marriage allowed Moore to silence Susie's testimony. It also, likely, protected him from prosecution for domestic abuse. Moore was a violent man. He had hit Susie in public and murdered the man who tried to protect her. Once married, it is almost certain this abuse continued. However, after Moore became Susie's husband, it became exceedingly unlikely he would ever be punished for domestic violence.

A 1782 caricature by James Gillray.

Historically, husbands had the right to physically chastise their wives. A husband was legally responsible for a wife's conduct, and this gave him the right to control her behavior, including with physical force or violence. This right of chastisement was sometimes known as the Rule of Thumb, in reference to the English common-law rule that a husband had the authority to beat his wife with a "rod not thicker than his thumb."

The right of chastisement, combined with coverture's prohibition on suits between spouses, meant husbands could not be prosecuted for most domestic violence. Abusing one's wife became a privilege of marriage. *The Comic Blackstone*, a satirical

1846 examination of the common law, mocked the chastisement right while simultaneously acknowledging its appeal:

> By the old law, a husband might give his wife moder-
> ate correction . . . but it is declared in black and white
> that he may not beat her black and blue, though the
> civil law allowed any man on whom a woman had
> bestowed her hand, to bestow his fists upon her at his
> own discretion. The common people, who are much
> attached to the common law, still exert the privilege
> of beating their wives . . . and a woman in the lower
> ranks of life, if she falls in love with a man, is liable,
> after marriage, to be a good deal struck by him.[22]

By the 1870s, women's rights advocates began citing the chastisement right as one of the reasons women needed the vote. Women's newspapers, such as the *Woman's Journal*, published stories of wife beatings, murder, rape, and incest to emphasize the frequency of such abuse and the need for reform. As one column in the *Woman's Journal* noted, "The instances here reported are only a few of many similar ones which crowd our daily papers and which show the need for a redeemed public sentiment in regard to this great crime."[23] Women's rights advocates cited these gruesome reports as proof that husbands could not be trusted to protect women's interests and that women needed their own right to participate in the enactment and enforcement of the law.

The increased attention to the problem of domestic violence did not lead to suffrage, but it did change the justification for the policy of judicial non-interference. The right of chastisement was replaced with a concern for marital harmony. The 1886 North Carolina Supreme Court case *State v. Edens* exemplified this new justification. In *Edens*, the court described the marital

Suffragist Margaret Foley distributing the *Woman's Journal and Suffrage News*.

home as an idealized private realm ruled by love and potentially harmed by outside interference. The court wrote:

> [The law] drops the curtain upon scenes of domestic life, preferring not to take cognizance of what transpires within that circle, to the exposure of them in a public prosecution. It presumes that acts of wrong committed in passion will be followed by contrition and atonement in a cooler moment, and forgiveness will blot it out of memory. So, too, the harsh and cruel word that sends a pang to the sensitive heart may be recalled, and relations that should never have been interrupted by an unkind or unwarranted expression again restored.

Non-interference in the name of marital harmony quickly became an accepted feature of the criminal justice system. Instead of punishing domestic abusers, family courts encouraged reconciliation. They also insisted family conflict, including violence, should remain private.[24] State legislatures helped further this goal by creating separate family and juvenile courts. These courts guaranteed that cases involving family violence were heard outside of the traditional criminal system. As law professor Reva Seigel notes, the changes ensured that the "ancient prerogative of marriage, chastisement did not die an easy death." Rather, these changes re-legitimized and more deeply entrenched the practice of judicial non-interference.[25] The history of marital rape is similar.

Marital Rape

Traditionally, the right to have sex with one's wife was one of the benefits of marriage. This was because marital sex was the only permissible form of intercourse and because a wife could not, legally, say no. The idea that marital rape was a legal impossibility originated in a seventeenth-century treatise authored by Lord Matthew Hale, the chief justice of England. In this treatise, Hale wrote, "The husband cannot be guilty of a rape committed by himself upon his lawful wife, for by their mutual matrimonial consent and contract the wife hath given up herself in this kind unto her husband, which she cannot retract." Hale provided no precedent for his theory of perpetual consent, but it was readily accepted into the common law.[26] Marriage became an absolute defense to rape.

By the nineteenth century, a husband's right of sexual access had expanded to include the right to prevent his wife from having sex with others. This meant, if a woman committed adultery, her husband could sue her lover for "criminal conversation" and receive monetary damages. He also had the right to recapture, restrain, and confine his wife to keep her from committing adultery and the right to seek a writ of habeas corpus (a document ordering a person's release) against any person who kept his wife from him. The husband's sexual monopoly over his wife even gave him a defense to murder.[27] The 1859 murder trial of Daniel Sickles established this "heat of passion defense."

Daniel Sickles was a New York City congressman who murdered the district attorney of New York after discovering he was having an affair with his wife. At trial, Sickles claimed a loss of control due to intense romantic jealousy. His attorney likened this argument to the already accepted defense of temporary insanity. According to Sickles's attorney, in such cases, deadly violence must be excused. "To kill in the name of jealousy is merely obedience to the will of nature."[28] Shockingly, the jury agreed, and Sickles was acquitted. Ten years later, the heat of passion defense became the core issue in the even more sensational New York murder trial of Daniel McFarland.

Harper's Weekly engraving of Daniel Sickles shooting Key.

In 1857, Daniel McFarland married Abby Sage. McFarland told Abby he was a successful lawyer and "a man of temperate habits, of the purest morals." However, neither was true. Shortly after their marriage, Abby discovered that McFarland was a broke land speculator and an alcoholic. Three months after their wedding, McFarland pawned Abby's jewelry to pay their bills. He also forced her to become an actress to support the family, and he began hurting her. Then, after ten years of marriage and abuse, Abby met Albert Richardson.

Albert Richardson was a journalist living in the same boardinghouse as the McFarlands. He was intelligent and kind, and he and Abby quickly became friends. McFarland grew jealous of this friendship, and one evening McFarland came home to find Abby standing by Richardson's door and flew into a terrible rage. He beat Abby throughout the night and into the next day, taking breaks only to go "to the nearest bar-room to drink, and then [to] com[e] in still more furious." Eventually, after more

Abby McFarland and Albert Richardson.

than a full day of abuse, Abby told McFarland she was leaving.[29] Recalling that night, Abby stated:

> As mildly and firmly as I possibly could, I began to talk with him. I told him decidedly that I should leave him forever; that I had borne with patience for many years great outrages from him; that he had made my life miserable, and had often put me in great dread of my life; that I could not endure it any longer; that by his outrageous conduct for the two days past, and by the language he had used when he found me at Mr. Richardson's door, he had added the last drop to my cup of endurance, and I should go away from him at once.

Abby left McFarland. In response, McFarland shot Richardson. Richardson survived this attack, and Abby filed for divorce. Sixteen months later, the length of time needed to establish residency in Indiana (one of the few states where divorce was

FIRST DAY OF THE M'FARLAND TRIAL—SCENE IN THE COURT-ROOM.—[FROM A SKETCH BY STANLEY FOX.]

First day of the McFarland trial — scene in the courtroom.

permissible), the divorce was granted. Unfortunately, as Abby and Albert were preparing to marry, McFarland shot Richardson a second time. This time, the shot was fatal. Richardson died, and McFarland was arrested for murder.[30]

McFarland admitted to killing Richardson. The only issue at trial was whether he had the right to do so. McFarland's lawyers argued that when Abby left McFarland, it made him crazy. They contended that when he shot Richardson, McFarland was acting under an "ungovernable impulse, uncontrolled by reason," and thus was neither morally nor legally responsible for Richardson's death. The jury agreed. After deliberating for less than an hour, McFarland was acquitted. Tellingly, the public supported this result.[31] Despite the abuse, most Americans blamed Richardson for stealing Abby away. McFarland was viewed as an honorable man who only did what love compelled him to do.

A Loophole for Statutory Rapists

Marriage provided husbands with a defense to rape and murder. It also became a defense to child sexual abuse. Historically, statutory rape laws only forbade sexual intercourse with a female under the age of ten or twelve (it varied slightly by state). Then, in the 1890s, social reformers began working to increase the age of consent. By the 1920s, all but one state had raised it to sixteen.[32] Nevertheless, there were two glaring exceptions to the new statutory rape laws. The first was that they only applied to virgins. The second was marriage. Despite growing concerns regarding child sexual abuse, marriage remained a loophole for men wishing to have sex with children.

One of the most famous examples of the child sex loophole was the marriage of Edward "Daddy" Browning and Frances "Peaches" Heenan. "Daddy" and "Peaches" were the couple's revealing nicknames for each other. The two met in the spring of 1926 when Browning was a fifty-one-year-old multimillionaire and Frances was a fifteen-year-old high school student. Browning liked young girls. Long before he met Frances, there were allegations Browning had molested his own adopted daughter. Then, as he and Frances started "dating," Browning came under increasing legal scrutiny.[33]

Vincent Pisarra, the superintendent of the New York Society for the Prevention of Cruelty to Children, believed Browning's interest in Frances was child abuse. He attempted to end the relationship by filing suit in New York Children's Court and having Frances's mother declared unfit. This would have invalidated her ability to consent to the marriage. Unfortunately, Browning discovered Pisarra's plan and thwarted it by marrying Frances one month after meeting her. Once married, Browning had the legal right to have sex with Frances.

Frances "Peaches" Heenan.

The Browning marriage lasted less than a year, and it ruined Frances's life. After a much-publicized divorce, in which Frances was vilified and denied a fair share of the marital assets, she had a short-lived career as a vaudeville actress and then three additional, unsuccessful, marriages. Frances died at age forty-six after a slip and fall in her bathroom.[34]

The Married Prostitute

Marriage shielded husbands from criminal prosecution for physical abuse, sexual abuse, and even murder. However, the marriage defense was not limited to men. Women also used marriage as a defense strategy, most commonly against charges of prostitution. In fact, during the late nineteenth century, marriage was such an effective defense that prostitutes could boldly advertise their services simply by including the word *marriage*. Consider the following solicitation : "A discreet young lady, cosy home, appreciates meeting generous gentleman, matrimony." Few readers would have thought this "discreet young lady" was looking for marriage. As a different advertiser explained, "The [newspaper editors] know I don't want to marry, and most of those who answer know it too."

Nineteenth-century prostitutes were able to advertise their services and circumvent the law by simply including the word *marriage*.[35] Then, in the early twentieth century, this leniency disappeared as Congress became increasingly concerned about the immigration of foreign prostitutes and their use of marriage to evade immigration restrictions. Initially, Congress attempted to address the problem of foreign prostitutes through the Immigration Act of 1907. The act barred foreign women from entering the US for "immoral purposes." One year later, the Supreme Court decided *U.S. v. Bitty* and upheld the act's "immoral purposes" ban, but also confirmed that this prohibition could be circumvented through marriage.

Bitty involved the arrest of Englishman John Bitty after he entered the United States with Violet Sterling, a twenty-one-year-old Englishwoman whose travel documents identified her as Betty Bitty. When questioned by the police, Bitty told the following story: "The girl [Sterling] worked for me [selling cigarettes] in London . . . [W]hen I started for New York she begged me not to leave her. I engaged passage for her as my niece, as I thought that would look better. I had taken a fatherly interest in her."[36] The police did not believe Bitty's story and charged him with violating section three of the 1907

Immigration Act, "import[ing] or attempt[ing] to import, into the United States, any alien woman or girl for the purpose of prostitution or for any other immoral purpose." Bitty objected to the charge. He noted that Sterling was not a prostitute, but the court held this made no difference. As the court explained, Bitty brought Sterling into the United States to "live with him as his concubine, that is, in illicit intercourse, not under the sanction of a valid or legal marriage."[37] According to the court, this satisfied the act's immoral purposes provision. The important difference was not between a "concubine" and a "prostitute," but between a wife and all other women.

The 1907 Immigration Act also created the Dillingham Commission. The purpose of this commission was to conduct a wide-ranging investigation of US immigration practices, including the immigration of prostitutes. In 1911, Congress published the Dillingham Commission's report and confirmed that marriage was routinely used to circumvent the 1907 act's immoral purposes provision. The report noted that, initially, immigration officials had attempted to bar foreign prostitutes by identifying them based on physical characteristics such as their dress or speech but that these efforts were abandoned after one hapless immigration inspector stopped the wife of a rich and important citizen and nearly accused her of prostitution.[38] The woman was gaudily dressed and unrefined, but she was not a prostitute. Luckily the mistake was caught before the woman discovered why she had been briefly detained. Nevertheless, the mishap highlighted the danger of using appearance or manner to identify prostitutes.[39] Afterward, female entry determinations were primarily based on marital status. Single women attempting to enter the US alone or with a male partner were turned away as likely prostitutes; married women were almost always granted entry.

The Dillingham report confirmed, marriage was the key to evading the 1907 act. However, in discussing the entry of foreign prostitutes the report also stoked "white slavery" fears. At the time, there was a widespread belief that large numbers of unwilling women were being tricked into sex work through false promises of marriage made by foreign or other racially "inferior" men. In 1907, a *Los Angeles Times* article titled "Jewish Girls Are Sacrificed: Sensational Disclosures from Chicago Ghetto" claimed, "Some [Jewish procurers] seek the company of Jewish maidens with avowed intention of honorable marriage. Others actually marry the girls and then force them to lead dissolute lives. Many . . . have married dozens of girls under various names and disguises." In 1909, *McClure's Magazine* ran a similar article titled "Daughters of the Poor." According to this article, "A network of Austrian, Russian, and Hungarian Jews dealt in women" and warned that these "lonely and poverty stricken girls . . . are very easily secured by promise of marriage."⁴⁰ The Dillingham report appeared to confirm these fears. The report noted:

> The Jews often import or harbor Russian, Hungarian, Polish or German women, doubtlessly usually of their own race . . . There are large numbers of Jews scattered through the United States, although mainly located in New York and Chicago, who seduce and keep girls. Some of them are engaged in importation.

Historian Nancy Cott notes that it was easy for Americans "to believe that 'racially' different and non-Christian groups were likely to commit such grotesquery." She writes, "Both Asians and Jews — the latter via the Old Testament — were tainted by association with polygamy . . . Also, both Jews and Asians

The Slaves of the Jews by J. A. Wales (a known anti-Semitic cartoonist), published in *Judge* magazine in 1882.

in their home cultures used arranged marriages, in which overt economic bargaining and kinship networks beyond the marrying pair played acknowledged parts."[41]

The racism underlying early-twentieth-century marriage trafficking fears was obvious. Nevertheless, there is little question that marriage was used to bring willing, and possibly unwilling, sex workers into the United States. As one Marseilles madam told the commission's agents, "All the bunch that I know [referring to the male facilitators], marry their girls. If the girl is young, you then have no trouble."

Marriage helped foreign prostitutes enter the United States. It also helped them avoid deportation after entry. Under an 1855 federal statute, the foreign wives of American citizens received automatic citizenship. Any American man could marry a foreign-born (though not Asian) woman and remove her from the reach of immigration laws.[42] As a result, marriage quickly became a common and effective tactic foreign prostitutes used

Men of the New Immigration Commission.

to avoid deportation. As the Dillingham report noted, "One of the great difficulties encountered in the deportation of alien prostitutes, has been the contraction of marriages to citizens of the United States as soon as warrant proceedings have been instituted." To illustrate this problem, the report highlighted one New York City police detective's unsuccessful efforts to deport "Jane Doe."

Doe was arrested for solicitation, but shortly after her arrest, she married an American citizen. According to Doe, the man "got 'dead stuck' on me, because I appeared to be a nice girl . . . I know how to behave, when necessary." When the detective arrived to order her deportation, Doe showed him her marriage certificate. She then boasted that the poor sucker who married her wasn't even around anymore. She told the detective, "I couldn't live with that man . . . he isn't making enough money. I don't want to go into the dressmaking business and earn $8 or $9 a week when I can make that every day on Broadway." Once

Doe proved she was the wife of an American citizen, the detective was forced to release her. The officer concluded his interview with the commission noting, "Almost every night I see the said Jane Doe (now Mrs. Doe) soliciting on Broadway and taking men to hotels in that vicinity."[43]

Women like Mrs. Doe convinced lawmakers that the connection between marriage and citizenship was promoting prostitution and degrading marriage. Responding to these concerns, Congress passed the Immigration Act of 1917. This statute decreed "that the marriage to an American citizen of a female of the sexually immoral classes, the exclusion or deportation of which is prescribed by this Act, shall not invest such female with United States citizenship if the marriage of such an alien female shall be solemnized after her arrest or after the commission of acts which make her liable to deportation under this Act."[44] The 1917 act ensured that marriage was no longer a defense to the deportation of foreign prostitutes. Nevertheless, it did not portend the end of the marriage defense. In fact, it proved to be the exception.

The Marriage Defense's Many Guises Today

Today, the connection between marriage and criminal defense continues. This is true for acts that are no longer criminalized, like seduction and breach of promise to marry, and for crimes like domestic violence and child abuse, which are now more vigorously enforced.

For example, a recent "offer" during the COVID-19 pandemic from the Robeson County, North Carolina, sheriff's office demonstrates the ongoing criminalization of jilters. In this "Pre-Valentine's Day special," the department offered to arrest "your ex" for Valentine's Day:

If you have an ex-Valentine with an outstanding warrant who is playing hide-and-seek now is the time to enjoy this offer. The weekend special offers a set of limited-edition platinum bracelets, free face mask, free hand sanitizer, along with free transportation provided by a state-certified chauffeur, free glamour headshot, a one-night minimum stay in our luxurious, freshly painted, 5-star accommodations with 24/7 security, and a unique Valentine's dinner.[45]

Jilting is no longer a crime, yet the Robeson police department was specifically targeting jilters for criminal punishment. Other historic morality crimes, such as fornication and cohabitation, also continue to have criminal repercussions. Some of the most common examples are parole restrictions.

In 2004, North Carolina refused to supervise the parole of Melissa Sheridan because she was cohabitating with her boyfriend in violation of North Carolina's no-longer-enforced 1805 anti-cohabitation statute.[46] To remain with her partner in North Carolina, Sheridan was told to marry.[47] Terry Gootee, judicial district manager with the 5th Judicial District's Division of Community Corrections, explained the parole decision, stating, "We cannot allow that person to break the law." Other states have issued similar parole denials. In 2006, West Virginia refused to release William Stanley because he planned to cohabitate with his fiancée. Stanley remained incarcerated until he was finally paroled to a religious program that required daily prayer sessions and memorization of religious materials.[48] Similarly, in 2007, a Texas court issued a parole condition for Briane Woods prohibiting her from residing with any person other than a spouse or blood relative. The court justified this parole condition by claiming Woods's mother's out-of-wedlock childbearing, and Woods's own decision to not "marry the father of her one-year-old child and her unborn baby," contributed to her criminal behavior.[49]

Sexual Harassment and the Marriage Defense

The punishment of non-marital sex also continues through a system of civil regulations. Sexual harassment regulations are the most prominent example. These rules were created to reduce gender discrimination in the workplace. However, many go beyond their stated anti-discrimination objectives to regulate sex, and sexuality more generally. Many employers now prohibit sexual conduct that would not amount to sexual harassment.[50] At the same time, sexual harassment is becoming even harder to discern, and this makes employers even more inclined to regulate employee sex. As law professors Melissa Murray and Karen Tani write, today "few sexual encounters are presumptively permissible or impermissible." Instead, "the legitimacy of every encounter turns on consent. But even (and perhaps especially) in this 'yes means yes' era, expressions of consent are subject to interpretation, and thus disagreement."[51] Regulation of such encounters is then further complicated by the fact that workplace romance is common and often highly successful.

Workplace romance statistics show that while it is often assumed most people meet online, in reality more people meet their spouse in the workplace than on an app. A 2023 *Forbes* survey "found that 43% of those who date a colleague end up marrying them." Nevertheless, the fear of sexual harassment suits means employers are now regulating a wider range of sexual behavior and often prohibiting employee relationships altogether.[52] Two recent cases concerning non-marital sex by public employees,

Seegmiller v. LaVerkin City and *Anderson v. City of LaVergne*, illustrate the growing regulation of employee sex.

Seegmiller concerned the non-marital sexual conduct of Sharon Johnson. Johnson was a Utah police officer involved in a contentious divorce. During an out-of-town police training conference, Johnson had "a brief affair with an officer from another department who was also attending the conference." When Johnson's estranged husband learned of the affair, he contacted her employer, the LaVerkin Police Department, and told them she had been raped. Johnson denied being raped, and no disciplinary action was taken against her lover. This inaction enraged Johnson's husband, who reported to the city council that Johnson was having an affair with the police chief. While investigating this allegation (which the husband later recanted), the city council learned about Johnson's conference relationship. Johnson was issued a formal reprimand based on a provision in the law enforcement code of ethics requiring an officer to "keep [her] private life unsullied as an example to all and [to] behave in a manner that does not bring discredit to [the officer] or [the] agency." She was also warned that further violations of the professional code would result in "additional discipline up to and including termination." After receiving this reprimand, Johnson sued the city. She argued that punishment for off-duty private conduct was a violation of her constitutional rights. The *Seegmiller* court disagreed and held that her reprimand was constitutional.

In *Anderson*, two employees of the LaVergne, Tennessee, police department, Michael Anderson, a police officer, and Lisa Lewis, an administrative assistant, began a romantic relationship. When the police chief learned of their relationship, he became concerned that "intra-office dating between employees of different ranks . . . might lead to sexual harassment claims against the department." In response, he issued an administrative order directing Anderson and Lewis to "cease all contact with each other" outside of the workplace. The couple ignored the order and continued their relationship. Shortly thereafter, Anderson was fired. He then sued the city, claiming his dismissal was a violation of his constitutional rights — and, like Johnson, he lost. The *Anderson* court concluded that the LaVergne Police Department's interest in avoiding sexual harassment suits was a legitimate government interest and that the decision to fire Anderson was constitutional.

Seegmiller and *Anderson* highlight the continuing regulation and punishment of non-marital sex. They also show that marriage remains an effective defense. In both cases, marriage would have negated the state's alleged concerns regarding the employees' sexual relationships. Unfortunately, such protection is not always desirable. While marriage protects the private sexual conduct of consenting adults like Johnson and Anderson, it can also shield employees actively engaging in sexual harassment. This problem has been particularly acute in cases involving same-sex sexual harassment. In these cases, courts have frequently dismissed claims when the alleged harasser was part of a heterosexual marriage.[53] The courts' reasoning in these cases is twofold. First, they appear to hold the false assumption that a person involved in a cross-sex marriage could never harbor same-sex desire, and second, they worry that a finding of same-sex sexual harassment would harm the harasser's marriage.[54] The 2010 case *Smith v. Hy-Vee Inc.* is typical.

Dru Smith, a female employee of a Hy-Vee grocery store, brought a sexual harassment suit against her colleague Sherri Lynch. Smith described a number of incidents that she claimed constituted sexual harassment. The first occurred after Smith observed Lynch "dry humping" a male Hy-Vee manager. After the manager left, Smith said, "God, Sherri, it's like you practically raped him." Lynch replied, "No Dani, if I were going to rape someone, it would be like this." Lynch then pushed Smith up against a wall and held her there while rubbing her hands and body up against Smith. Smith also described a different incident in which Lynch "rubbed her fingers against Smith's fingers and told Smith '[t]hat's what a penis feels like.'" Smith testified that throughout her employment, Lynch repeatedly made sexually suggestive remarks and that she had "smacked [Smith] on the buttocks approximately six times." Lynch had repeatedly fondled and groped Smith, but the court denied the sexual harassment claim because it held Lynch's conduct was not "motivated by a particular attraction to Smith." In reaching its decision, the court emphasized that Lynch has "been married to the same man for sixteen years and [had] two daughters."[55] The court appears to have been influenced by both Smith's heterosexual marriage and a reluctance to upend the lives of her husband and children.

Hy-Vee was not unique. That same year, the Nevada Court of Appeals issued a similar decision in *Sillars v. Nevada*. *Sillars* involved a same-sex sexual harassment claim against a female state employee named Patsy Cave. The plaintiff, Elizabeth Sillars, had been training Cave, and the two struck up a friendship. One night, Cave visited Sillars's house and while drinking, confessed she "had feelings for someone in the office." Sillars named several male employees, and Cave began to cry. A few days later, "Cave called Plaintiff in tears stating, 'I don't want you to think bad of me.' She then asked if she could come to Plaintiff's home and talk to her, but Plaintiff said, 'No, it's late at night.'" After this incident, Sillars noticed that Cave would often stand too close to her and that she would stare at her breasts. At trial, Cave denied having feelings for Sillars, and the court accepted this denial, citing Cave's marriage as proof. According to the court, there is "no evidence demonstrating that Cave is homosexual. Instead, Cave is married and has several children. There is no evidence that she has ever been in, or intends to be in, a homosexual relationship, and Cave denies having romantic feelings for Plaintiff." Sillars's sexual harassment claim was dismissed.

One of the most shocking examples of the marriage defense in a same-sex sexual harassment decision is the 2004 Louisiana case *Kreamer v. Henry's Marine*. In *Kreamer*, the plaintiff, Thomas Kreamer, a deckhand, alleged harassment by his male co-worker, Carroll Carrere. Kreamer testified that Carrere grabbed him by the crotch on eight occasions and that on one of these occasions, Carrere told Kreamer that "he would like to compare packages." Other incidents cited by Kreamer included Carrere blowing kisses at him, putting a hot Zippo lighter between his legs, and staring at him while he slept. Regarding the sleeping incident, Kreamer testified that he woke one morning to find Carrere standing next to his bed just looking at him. When he told Carrere to "get the hell out," Carrere left without saying a word. When Kreamer saw him later, Carrere whistled at him and made "offensive gestures." Kreamer also described an event that occurred toward the end of his employment. According to Kreamer, "Carrere approached [him] from behind as he was bent slightly over the engines, grabbed his sides and said he 'would like to f**k that piece of ass.'" Despite all this testimony, the court denied Kreamer's sexual harassment claim. It concluded that this evidence, "as a whole, reveals an intent of Carrere to humiliate plaintiff for reasons unrelated to a sexual interest, rather than an actual intent to have sexual contact." The court then cited Carrere's heterosexual marriage as proof that Carrere could not have sexually desired Kreamer.[56]

Sexual harassment claims no longer require a finding of desire. In 2020, the US Supreme Court decided *Bostock v.*

Clayton County and held that terminating an employee because of their sexual orientation, or perceived sexual orientation, is a form of sex discrimination. *Bostock*, combined with the court's earlier decision in *Oncale v. Sundowner* (finding that same-sex sexual harassment claims can be actionable), suggests a same-sex harassment case does not require the harasser to be attracted to the victim but can be based solely on the victim's sexual orientation. As a result, *Bostock* may lessen the importance of the marriage defense in same-sex harassment cases, or it may not. None of the above cases included allegations that the victim was harassed because of their sexual orientation. Rather, all involved allegations of explicit desire that were undermined by the defendants' heterosexual marriages.[57]

Marriage and Domestic Violence

In the same-sex sexual harassment cases, marriage provides a problematic yet often effective defense. In the criminal context, the harms of this defense are even more pronounced. Nevertheless, states remain reluctant to eliminate or even limit it. In Arizona, it took the gruesome murder of Penny Williams to convince the legislature that the marital testimonial privilege should only apply to post-marital acts. Many states have not taken even this minimal step.

The Williams case began the morning of November 29, 1978, when the body of Penny Williams was found in the front seat of her automobile near Pantano Wash in Tucson, Arizona. Penny had been stabbed multiple times in the head and neck. The words THE BITCH were printed in dust on the side of the car. Three weeks later, the police received a call from Rita Sipler, the girlfriend of Penny's ex-husband, Scott Williams. Sipler told the police that

Williams had confessed to murdering Penny, and based on this information, Williams was arrested. Sipler was the state's chief witness. However, shortly before the trial commenced, Williams married Sipler. He then asserted the marital testimonial privilege to prevent her from taking the stand. Although the court granted Williams's request, it criticized the privilege, writing, "If it is, perhaps, overly sentimental to wish that marriage should be made in heaven, it is foolish to encourage it to be made on the courthouse steps."[58] The Arizona legislature agreed. Two years later, it limited the privilege to acts occurring after marriage.[59] Other states still do not have such limitations.

In the 2017 Georgia case *U.S. v Davis*, the court confirmed the privilege's continuing applicability to premarital acts. *Davis* involved the prosecution of Joshua Davis, a Brinks armored truck driver and ATM technician. On October 15, 2015, while Davis and his colleague were servicing ATM machines, Davis stole hundreds of thousands of dollars. Davis's colleague did not know of the thefts, and when their truck ran out of gas at the end of their shift, he agreed to stay with the truck and wait for the tow. Davis thanked him and called his girlfriend, Philicia Morris, to pick him up. Then, shortly after Davis left with Morris, his partner called to tell him the police were at the truck and that they were looking for a black bag with money in it. Overhearing this exchange, Morris confronted Davis, asking, "What money, what are you talking about . . . you got money on you or something?" Later, when speaking with the police, Morris told them Davis had answered "yes." She then explained she "freaked out" and "told him to . . . just get it out of [her] car." Davis stuffed the stolen money into a pink bag he found in her car and "threw it out" the car window. Morris then drove Davis back to the Brinks truck where the police were waiting. Later that day, she gave a statement to the FBI, and based on this testimony, Davis was arrested. Shortly thereafter, Davis married Morris and invoked the marital testimonial privilege. Although the government objected, the court upheld the privilege, declaring it vital to protecting "the harmony and sanctity of marriage." The court wrote that there is a "*natural repugnance* in every fair-minded person to compelling a wife or husband to be the means of the other's condemnation, and to compelling the culprit to the humiliation of being condemned by the words of his intimate life partner."[60]

The *Davis* court believed the testimonial privilege fostered marital harmony, but case law shows it is more likely to perpetuate marital violence. Domestic violence exceptions to the testimonial privilege are now universal, specifically because domestic abusers routinely asserted this privilege to avoid prosecution.[61] Unfortunately, even with these exceptions, the spousal testimonial privilege may still be fostering domestic violence. Consider the 2020 Indiana case *U. S. v. Schambers*.

Kenneth Schambers was a convicted felon rearrested for parole violations. While in prison, Schambers sought permission to marry his girlfriend. Permitting the marriage would lead to the exclusion of the girlfriend's testimony, yet the court still granted the request. According to the court, the "concern that the Defendant's request will result in a key witness invoking the adverse spousal testimonial privilege is not enough" to justify infringing his constitutional right to marry. The court then discussed this marital right at length but made only a passing reference to the fact that "among other violations" the defendant was also charged with "Domestic Battery."[62] While details in the opinion are sparse, it appears clear that Schambers was a violent man who would not have hesitated to use threats to obtain his girlfriend's marital consent.

Advocates for victims of domestic abuse note that the testimonial privilege creates a strong incentive for criminal defendants to force — through physical violence or emotional abuse — an unwilling partner to marry them. Dorothy J. Lennig, director of the legal clinic at House of Ruth (a domestic violence shelter in Maryland), testified before the Maryland legislature that coercive marriages are common among abusive men. She noted, "We at the House of Ruth have had multiple clients where their abusers have intimidated them, leaned on them, scared them, forced them into getting married before the trial so they would invoke their spousal privilege."[63] It is therefore ironic that courts continue to uphold the testimonial privilege as respecting the sanctity of marriage and fostering marital harmony.

The testimonial privilege is not the only way marriage continues to benefit abusers. Judicial protection orders offer another example. These protection orders prevent individuals from engaging in violent or threatening acts, harassment, contact, communication, or being in physical proximity to another person. Between 1970 and 1993, most states enacted special laws and proceedings relating to domestic violence protection orders, and they quickly became the most widely used legal remedy against domestic violence. Nevertheless, throughout the 1990s, many courts refused to grant domestic protection orders in the name of marital harmony. At one such hearing, the judge began the proceedings with the comment, "Well, well, well, we had a little domestic squabble, did we? Naughty, naughty. Let's kiss and make up and get out of my court."[64] In another case, the petitioner testified that her husband had repeatedly punched her in the face and presented photographs of her injuries. The judge still denied the protection order, stating:

> I am authorized to award you a civil protection order, which could order him to stay away from you and stop hurting you. But I'm not going to do that today.

> Because you have children together, you're going to
> have to find some way to cooperate with each other
> to raise them. So, I want you to go home and try to
> work things out in private. And I suggest that you go
> see a movie I saw recently, called "Mrs. Doubtfire,"
> where Robin Williams and his wife decide to sepa-
> rate, but still manage to find a creative way to work
> together when it came to their children.[65]

Studies on domestic violence from this period confirm that married abusers routinely received lesser penalties than unmarried abusers. The 1992 DC Gender Bias Task Force Report noted that 70 percent of respondents received shorter sentences in criminal prosecutions where perpetrator and victim were married as compared with violence between strangers. This report also showed that married perpetrators were significantly more likely to receive lighter sentences than those who committed domestic violence outside of the marital relationship.[66] A 1993 report compiled by the Missouri Gender Bias Task Force demonstrated a similar prejudice. This report revealed that judges imposed lighter sentences on defendants convicted of domestic violence crimes than those convicted of assaulting non-intimate-partner strangers and that the greatest reduction was for married perpetrators.[67]

Today, judges, police, and even victims' friends and family remain reluctant to punish marital violence as harshly as non-marital abuse. In her 2021 article, "The Role of Place and Sociodemographic Characteristics on the Issuance of Temporary Civil Protection Orders," sociologist Anne Groggel found that "judges are more likely to issue temporary orders for unmarried victims who cohabit with their abusers than married victims." Groggel blames this difference on a continuing concern for marital harmony, writing that "judges seek to preserve existing marriages and are therefore more reluctant to grant protection orders for married victims than their unmarried counterparts, even after accounting for the recency and severity of abuse."[68]

Sentencing decisions also continue to be influenced by marital status. The 2004 Canadian study "Sentencing Outcomes: A Comparison of Family Violence and Non-Family Violence Cases" found that offenders convicted of violence against their spouse were significantly less likely to receive prison sentences than non-married offenders. It also showed that estranged male spouses were more likely to be imprisoned for domestic violence than current spouses.[69] Moreover, this differential treatment is not limited to legal actors. In their 2005 study on community-based domestic violence norms, sociologists Catherine Taylor and Susan Sorenson showed that non-married domestic violence victims received greater support than married victims for leaving the relationship and for seeking legal interventions. Married victims were likely to be counseled to "try and work things out."[70]

The Marital Rape Exception

The differential treatment of married and unmarried violence is particularly stark with respect to sexual assault. Until the 1990s, most states refused to treat marital rape as a crime and justified this decision with appeals to marital harmony.[71] In the 1981 marital rape case *People v. Brown*, the Supreme Court of Colorado exemplified this view when it wrote that the marital rape exception was beneficial, because it "may remove a substantial obstacle to the resumption of normal marital relations" and "encourag[e] the preservation of family relationships."[72] The

1984 Virginia case *Kizer v. Commonwealth* made similar appeals to marital harmony while also exposing the hollowness of this justification.

Edward and Jeri Kizer were a married couple who had been having marital difficulties for many months. After various attempts at reconciliation, Edward finally moved out. A few weeks later, he met with a friend, and the two discussed "the rape laws of Virginia." Specifically, they discussed the marital rape exception. The friend testified that Edward said, "He was kind of hard up for sex" and that, because he knew he could not be prosecuted, he thought he "ought to go over there and rip [the wife's] clothes off her and take it." The next day, that is what Edward did. He went to Jeri's home, forced his way inside, and raped her in front of their young child.[73] Edward was then convicted of rape, but his conviction was overturned. The appeals court held that it was not clear the "husband perceived, or reasonably should have perceived, that the marriage actually was ended." Consequently, Edward could not be convicted of rape.

Marriage is no longer an absolute defense to rape, yet it continues to provide significant protections. In many states, the bar for prosecuting sexually abusive spouses is higher than for non-spouses; proof of additional elements, such as force or resistance, is often required.[74] Other states maintain distinct reporting requirements for spousal rape. These include requiring that victims immediately report marital rape or lose their right to press charges. Marital rape is also, frequently, punished less severely than non-marital rape. In Maryland, until 2023, a spouse could not be charged with first- or second-degree rape, the two most serious charges.[75] In South Carolina, marital rape convictions can receive no more than ten years, while non-marital rapes can receive up to thirty,[76] and in Virginia, when the offender is the spouse of the victim, the judge may suspend a guilty judgment and order counseling "if the court finds such action will promote maintenance of the family unit and be in the best interest of the complaining witness."[77]

The different treatment of marital and non-marital rape is also apparent in cases involving capacity to consent. Many states exempt spouses from prohibitions forbidding sex with a mentally incompetent person.[78] In 2015, the issue of spousal consent and mental competence garnered national attention when seventy-eight-year-old former Iowa legislator Henry Rayhons was charged with rape. Rayhons's wife, Donna, was suffering from Alzheimer's, yet he continued having sex with her even after being informed that she could no longer consent. State prosecutors argued that sex with Donna was rape, but at trial the jury sided with Rayhons. Donna was Rayhons's wife, thus, her inability to consent to sex appears to have been deemed irrelevant.[79]

Heat of Passion

The greater tolerance for marital violence is also apparent in the continuing acceptance of the heat of passion defense. Throughout the 1990s, courts routinely excused marital violence as an understandable and forgivable reaction to marital infidelity. In one 1993 New Hampshire case, an estranged husband violently assaulted his wife after discovering her camping with another man. The husband was convicted of assault but sentenced to only twenty-eight days in prison and permitted to serve this time on the weekends. According to the judge, although the couple had been separated for a year, the victim was still legally the defendant's wife, thus "I can't conclude that [the attack] was completely unprovoked. I think that would provoke the average man."[80] The same year, an Ohio man with a record for murder, rape, and armed robbery entered his estranged wife's home and found her in bed with another man. He beat her with a crowbar and knocked out her daughter's teeth when the girl attempted to call 911. The Ohio court sentenced the man to the state-mandated fifteen years but released him after seven months. The judge explained, "The guy walked into his house with his wife in his bed with another guy. It's enough to blow any guy's cool if he's any kind of man."[81] One year later, in 1994, Kenneth Peacock shot his wife in the head several hours after finding her in bed with another man. Peacock pleaded guilty to voluntary manslaughter, yet the Maryland judge was reluctant to sentence him. The judge likened the case to a drunk driving accident, declaring, "The most difficult thing that a judge is called upon to do . . . is sentencing noncriminals as criminals." The judge added, "I seriously wonder how many married men, married five years or four years would have the strength to walk away, but without inflicting some corporal punishment . . . I shudder to think what I would do."[82]

The idea that a husband should be excused for a violent response to infidelity remains widespread. In nearly all US jurisdictions, a husband who commits violence upon discovering his wife in the act of adultery can receive a mitigated sentence or charge. Marriage remains the key to this defense. Courts are much more likely to find the defense inapplicable when an unmarried man is subject to infidelity. It is a wife's disloyalty, either through actual adultery or sometimes just a desire to leave the marriage, that is treated as uniquely provoking.[83] The 2007 case *People v. Le* is one more recent example.

In Le, Johnny Viet Le killed his wife's lover, Truoung (known as Thang). When Le first discovered the affair, he confronted his wife, Pham, who promised to stop. Despite her promise, the affair continued. When Le learned of the affair again, Pham again promised to end it. When Le discovered for the third time that the affair had not ended, he told Pham he wanted to meet Thang. Pham objected, and Le became very angry. He arranged the meeting without Pham's help (he pretended to be a potential customer) and then butchered Thang with a meat cleaver. Le was arrested and convicted of second-degree murder. On appeal, the conviction was reversed. The California Court of Appeal held that the evidence supported a finding that Le was provoked, and the jury should have received an instruction on voluntary manslaughter.

The *Le* court sympathized with Le and viewed his violence as uncharacteristic and understandable. In describing Le, the court wrote, he is a "47-year-old man with a peaceful disposition and no criminal record." It was his wife who was presented as the real culprit. Pham's insults toward Le on the day of the murder were described "as the spark that caused this powder keg of accumulated provocation to explode."[84] According to the court, this provocation caused Le to act "rashly and under the influence of intense emotion that obscured [his] reasoning or judgment." Consequently, the court held that a manslaughter instruction was appropriate. Notably, in reversing Le's conviction, the court emphasized how much Le loved Pham and how horrible it was for him to discover she "still loved Thang." Le hacked a man to death with a meat cleaver, but because his wife cheated, the court found him sympathetic.

Ironically, while marriage excuses violence and protects abusers, it is often touted as doing the opposite. In their 2014 *Washington Post* article, "The Best Way to End Violence Against Women? Stop Taking Lovers and Get Married," law professors Brad Wilcox and Robin Wilson argued that women can avoid physical and sexual violence by getting married. They noted that married women are victimized less than other women and suggested this statistical difference was because marriage "cause[s] men to behave better." Wilcox and Wilson claimed that married men are less violent than unmarried men because they "tend to settle down after they marry, to be more attentive to the expectations of friends and kin, to be more faithful, and to be more committed to their partners — factors that minimize the risk of violence." The article presented marriage as the cure for male violence, and domestic violence victim advocates were quick to criticize this claim.[85] As one wrote, "The last thing that women in abusive relationships need is to be told that they can turn a bad man good by marrying him."[86]

The freedom to commit abuse is rarely acknowledged as a marriage incentive. One exception is mail-order marriage. In the context of mail-order marriage, the idea that men are marrying to abuse is widely accepted. In 1999, an Immigration and Naturalization Service report on the international mail-order bride industry stated:

> While no national figures exist on abuse of alien wives, there is every reason to believe that the incidence is higher in this population than for the nation as a whole. Authorities agree that abuse in these marriages can be expected based on the men's desire for a submissive wife and the women's desire for a better life.

Organizations such as Tahirih Justice Center, which works to end violence against women, have also suggested that men seek mail-order marriage to perpetuate abuse. Layli Miller-Muro, the executive director of Tahirih Justice Center, stated, "[The mail-order-bride] industry predominantly places women at a disadvantage where the man is the paying client and the woman advertised as a product, a commodity." According to Muro, this creates a "presumption of power and a potentially very dangerous recipe for abuse." In 2005, Congress responded to these fears with the International Marriage Broker Regulation Act (IMBRA). The act accepts the idea that men seek mail-order marriage to perpetuate abuse, and it provides mail-order brides with special rights and protections to reduce that possibility.

Whether mail-order brides are more likely to be abused than other wives is hotly debated.[87] Nevertheless, the discussion surrounding mail-order marriage and abuse shows that, in this context, abuse is recognized as a potential marital motivation. The other obvious example is child marriage. It is now widely assumed that most child marriages are motivated by adult men's desire to legally engage in child sexual abuse. As historian Nicolas Syrett writes in his book *American Child Bride*, "Contemporary observers may recoil when an older man marries a much younger girl . . . because they suspect him of pedophilia." He notes, "Marriage, in this analysis, is simply a back door to that which is illegal outside of it."

Child Marriage

Sex with a child is a strict liability crime. This means the child's "consent" is irrelevant. The well-known adage "sixteen will get you twenty" (meaning sex with a sixteen-year-old will subject you to a twenty-year jail sentence) is a recognition of the strict liability aspect of state statutory rape laws.[88] Still, marriage remains an effective defense, and until relatively recently it was a defense actively promoted by many states. A disturbing

1997 law review article about child marriage in Orange County, California, revealed that a county social service agency routinely advised pregnant teenagers, some as young as thirteen or fourteen, to marry their statutory rapists. According to the article, agency officials promised not to report the fathers of these girls' babies to law enforcement authorities if the parties agreed to marry. Such tactics worked. After being "shaken by threats of arrest," most men agreed to marry the children they had impregnated. The article also revealed that once the threat of jail had passed, many of these men abandoned their child brides.[89]

Today, anti-child-marriage advocates, many who are former child victims themselves, have been slowly changing state child marriage laws. Sherry Johnson is one such advocate. Johnson was eight years old when she was raped by an adult member of her church in the late 1960s. When she became pregnant at ten, the police started an investigation, but the investigation ended when Johnson's parents and the church elders pressured her to marry her rapist. "They took the handcuffs from handcuffing him," she said, referring to the risk he faced of arrest for rape, "to handcuffing me."[90] Eventually, Johnson divorced her rapist and began working to protect other children from sharing a similar fate.

Due to the efforts of advocates like Johnson, states are increasingly restricting child marriages. Some have done so by limiting underage marriage to parties within a similar age range. Florida requires that the spouse of a child bride be no more than two years older than the child, while Arizona sets a three-year age gap.[91] Other states have restricted child marriages by raising the age of consent. Recently, both Virginia and New Jersey have raised the age of consent to eighteen.[92] These changes are encouraging, but they are not universal. Many states continue to permit underage marriage and allow child sexual abusers to avoid prosecution.[93] In addition, the problem of underage marriages may soon become worse. In 2022, the US Supreme Court eliminated the constitutional right to abortion. Shortly thereafter, many states began banning access to abortion. Without abortion, there will be fewer options to hide the evidence of child sex crimes. This may become an increasingly powerful reason to marry, but it also underscores the deep-seated problems with the marriage defense.[94]

When most women were at the financial and sexual mercy of men, the criminal defense benefits of marriage were justifiable. The availability of the marriage defense could force reluctant men into marriage or allow vulnerable women to leave dangerous relationships. However, the connection between marriage and criminal prosecution was always an imperfect solution to women's economic, legal, and sexual vulnerabilities. The defense protected vulnerable women from certain harms but exacerbated others. Today, the positive aspects of the marriage defense have largely disappeared. Its primary benefits are for those wishing to abuse, and, sadly, many still marry for these protections.

chapter five

The Married Parent

Maternity is a matter of fact. Paternity is a matter of opinion.

— AMERICAN PROVERB

Shortly after the conclusion of World War I, a young English-woman, known as E.A., arrived at Ellis Island with her three-month-old baby. As a single woman with a child, E.A. was detained by immigration officials as potentially "immoral." Then, after a hearing before a board of special inquiry, she was ordered deported. Just before E.A. was removed, Mrs. C.B. of Baltimore, the wife of the baby's father, intervened and filed an appeal. Mrs. C.B had sent E.A. the money to travel to the United States, and she testified that she and her husband wished to adopt the child. She also noted that she was fully aware the baby was the result of an affair between Mr. C.B. and E.A. that occurred while he was serving with the US armed forces in England. Despite the affair, Mrs. C.B. defended E.A.'s virtue. She described E.A. as "far removed from the deadline of immorality laid down by the immigration laws" and pronounced her "a lovable, refined girl." In further defense of E.A.'s morality, Mrs. C.B. noted that her brother-in-law, G.B., was willing to marry her. In a separate affidavit, G.B. confirmed Mrs. C.B.'s claim, writing, "I am perfectly willing to marry [E.A.] and be her faithful husband as long as I live for I know that her moral character is good." Mrs. C.B. concluded her plea to the immigration authorities by averring that she strongly supported a marriage between E.A. and G.B. and that it "would never disturb her happiness with her husband."[1]

The *New York Times* article on the E.A./C.B love triangle —
"Romance of War Puzzles Officials" — presented the story as
baffling. Yet C.B.'s actions were perfectly rational given America's
harsh immigration laws and non-marital fathers' limited parental rights. C.B. cheated on his wife while stationed abroad. His
girlfriend, E.A., became pregnant, but because C.B. was married,
he could not marry E.A. More important, because he was not
married to E.A., C.B. had no rights to the child. To gain rights
to his son, C.B. needed to adopt him. He also needed E.A. to
agree, but it appears E.A. would only agree to the adoption if
she remained part of her son's life. Therefore, the question was
how to bring both E.A. and the child to America. As an unwed
mother, E.A. fell afoul of the immoral purposes provision of the
1907 Immigration Act. The C.B.s solved this problem by having
C.B.'s brother agree to marry E.A.

The specific situation of the C.B.'s was rare, but the custody
problems facing non-marital fathers like C.B. were common.
Historically, paternal rights were established through marriage,
and men had no rights to the children they fathered outside of
wedlock. Thus, American custody law proceeded as follows: "The
mother is the woman who bears the child, and the father is the
husband of the mother."[2] Obviously, this was not always biolog-
ically true, but legally it was correct. As a result, marriage was
crucially important in securing the custodial rights of fathers.

Parental Rights Under the Common Law

Under common law, a man had complete authority over any
children born of his wife. His authority was so absolute that he
could even convey custody of the child to a third person without
the mother's consent and over her objection.[3] Conversely, a man
had no legal relationship to a child he sired out of wedlock.[4] A

non-marital father could not even effectively adopt such a child. The nineteenth-century inheritance case *Safford v. Houghton's Estate* highlights this problem. In *Safford*, the father had a child outside of marriage and then adopted him. The adoption meant the child could inherit from the father, but as the *Safford* court explained, it did not make the child legitimate, and thus it did not make him the legal heir of his biological grandfather. The court held, "To Abel Houghton, the father, and to all other kindred of George F., Frederick remained as before the adoption — an Ishmael — *filius nullius* — base-born, with no heritable quality in his blood."[5]

Although fathers could not legitimate their non-marital children through adoption, they could do so through marriage. This different treatment was intentional. As legal historian Lawrence Friedman explains, "Only 'families' in the traditional sense could have babies. If you wanted sex, you were supposed to get married. If you wanted babies, you were supposed to get married. Sex and babies were otherwise (officially) off limits."[6] Limiting paternal rights to marriage helped facilitate men's willingness to marry. However, this was only one of the parental benefits of marriage. An equally important benefit was the legal presumption that all husbands, regardless of biology, were the fathers of their wives' children.

The marital presumption was a legal fiction created to deal with the fact that, for most of history, men could rarely be certain they were the genetic parent of their children.[7] The presumption had been part of English common law for centuries, but it was only codified in the late eighteenth century as cuckoldry fears increased.[8] By linking marriage to legal fatherhood, the marital presumption ensured men could "guarantee" their paternity and justified the wisdom of assuming responsibility for children that might not be their biological progeny.[9]

In contrast with the robust parental rights of husbands,

The Cuckold Departs for the Hunt. Metal print by Isaac Cruikshank.

the rights of unmarried fathers were almost non-existent. Non-marital children were *filius nullius*, meaning, literally, the "children of no one." Technically, both unmarried fathers and unmarried mothers lacked legal rights to their children, but in practice, only unmarried fathers lacked such rights.[10] The vicious legal battle between Tillatha Catherine Bennett and her gold miner husband Isaac Graham highlights the stark difference between the rights of married and unmarried parents during the first half of the nineteenth century.

In 1845, twenty-one-year-old Tillatha Bennett wed forty-five-year-old Isaac Graham. The relationship quickly turned violent, but by that time Bennett was already pregnant and could not leave without forfeiting custody of her child.[11] Bennet remained with Graham for five years. Then, one day, a young man arrived at the homestead. The man was Graham's son from his first marriage, and he revealed that his mother was still very much alive. The Graham-Bennett marriage was bigamous. This meant Bennett was an unmarried mother and, under the law, the sole

Issac Graham.

legal custodian of her children. Shortly thereafter, Bennett fled with her two children (and most of Graham's gold). Eventually, Graham tracked her down and took the children back to California. Bennett then followed and sued for custody.

Initially, Bennett did not raise the bigamy defense (presumably she was reluctant to officially declare her children bastards). Instead, she claimed her actions were justified by Graham's cruelty. She published a letter in a San Francisco newspaper detailing Graham's abuse and wrote she had fled because she was "so tired of being beat and having Bowie knives drawn over me . . . for twice that old brute Graham drew his Bowie knife across my throat until blood ran down my breast and I expected every day he would kill me." The abuse Bennett suffered was horrendous, but it did not entitle her to custody. Eventually, with no other option, Bennett argued that Graham lacked paternity rights because their marriage was bigamous.[12]

Initially, Bennett's bigamy argument was successful.[13] The lower court agreed that because Graham's first wife was alive when Bennett and Graham married, their marriage was void. Bennett was granted sole custody of the children, and Graham appealed. The California Supreme Court then reversed the lower court's decision, holding that despite Graham's living first wife, his marriage to Bennett was valid. The court defended its dubious legal decision, claiming it was unwilling to condemn the children to bastardy. However, the real reason may have been less altruistic.

Graham was a violent man. Only a few years earlier, he had led a successful coup against the Mexican governor of Northern California and then planned a second insurrection against his replacement. Graham's son was similarly violent. After Bennett fled with the children, he shot at her mother and then murdered her brother. The court had good reason to worry about angering Graham. This may be why, despite the parents' obviously bigamous marriage, the court declared the Graham-Bennett children legitimate. Then, once it did so, all other factors, including Graham's violence and abuse, became irrelevant.[14] As the legal father, Graham was entitled to custody.

The rule that a husband's parental rights were absolute derived from the 1804 English case *Rex v. De Manneville*. In *De Manneville* the court gave custody of a nursing infant to its father despite the uncontested claim that the mother had only separated from the father to escape his horrendous abuse. The court also ignored the fact that De Manneville was a convicted criminal and Jacobite traitor and had broken into the mother's family home, literally grabbed the infant from her breast, and fled with it into a terrible storm. All that mattered was marriage. Because De Manneville had married the mother, he had the right to the child. As Lord Eldon, the lord chancellor deciding *De Manneville*, stated, "The law is clear that the custody of a child, of whatever age, belongs to the father [and] the father's rights extend to the hour of a child's birth."

American courts cited *De Manneville* for the proposition that married fathers should always receive custody of their children.[15] Still, they were often more open to considering parental conduct than their English peers.[16] In his 1884 *Commentaries on Equity Jurisprudence*, Supreme Court justice Joseph Story notes the presumptive authority of the married father to custody, but also suggests limitations:

> For although in general parents are entrusted with the custody of the persons and the education of their children, yet this is done upon the natural presumption that the children will be properly taken care of, and will be brought up with a due education in literature and morals and religion, and that they will be treated with kindness and affection. But whenever this presumption is removed, whenever (for example) it is found that a father is guilty of gross ill-treatment or cruelty towards his infant children; or that he is in constant habits of drunkenness and blasphemy, or low and gross debauchery; or that he professes atheistical or irreligious principles; or that his domestic associations are such as tend to the corruption and contamination of his children; or that he otherwise acts in a manner injurious to the morals or interests of his children, — in every such case the Court of Chancery will interfere and deprive him of the custody of his children, and appoint a suitable person to act as guardian and to take care of them and to superintend their education.

As Story notes, American courts presumed paternal custody but would consider giving custody to a more suitable person, if justified by the circumstances. Typically, this meant the child's mother.

The Rise of Maternal Rights

The idea of giving custody of children to mothers, not fathers, was supported by the nineteenth century's separate-spheres ideology. Often termed the cult of domesticity, these beliefs identified women with the home and family and supported the idea that maternal instincts made women the natural custodians of young children. The highly publicized 1840 Pennsylvania custody case *D'Hauteville v. Sears* was the first to argue for a maternal preference. The case involved a custody dispute between Ellen Sears, the daughter of a wealthy Boston merchant, and the Baron Gonzalve D'Hauteville, a Swiss nobleman. The couple met and married in Europe, but the relationship quickly deteriorated. Sears didn't like living in Switzerland and considered her husband a bully and a tyrant. D'Hauteville was similarly unhappy. He thought his wife was too independent-minded and neglected her wifely duties. He also didn't like the fact that his mother-in-law had been living with the couple since the wedding. Sears became pregnant, but by the time she returned to the US to give birth, the two were barely speaking. After the baby was born, she decided to stay.

As a married mother, especially one who had deserted her husband, Sears did not have the law on her side. The law presumed a marital child belonged to the father. Therefore, Sears's only option was to challenge this presumption. Sears claimed custody decisions should be based on the parents' relationship to the child, not marriage. She also argued that young children, in particular, needed the special care only a mother could provide. Surprisingly, the court agreed. According to the court, "Everyone knows that a father is unfit to care for an infant; physically unfit and unfit by reason of his avocations." It then declared, "No substitute can supply the place of [a mother]." Consequently, against all odds, Sears won.[17]

Family Prayer, circa 1871, by Currier and Ives.

As the nineteenth century progressed, women were increasingly considered the preferred caretakers of young children, and only deeply unwomanly behavior, usually related to accusations of immorality, could overcome the maternal preference. In the 1854 case *Lindsey v. Lindsey*, the Georgia Supreme Court explained this morality exception and why it defeated the maternal presumption. In *Lindsey*, the court refused to give custody of a child to an adulterous mother despite recognizing the woman had only left her husband after suffering terrible abuse. The court wrote, "In the eye of an omniscient God, the weak and erring woman may not be, (to say the least,) the more sinful and degraded of the two. But . . . in the opinion of society, it is otherwise." According to the court, having violated the marriage contract, an adulterous wife inevitably found herself reduced to "utter and irredeemable ruin, where her associations are with the vulgar, the vile and the depraved. If her children be with her, their characters must be, more or less, influenced and harmed by the circumstances which surround them." As a result, even if her actions were justified, an adulterous mother still could not be given custody of her children.[18]

Barring immorality, women became the favored custodians of children, and this maternal preference even included unmarried women. By the late nineteenth century, adoption by single women, many of whom had lost fiancés and sweethearts during the Civil War, became accepted and encouraged. "Leftover women" and "leftover children" were considered the perfect match.[19] In 1912, *Harper's Bazaar* exemplified this view when it published a glowing profile of Mary Hildreth, an unmarried, adoptive mother of ten children living in New Hampshire. Hildreth adopted her first child in the late 1880s after a friend, "to whom she was deeply attached," married and had a child. According to the article, Hildreth fell in love with her friend's new baby and decided that "she could not endure to be without a possession so wonderful and desirable." She then adopted a child about the same age and, as the article noted, "the two women — one married, one not — spent the next few years comparing infant accomplishments." The story ended by noting that Hildreth "could not love the children more if they were her own."

As unmarried adoption became acceptable, some social reformers began advocating for the elimination of distinctions between marital and non-marital families more generally. These reformers recognized that such differences harmed children, especially laws related to illegitimacy. Reformers contended that "there may be illegitimate parents, but there can be no illegitimate children."[20] In 1920, two regional conferences were organized by the Children's Bureau and the Inter-city Conference on Illegitimacy to consider ways to eliminate the distinctions between marital and non-marital families. One proposal was the Uniform Illegitimacy Act. This act would have entitled unmarried children to parental support, but it never gained widespread support.[21]

Although some child welfare advocates sought to reform illegitimacy laws, others were highly resistant. Despite acknowledging the problems with marriage-based parental rights and obligations, these men and women believed that such changes could not be made without undermining the marital family. In 1919, Bradley Hull, a social justice reformer and an attorney with the Cleveland Humane Society, exemplified such views when he argued against illegitimacy reform, warning, "If you put the illegitimate child on a basis of equality with the child born of the man wedded wife, there is a great source of danger." According to Hull, the question was whether "the child or the home [is] to be the unit of the state? If you're going to make, as far as the economic basis is concerned, the status of the unmarried mother and her child equal to that of the married woman and her child, you're going to do something to unsettle society." A few years later, child welfare advocate Emma O. Lundberg made a similar assessment. She declared, "In practically all states, up to the present time, it has been held incompatible with the interest of the legal family to place the child of illegitimate birth upon and equally with the children born in wedlock."[22]

Reforming Illegitimacy Laws

As attempts to reform state illegitimacy laws failed, support for the marital family grew, and even the prior approval of single-parent adoption began to wane. In the 1920s and '30s, motherhood was still viewed as women's primary role. However, as adoption historian Julie Berebitsky notes, "Now it was understood as part of the experience of the sexually satisfied and emotionally fulfilled wife."[23] Single women were increasingly viewed as abnormal and potentially sexually deviant, and child welfare experts began arguing that these women should not be allowed to adopt. By 1945, child welfare workers attending the National Conference of Social Work openly described "unmarried people" as "obviously disqualified [from adopting]" and grouped them with the "mentally ill" and "alcoholics."[24] It was not until the late 1960s that the different treatment of marital families and non-marital families was finally, seriously, questioned.

In 1968, the US Supreme Court decided *Levy v. Louisiana*. *Levy* was a wrongful death suit brought by five non-marital children after the death of their mother by her doctor's alleged negligence. The lower court rejected the children's claim, holding that the state statute only applied to a "legitimate child." On appeal, the Supreme Court reversed. The court held that the children's illegitimacy had no rational relation to the wrong inflicted on the mother, and thus the statute violated the Equal Protection Clause of the Fourteenth Amendment. The *Levy* court also forcefully rejected the doctrine of *filius nullius* and the idea that illegitimate children are "non-persons." As Justice Douglas poignantly noted, "They are humans, live, and have their being," therefore they are entitled to equal protection under the law.

Shortly after deciding *Levy*, the court decided *Glona v. American Guarantee*. *Glona* was another wrongful death case, but this one was brought by a mother for the wrongful death of her non-marital son. The lower court held that because Glona's son was born out of wedlock, she had no right to bring an action for his death. The Supreme Court reversed and once again held there was no justifiable basis for the distinction between marital and non-marital children.

Levy and *Glona* were limited to the role of illegitimacy in the wrongful death context, but four years later, in *Stanley v. Illinois*, the Supreme Court expanded on these rulings when it struck down a state law forbidding unmarried fathers from receiving custody. *Stanley* concerned the parental rights of Peter

Stanley, an unmarried father who had lived, off and on, with his girlfriend, Joan Stanley, and their three children for eighteen years. When Joan died, Stanley sought custody of their children. However, because he had never married Joan, Illinois refused to recognize him as a legal parent. Stanley was denied custody, and his children became wards of the state. Stanley then challenged the constitutionality of the Illinois custody law and won.

Stanley v. Illinois was a major victory for the rights of unmarried fathers, but it was not a rejection of the long-standing connection between marriage and parenthood. Despite ruling for Stanley, the court largely agreed with the state's argument that "the presence or absence of the father from the home on a day-to-day basis and the responsibility imposed upon the relationship" typically distinguished married fathers from unmarried fathers and justified giving them greater rights.[25] The *Stanley* court simply held that in the rare case that an unmarried father behaved like a married father — living with and caring for his children — then such a man could also be entitled to parental rights. The court did not find that married and unmarried fathers needed to be treated equally.

Five years later, the Supreme Court decided *Quilloin v. Walcott* and confirmed that when determining parental rights, marriage still trumped biology. *Quilloin* concerned an unmarried father's objection to his child's adoption by the mother's new husband. The trial court denied Quilloin's request to prevent the adoption, and on appeal the Supreme Court affirmed this decision. *Quilloin* described the unmarried father in *Stanley* as the exception and held that marriage, not biology, remained the primary means of conferring paternal rights. Quilloin, unlike Stanley, had not behaved like a married father. He had not lived with his child or the mother. Therefore, the court held it was not discriminatory to distinguish an unmarried father like Quilloin from marital fathers.[26] Unmarried fathers could possess parental rights, but in most cases the rights of married fathers remained greater.

Marriage and Contraceptives

The Supreme Court's 1965 decision in *Griswold v. Connecticut* also highlighted the connection between marriage and parental rights. In *Griswold*, the court held that married people, but not single people, had the right to use contraceptives and thus, control the decision to become a parent. This victory was the culmination of a decades-long campaign to legalize contraceptives for married couples.

One of the earliest marriage-based contraceptive arguments was made in 1918 by family planning pioneer Marie Stopes in her controversial book *Married Love*. Stopes's book intentionally focused on married couples. Both the explicitly marriage-focused title, and the opening sentence — "Every heart desires a mate" — set the book's marital tone. By linking contraceptives to marriage, Stopes redefined this taboo subject as acceptable and necessary — at least for married couples. She even suggests that her own marriage might have been saved if she had possessed greater sexual knowledge. "In my own marriage I paid such a terrible price for sex-ignorance that I feel that knowledge gained at such cost should be placed at the service of humanity."[27]

Less than a decade after *Married Love* was published, Margaret Sanger released her similarly groundbreaking book *Happiness in Marriage*. Like Stopes, Sanger focused on contraceptive use by married couples and specifically argued that birth control was essential to creating strong and healthy marriages.[28] Together, Stopes and Sanger helped change the public's perception of marital contraceptive use. By the 1930s, polls showed that

MARRIED LOVE

By Dr. MARIE STOPES.

Price 6/6, *post free, from :*

HEALTH PROMOTION Ltd.,

186, Efficiency House, Paternoster Sq., E.C. 4

most Americans supported marital birth control. In 1965, birth control advocates used this long-standing support for marital contraception to successfully challenge the constitutionality of Connecticut's contraceptive ban.[29]

Griswold involved a state ban on contraceptive use. The state defended the law, arguing that it helped deter promiscuity and other forms of sexual immorality. The *Griswold* court disagreed. The court found these arguments could justify a prohibition on contraceptive use outside of marriage but were inapplicable to married couples. It held that contraceptive use was different within marriage. When spouses used contraceptives, they were transformed into something moral, appropriate, and constitutionally protected.

Griswold established a constitutional right to contraceptive use for married couples, and shortly thereafter, in *Eisenstadt v. Baird*, the court extended this right to unmarried partners. *Eisenstadt* eliminated *Griswold*'s marital requirement. However, the case did not portend a rejection of the marital preference more generally. Eisenstadt could have cast doubt on the use of marriage as a criterion for numerous other parental rights and benefits, but it did not. As law professor Susan Frelich Appleton has written, "Despite *Eisenstadt*'s promise to make marriage irrelevant for important decisions in intimate life, marriage has persisted as the holy grail in family law."[30]

Marriage and Parental Rights Today

One of the most famous modern examples of marrying for parental rights was the 1996 marriage of Michael Jackson and Debbie Rowe. Initially, the public didn't know what to make of the Jackson-Rowe marriage, and their union was largely greeted with confusion. Unlike Jackson's earlier marriage to Lisa Marie Presley — a lavish affair and very public — the Jackson-Rowe marriage was secretive. Jackson didn't even confirm the marriage until months later. Nevertheless, when considering the very different purpose of this marriage, Jackson's behavior makes sense. Jackson married Rowe to become a father, and years later Rowe confirmed that the couple only wed after she offered her womb as a "gift."

Jackson was wealthy and famous. Undoubtedly there were other ways he could have become a parent. Still, marrying Rowe was probably the most effective. Marriage is the only legally binding agreement guaranteeing a man's parental rights before birth. Any non-marital parenting agreement with Rowe (or any other woman who agreed to bear his child) would have been risky. Adoption would also have been difficult given Jackson's scandal-plagued history; even surrogacy could have been problematic if Jackson was not (as is frequently suggested) genetically related to his children.[31] Marriage solved all these problems. Upon marriage, Jackson became the presumed father of Rowe's children, and once she gave birth, no additional steps were needed for him to assume legal and physical custody. Moreover, by marrying Rowe, any doubts surrounding her children's genetic paternity became legally irrelevant. Jackson was the father.

Historically, the marital presumption benefited husbands, like Jackson, men who may or may not have been the biological fathers of their spouses' children. At a time when paternity could rarely be proved, this presumption made sense. However, paternity tests are now highly accurate. Consequently, the presumption is no longer about providing a practical solution to the question of paternity. Rather, its continuation is an intentional choice to elevate the rights of marital fathers over non-marital fathers. Notably, in the 1988 Supreme Court case *Michael H. v. Gerald R.*, the court had the opportunity to eliminate the marital presumption — and it declined.

Michael H. involved a love triangle. Carol, who was married to Gerald, had an affair with Michael and became pregnant. After waffling back and forth between the two men, Carol ultimately chose to raise the child with Gerald. Michael then sought custodial rights, and the court refused his request. Despite recognizing that Michael was almost certainly the biological father (genetic testing was still relatively new), the court protected Gerald's paternity rights. According to the court, the purpose of the marital presumption was to safeguard marriage and marital harmony. The court held that the invention of accurate paternity testing did not undermine the marital presumption. Marriage trumped biology.[32]

The marital presumption has weakened since *Michael H.*, but it remains a significant benefit of marriage. In most states, rebutting the presumption is extremely difficult. Even if a man obtains a DNA test indicating he is a child's biological father, it doesn't mean he has the right to present this evidence to the court.[33] At least six states have statutes denying genetic fathers' standing to challenge the paternity of a marital child. Moreover, even in states where such challenges are permissible, a court can refuse to allow a paternity challenge if it determines it would not be in the child's best interest.[34] In addition, even if a court permits a paternity challenge and hears DNA evidence, it can still determine that it is in the child's best interest for the husband to maintain his status as the legal father.[35]

A 2015 study on the use of marriage as a "risk reduction

strategy" showed that men are aware of marriage's parenthood benefits and that they will marry for them. Many of the study's male participants "felt that taking advantage of [legal] benefits is a legitimate reason to marry, particularly when expecting a child."[36] These men cited securing paternity rights as "the big advantage of marrying." Notably, the most highly educated male participants were especially cognizant of the fact that "marriage was the best way to secure parental rights." One man noted that he and his partner had initially planned to enter into a registered partnership because they didn't want "the fuss" of marriage. "But then we started to look closely at all the arrangements and yes, marriage is a good institution. Everything is covered at once and everything is cared for."[37]

The study also revealed that the more paternity motivates men's marital decisions, the more men are willing to "pay" women for mating opportunities. Notably, the men least able to offer attractive compensation to potential wives were also the most disapproving of marrying for parental rights. These less-well-off participants described marrying for parenthood as too strategic and complained that people in such marriages were not marrying for the right reasons. As one participant noted, "When you are expecting a child you shouldn't get married because of the mere fact that marriage is securing your rights, because then you are only marrying for the child, and not because you yourself are ready."[38]

Single Status and Moral Fitness

Single men are not the only ones who marry for parental rights. Marriage can also play an important role in divorced parents' custody disputes, especially when there are accusations of immorality. In the past, arguing that a mother was morally unfit was one of the few ways a father could successfully challenge the maternal custody presumption. Today, such accusations (often involving unmarried cohabitation) continue to provide fathers with one of the most effective tools for gaining custody.[39]

Cohabiting parents are often dismayed to find they have few defenses against charges of immorality. For example, in the 1990 Michigan case *Helms v. Helms*, a mother lost custody of her children due to her unmarried cohabitation despite prior case law holding that unmarried cohabitation did not constitute immorality. The *Helms* court simply distinguished the prior cases based on the fact that the mother in *Helms* was cohabitating *and* pregnant. The court held that this difference made the prior cohabitation cases inapplicable and then awarded custody of the children to the father.[40] Similarly, in the 2000 case *Ulvund v. Ulvund* an unmarried mother was living with her same-sex partner, and due to same-sex marriage bans, the couple could not marry. Therefore, to avoid possible accusations of immorality, the mother refrained from all displays of affection toward her partner in front of the child. Unfortunately, not only were such precautions ineffective, they were also actually detrimental. In considering the father's change in custody petition, the *Ulvund* court held that the mother's lack of affection toward her partner was unnatural and harmful. It then placed the child with the father, noting, "He and his wife do express affection for each other in their home."[41]

More recent cases confirm the continuing difficulties facing unmarried parents in cohabiting relationships. In the 2010 Mississippi case *Brumfield v. Brumfield*, the state appellate court held that the mother's non-marital sexual relationships were relevant to its custody determination while also holding that the father's domestic violence — he had beaten the mother with a belt — was immaterial. According to the court, the father's actions need not be considered because it was "only" a single occurrence.[42] One year later, in *Masters v. Masters*, the Mississippi court again held that non-marital relationships could justify a change in custody. In *Masters*, the non-custodial father sought a change in custody based on the fact that the mother had lived with three different men in the nine years since the couple's divorce. The appellate court agreed that such non-marital cohabitation could warrant a change in custody and remanded the case to the trial court to consider the effects of mother's "unstable marital and extramarital relationships" upon the child's welfare.[43]

Remarrying for Custody

Given the fact that unmarried parents, especially mothers, are vulnerable to accusations of immorality, many have decided that the best way to neutralize this threat is to marry. The 1990 Arkansas case *Holmes v. Holmes* is illustrative. In *Holmes*, the father sought a change in custody based on the fact that the mother "had engaged in extra-marital affairs" while married to her second husband (not him), and that she began cohabitating with another man after her second marriage had ended. The court agreed with the father that the mother's unmarried cohabitation was concerning, and it appeared poised to order a change in custody. Then, recognizing she was about to lose custody, the mother quickly assured the court that she and her boyfriend intended to get married. By the rehearing they were married and the court held there was no longer any reason to order a change in custody. According to the court, the mother's "recent marriage was sufficient to overcome her previous, unstable conduct."[44]

The 2004 Arkansas case *Powell v. Marshall* is similar. In *Powell*, the court noted that the mother "has lived for an extended period of time with a person who was not her husband

[and] continued to cohabit with [this man] after the filing of the Petition for Change of Custody." The trial court then granted a change in custody based on this non-marital cohabitation, and the mother appealed. While the appeal was pending, the mother married her boyfriend. The appellate court then held the mother was "no longer out of compliance with the court orders," and the change in custody decision was reversed.[45]

As non-marital cohabitation has become increasingly common, some parents have challenged the continuing judicial preference for marriage over cohabitation. The 2016 Utah case *Robertson v. Robertson* is one example. In *Robertson*, both the mother and father were in non-marital cohabitating relationships, which the court viewed as extremely concerning. Consequently, once the mother married her boyfriend, she was quickly declared the more "moral parent" and awarded custody.[46] The unmarried father then challenged this custody determination. He argued there has been a "significant shift in culture" over the past thirty years and that his decision to cohabitate should not reflect negatively upon his moral standards. The appellate court disagreed. It dismissed the father's argument, stating, "In concluding that the moral standards factor weighed in favor of [the mother] . . . We agree with the trial court."

The Mystifying Curative Power of Marriage

Marriage can negate intrusive and arguably unwarranted morality concerns that threaten parental custody. It can also protect parents in cases where moral fitness concerns are clearly justified. For example, in the 1990 New Mexico case *Leszinske v. Poole*, the mother entered a sexual relationship with her uncle while married to her children's father and continued the relationship after the parties' separation. The father then sought

custody on the grounds that the mother's incestuous relationship could prove damaging to the children. Shockingly, the court
denied the father's request. According to the court, an incestuous relationship is only concerning outside of marriage. Once
the mother married the uncle, which she had to do in a foreign
jurisdiction because no US state would permit the marriage, the
court dismissed the change in custody petition.[47]

An even more stunning example of the curative power of
marriage is the 1998 Alabama case *K.T.W.P. v. D.R.W.* Here
the mother and her new husband were literally having sex in
front of the child. The couple shared a bedroom with the child
and engaged in sexual relations as she slept. When learning of
this sleeping arrangement, the child's father sought a change in
custody. During the hearing, the court asked the stepfather if
the child ever witnessed their sexual activity, and he flippantly
replied, "Well, that's part of living with a man, sleeping with a
woman."[48] The mother also admitted that she and the stepfather
had sexual relations with the child in the room, but justified it by
stating "not while she was watching." Unmarried parents have
lost custody for far less, yet the *K.T.W.P.* judge just shrugged and
told the mother — and the father! — that in the future, they
should both try not to have sex in front of the child.[49]

The custodial advantages of remarriage for fathers also extend
to cases where morality is not at issue. In a typical custody
dispute between a mother and a father, courts will weigh the
relative merits of the two parents. However, if the father is
remarried, many courts will also compare the mother against
the stepmother.[50] This is especially true when the stepmother,
but not the mother, is a homemaker. The 1990 Arkansas case
Puzzuoli v. Puzzuoli is typical. In *Puzzuoli*, the court declared
both parents fit, but awarded custody to the father because his
new wife was a homemaker. The court found the father's home
preferable, because the child would be cared for by a stepparent

as opposed to the day care center his mother planned to use. By giving custody to the father, the court stated the child would now be "part of a family."[51]

The 2001 Alaska case *West v. West* is similar. In *West*, the court held that because the father planned to get remarried, he could provide a better home environment, meaning a "two-parent household," than the unmarried mother. In explaining its decision, the court noted, "It's likely that [the father] will remarry . . . And that's a situation that, I think, is very positive because of the number of adults it provides in a household for child-rearing. It's likely that's going to happen. I think highly likely in the near future. And that there would be two adults in that household, part of the immediate family, that would be available most of the time."[52] The *West* court then granted custody to the father.

More recent cases also demonstrate the continuing custodial benefits of remarriages. For example, in the 2017 Indiana case *Meyers v. Meyers*, the court that held the father's remarriage was a substantial factor in its decision to order a change in custody. It noted, "Father has a stable income, a stable home, and stable relationship with his new wife. This Court recognizes that this change of custody will be difficult on the children; however, this will result in the long-term emotional and psychological well-being of the children."[53] Likewise, in the 2018 Alabama case *Sylvester v. Cartee*, the court granted the newly remarried father's change in custody petition because he had remarried, and thus, his household was now the more "stable and suitable home environment."[54]

Social science research also confirms that fathers can gain a custodial advantage through remarriage. In their article "Effects of Divorce on Parents and Children," researchers E. Mavis Hetherington, Martha Cox, and Roger Cox examined a group of seventy-two middle-class white divorced families with a child in nursery school. All the families began the study with primary custody awarded to the mother. Over the next six years, six families experienced a change in custody, and in five of these six families, the change in custody followed the father's remarriage.[55]

Marriage can help parents gain or keep custody of their children, but its parenthood benefits are not limited to those who already have children. Marriage also helps those seeking to become parents, particularly those struggling with infertility.

Fertility Treatment Benefits

The first documented successful fertility treatment occurred in 1785, after the famed Scottish surgeon Dr. John Hunter was approached by a man unable to impregnate his wife. The man hoped Dr. Hunter could help, and Hunter agreed to try. Hunter collected a sample of the man's sperm and inserted it into the wife's reproductive tract. Nine months later, a baby was born.[56] Hunter had demonstrated that artificial insemination could work, but nearly a century passed before a woman was impregnated with donor sperm.

The first case of donor insemination took place in 1884, when Dr. William Pancoast of Jefferson Medical College in Philadelphia helped a childless couple conceive a baby. Pancoast invited the couple into his classroom and sedated the wife. He then obtained semen from the "best looking member of the class" and inseminated the woman while an audience of medical students sat in observation. According to his later published report, the insemination was successful and the woman subsequently gave birth to a baby boy. The mother was never told the truth of her son's conception, but the husband knew and was reputedly delighted.[57] Years later, the son serendipitously learned

John Hunter: Founder of Scientific Surgery by Robert Thom.

of his novel beginnings when he met one of the former medical students who had witnessed his conception.

Donor-conceived children remained rare until the mid-twentieth century, when technological advances enabled the use of frozen semen.[58] However, as artificial insemination (AI) became more common, it also became divisive. By 1945, the moral questions relating to AI were considered so pressing that when doctors and lawyers in the Chicago area planned their first Symposium on Medicolegal Problems they included AI on the agenda because "there is no subject at this time which is more controversial."[59] The debate over AI stemmed from the use of donor sperm and the concern that such insemination was a form of adultery.

The first case to address the question of AI and adultery was a 1921 divorce decision from Canada. The case, *Orford v. Orford,*

involved a married woman who became pregnant while she and
her husband were living apart. Given their separation, the child
could not have been Mr. Orford's, and Mrs. Orford was accused
of adultery. Mrs. Orford objected to the charge by claiming her
pregnancy was the result of artificial insemination. The judge
didn't believe Mrs. Orford (who was probably lying) and ruled
the child was the product of an extramarital affair. Nevertheless,
the court noted it didn't actually matter whether Mrs. Orford
was telling the truth because there was no legal difference
between adultery and artificial insemination. According to the
court, even if it had accepted Mrs. Orford's claim, she still would
have been guilty of adultery.[60]

American courts adopted the *Orford* reasoning and for
decades afterward held that donor-conceived children were
illegitimate.[61] Finally, in 1968, this view began to change. That
year, the Georgia legislature passed a statute legitimizing donor
insemination for married couples, and a California court upheld
the legality of AI. In both instances, the approval of AI was tied
to marriage. This link was especially clear in the California court
case *People v. Sorenson* in which the husband was described as a
man who, "unable to accomplish his objective of creating a child
by using his own semen," purchased semen from a donor "to
inseminate his wife to achieve [t]his purpose."[62] The *Sorenson*
court recognized that AI did not harm marriage, rather it could
help men fulfill their husbandly roles.

The reconceptualization of AI as marriage assisting, rather
than threatening, helped ease the moral concerns surrounding
the procedure. Soon, other courts and legislatures began adopting this view, and AI became widely accepted within the context
of the marital family. Nevertheless, its use outside of marriage
was treated very differently. Throughout the 1980s, many states
explicitly limited AI to married couples, and even in states without an outright ban, the unmarried were still routinely denied

access to this procedure.[63] A 1985 *Harvard Law Review* article on AI noted "that only about ten percent of the doctors who perform artificial inseminations are willing to do so for unmarried women."[64] Similarly, a 1987 survey conducted by the Office of Technology Assessment on Artificial Insemination Practice in the United States also confirmed that fertility clinics routinely refused to treat single women.[65]

Today, approximately one-third of AI consumers in the US are unmarried women. However, accessing this technology remains much more difficult for the unmarried. Some states continue to limit AI to married couples.[66] Others do not have specific prohibitions but permit doctors or clinics to deny treatment based on a preference for married parenthood.[67] In the 2008 California case *North Coast Women's Care Medical Group v. Superior Court*, Guadalupe Benitez challenged a California fertility clinic's right to discriminate based on marital status, and although she prevailed on other grounds, her marital discrimination was dismissed.

Benitez and her partner were a same-sex couple who sought reproductive assistance from North Coast Medical. However, because Benitez was unmarried (same-sex marriage was not yet legal in California), her request was denied. The defendant doctors claimed that providing artificial insemination treatment to an unmarried person violated their Christian religious beliefs. The lower court ruled in favor of the clinic and held that marital status discrimination was permissible. On appeal, the California Supreme Court agreed. It held that state law did not prohibit marital status discrimination but reversed the lower court's decision because it concluded the clinic had also discriminated based on Benitez's sexual orientation. Sexual orientation discrimination was forbidden, but marital status discrimination was fine.[68]

Shortly after the *North Coast* decision, California banned marital status discrimination. Other states have similar prohibitions. However, even these protections do not ensure that the unmarried have equal access to fertility assistance. In her article "I Got Inseminated in a Burger King Bathroom," journalist Joy Wright reveals how difficult it was for her to get artificially inseminated as an unmarried, gay woman. In the article, Wright notes that "sperm is not a scarce commodity," but that didn't mean she could "get [her] hands (or other parts) on any of it." Wright initially purchased frozen sperm from a sperm bank, but she soon ran out of money. "Do you know how expensive frozen sperm is?" she wrote. It was so expensive that Wright's friends helped her out by throwing her "a big sperm party — not a party where people brought sperm, which might have been a great idea, but a fundraiser to buy the stuff."[69]

Given Wright's limited income and inability "to obtain sperm by the traditional no-money-down method," Wright was willing to consider extreme options, and when a stranger she met at a wellness retreat offered to provide her with sperm, she eagerly accepted. The man lived hours away from Wright, so they would meet at a Burger King halfway between their respective homes, and Wright would inseminate herself in the restaurant's bathroom. Ultimately, these insemination attempts were unsuccessful, and Wright eventually adopted. Nonetheless, her story highlights the difficulties single women continue to face when trying to access AI.[70]

Fertility treatments are expensive, and insurance is often limited to married couples.[71] Currently, only seventeen states mandate that private insurance plans provide some fertility coverage, and of these one-third limit it to married couples.[72] Without a state mandate, many private insurance companies refuse to cover the unmarried. In 2022, OSF HealthCare, a private insurance company that operates 15 hospitals and 132 other facilities in Illinois and Michigan, made headlines when it narrowed its definition of *infertility* to "the inability for a married couple of the opposite sex spouses to conceive." The company readily admitted its goal was to assist only "married opposite sex spouses" to have children.[73] OSF is a private company. However, federal and state government fertility coverage is also, often, restricted to the married. For example, the federal government covers fertility services for veterans, but only married ones.[74] Similarly, Utah recently expanded its public employees' insurance program to cover fertility treatments — but again, only for spouses.[75]

For those seeking fertility coverage, marriage is often the best option. In 2010, Marsha Greene quickly realized the difficulties she would face in seeking fertility treatments as an unmarried woman in Maryland. Greene and her partner were both divorced and neither wanted to remarry, but they both wanted to start a family. Unfortunately, Greene had diminished ovarian reserves and extremely low odds of conceiving naturally. Her doctors recommended fertility treatments. She was advised to begin with IUI (intrauterine insemination) and was told that if that didn't work, she should move to IVF (in vitro fertilization), which can easily run $10,000 a round. Greene had insurance, and it covered fertility treatments, but the coverage was limited to married couples. When she spoke with her insurance company, she was bluntly informed they were "unable to cover any procedure, unless it is carried out with my spouse's sperm." As long as Greene remained unmarried, she'd have to pay out of pocket. "I can afford to do this maybe three times, so I am hopeful that it will work quickly," she said. If it didn't, Greene noted she would likely get married.[76]

Marriage and Adoption

Marriage's parenthood benefits also extend to adoption. Although no state currently requires adoptive parents to be

married, many still give married couples preference.[77] Private
adoption officials also routinely prefer married couples over
single parents.[78] In her article on Louisiana adoption services,
attorney Eden Bubrig recounts an interview with "Miss J," a
single woman in her forties who attempted to adopt a baby
through the Adoption Services of Catholic Charities, a non-profit
adoption agency in Louisiana. Miss J told Bubrig that she was
forcefully discouraged from attempting to adopt because she was
single. "They told me I was basically wasting my time and a lot of
my money. Because I was unmarried, I wouldn't even be considered. That was the only thing they knew about me, and at that
point, that's all they needed to know to make their decision."[79]

Bias on the part of birth mothers can also make it harder
for the unmarried to adopt, and most are keenly aware of
this marital preference. Consequently, potential adoptive
parents may marry to increase their adoption odds.[80] On the
online message board Wedding Wire, a woman named Kelly
explained how such considerations influenced her own marital decision. The thread began with the question, "Why get
married?" Kelly responded that in her case, it was to adopt a
child. Kelly notes that initially she and her partner were not
inclined to marry. The couple preferred a relationship that
was "more free spirited" and lacking in government involve-
ment. However, they changed their minds when they started
thinking about the adoption benefits of marriage. Kelly wrote,
"While it's not a requirement to be legally married to adopt it
greatly increases the likely hood [sic] the process will go well.
We decided we had more to gain from marriage than not,
especially long term."[81]

Kelly was in a romantic relationship when she decided to
marry, but platonic partners also marry for parenthood benefits.
In 2009, Dear Abby received the following letter from a woman
and her friend who wished to adopt:

Dear Abby: I consider my best friend, "Randall," to be my platonic soul mate — like a brother, only closer. Randall is gay. I am a straight female. We have no romantic interest but a deep and meaningful love nonetheless. We have talked about raising children together. In some states, there is an adoption requirement that the parents be married. Would it be considered duping friends and family to have a "real" wedding?

— Platonic in Michigan[82]

International adoptions are also easier for the married. In many foreign countries singles are barred from adopting.[83] Many organizations that help finance international adoptions also restrict their services to the married.[84] In her book *A History of Marriage*, Elizabeth Abbott recounts the marriage of Heather and Greg, which took place to facilitate an international adoption. The couple had lived together for fourteen years, but only married once they decided to adopt a child from China. In her wedding vows, Heather highlights their adoption plans. Standing at the altar, she tells Greg: "You're good with words. I'm good with pictures. So I won't say anything and I'll paint you a picture instead . . . I'll paint a plane flying to an unknown country to find an unknown child . . ." Heather had loved Greg for fourteen years, but she married him to adopt a baby.

Marriage's adoption benefits also extend to stepparent adoptions. When a spouse seeks to adopt their partner's child, the process is streamlined. Fitness determinations, home studies, and other procedures are usually not required. Even more important, such adoptions don't require terminating the custodial parent's rights. In contrast, when an unmarried person wishes to adopt their partner's child, the process is often difficult and sometimes impossible. In many states, an unmarried person cannot adopt their partner's child without terminating the partner's parental rights.[85] In other states, termination is not required, but an unmarried co-parent will still need to prove parental fitness, which can mean home studies, criminal background checks, waiting periods, and multiple adoption hearings. In the case of donor-conceived children, which are common in same-sex relationships, the unmarried partner may also need affidavits from a doctor or cryobank attesting to the facts of a child's conception.[86]

The importance of marriage for second-parent adoption was highlighted in *Obergefell v. Hodges* (the case extending the constitutional right to marriage to same-sex couples). Two of the *Obergefell* plaintiffs, April DeBoer and Jayne Rowse, were a same-sex couple living in Michigan. They were also the adoptive parents of four special-needs children. However, because Michigan law stated that only married couples or single people were permitted to adopt, the DeBoer-Rowse children only had one legal parent. DeBoer and Rowse joined the *Obergefell* litigation to secure legal rights to their children. As Rowse stated, "[We're] just two parents that want to take care of our kids and if that means going for marriage, that's what it is."[87]

In his *Obergefell* opinion, Justice Kennedy detailed the DeBoer-Rowse story and praised the women for their efforts to achieve "the certainty and stability all mothers desire to protect their children." He then highlighted the unfairness and danger of their situation, noting that if something happened to one of the mothers, "the other would have no legal rights over the children she had not been permitted to adopt." Kennedy wrote that, because their parents could not marry, the DeBoer-Rowse children were forced to "suffer the significant material costs of being raised by unmarried parents, relegated through no fault of their own to a more difficult and uncertain family life." Ultimately, Kennedy concluded that one of the most important reasons same-sex couples must be given the right to marry was because, "without the recognition, stability, and predictability marriage offers, [same-sex couples'] children suffer the stigma of knowing their families are somehow lesser."

Reaffirming the Preference for Married Parents

Obergefell ended the custodial uncertainty faced by unmarried couples like DeBoer and Rowse, but it did so by reaffirming the long-standing notion that non-marital life, and particularly non-marital child-rearing, is inferior. As critics like law professor Katherine Franke have noted, *Obergefell* accepted the idea of "the non-married parent . . . as a site of pathology, stigma, and injury to children."[88] Consequently, while the fight for same-sex marriage highlighted the inequality of attaching parental rights to marriage, the *Obergefell* decision ultimately helped further entrench this practice.[89]

The rights and benefits that attach to marriage are intentionally designed to create inequality between married and unmarried parents. As law professor Elizabeth Bartholet has noted, parenthood is the only area "that our system proudly proclaims not simply the right to discriminate [on the basis of marriage] but the importance of doing so."[90] This unfairness is then exacerbated by the fact that marriage rates are not uniform across demographics. Rich, white couples, those already at an economic and social advantage, are the group most likely to marry and thus the group most benefited by the marital parenthood preference.[91] As law professor Dorothy Roberts notes, encouraging and protecting marital parenthood works in tandem with "the devaluation of minority childbearing."[92] Similarly, law professor Nancy Polikoff argues that the preference for marital childbearing is particularly harmful for same-sex couples because they have few other ways to form a legal family. According to

Polikoff, recognizing only the parentage of married same-sex partners "revives the discredited distinction between 'legitimate' and 'illegitimate' children."[93]

As long as marital and non-marital families are treated differently, marriage remains a reasonable and rational decision for those seeking to secure greater parental rights. However, not all parents can or wish to marry. By encouraging the link between marriage and parenthood, the law neglects unmarried families and exacerbates their vulnerabilities. As child welfare advocates have long argued, children are most protected when they are treated equally, without regard to their parents' marital status. Protection, not marriage, should be the ultimate goal. Currently, it is not.

chapter six

Marrying for Money Part Deux

When you marry for money, you'll earn every cent.

— AMERICAN PROVERB

When Donald Trump became president, many long-standing presidential conventions were dismissed. One of the most surprising was the delay in having his family join him in the White House. Years later, it was revealed that this delay was a bargaining tactic. Publicly, Melania claimed she was waiting because she didn't want to interrupt their son Baron's school year. Privately, she was using the delay, and the ensuing bad publicity, to successfully pressure Trump into renegotiating her prenuptial agreement.[1]

That Melania signed a prenup is unsurprising. She was Trump's third wife, and, as everyone understood, she was marrying for money.[2] When they met, Melania was a young, beautiful, and only moderately successful model. Trump was an aging millionaire. From the beginning, money permeated their relationship. In 2004, when Trump proposed, he "iced" the deal with a $2 million engagement ring. When Melania walked down the aisle, it was in a $100,000 pearl-and-diamond-studded wedding gown. When she said, "I do," she was given a $500,000 diamond-encrusted wedding band, and when she greeted her guests, it was in front of a $50,000 wedding cake.[3]

During the wedding reception at Trump's Mar-a-Largo resort, a small plane crisscrossed the sky with a banner that read, MELANIA, YOU'RE HIRED. These words echoed Trump's catchphrase from his TV show *The Apprentice.* The statement also implied that

Melania Trump White House portrait.

being Trump's wife was a job and that Melania would be paid and she has been. In a *New York Post* story about Melania's marital life, it was noted that "most days, the lobby [of Trump Tower] is brimming with wardrobe boxes delivered for Melania." A different article estimated her shoe collection at more than $100,000 and her jewelry collection is worth many millions. The most stunning piece in her collection is a $3 million, twenty-five-carat diamond ring she received from Trump on their tenth wedding anniversary. It is prominently featured in her official White House portrait.[4]

People Marry for Money

Melania Trump may be the most famous modern-day gold digger, but she is far from alone. Marrying for money is no relic of the past. In fact, the practice may be growing. As chapter 1 detailed, historically women were expected to marry for money.

Then, in the early twentieth century, acceptance of this practice largely disappeared, but the desire and the need to marry for money did not.[5] Today, money remains a primary marriage motivation for many Americans.

In 2009, Prince & Associates, a Connecticut-based research firm focusing on the wealthy, polled a nationwide sample of 1,134 people and found that two-thirds of women and half of men would marry "an average-looking person" they liked for money.[6] Similarly, a 2011 study by the websites ForbesWomen and YourTango found that 75 percent of women said they would not marry someone who was unemployed, and 41 percent said they wouldn't marry someone who earned significantly less than them.[7] Most recently, a 2019 survey released by Merrill Edge, an online discount brokerage and division of Bank of America, revealed that 56 percent of Americans would choose money over love, valuing a partner who provides financial security more than one for whom they are "head over heels."[8]

Money remains such an important relationship factor that many singles will refuse a first date if the potential partner appears to lack funds. A revealing 2016 poll conducted by the online dating service Match.com showed that owners of older smartphone models are 56 percent less likely to get a date than singles who own the latest, and most expensive, technology.[9] Men, in particular, understand the role money plays in their dating prospects. A 2022 survey conducted by the personal credit company Credello found that a shocking 41 percent of men were willing to take on substantial debt in order to financially impress a new love interest.[10]

"People want the money, it's not a big secret," explains Russ Alan Prince, an expert on the wealthy. In an article on marrying for money, Prince notes that people are well aware of the ways their lives could improve with additional funds and describes the calculus as something like the following: "If I had a million dollars, I don't have to do this nonsense job anymore." According to Prince, "It's not a sin to want the good life. Let's be realistic. Money doesn't buy happiness, but it solves a lot of problems."[11] Economist Laurence Kotlikoff echoes these sentiments. In a 2022 opinion piece for CNBC, Kotlikoff writes, "We humans have the capacity to fall in love with lots of people. And there's no shame in targeting your swooning on someone who can provide you with a higher standard of living . . . Put it this way: If two people are the same in most respects, except one earns twice as much as the other, don't flip a coin. Go for the higher earner, and yes, marry for money."

Single women frequently heed this advice, and many will actually move to be closer to rich men. In her article "Sex and the City," economics professor Lena Edlund notes it is no coincidence that cities with the highest proportion of wealthy men also have some of the lowest male-to-female ratios.[12] The national average is 97 men to 100 women, yet in Boston and

New York the ratio is 94 men to 100 women, and in Philadelphia and DC, it's a paltry 90 men to 100 women. Rich men are aware of their "buying power" on the dating market. A 2016 study published in the journal *Frontiers in Psychology* showed that the more money men had, the less satisfied they were with their partner's physical appearance.[13] However, the practice of using money to interest a spouse is not limited to the wealthy. It is present at all income levels and becomes particularly widespread when women are scarce.

A 2012 study found that reading a single article about female scarcity was enough to change male financial behavior and convince them to significantly increase the amount of money they spent on a potential marriage partner. This study also confirmed that scarcity effects were not limited to men. When the female participants read the same articles, they also expected men to raise their spending.[14]

For some, marrying for money can be a path to riches, but for others, it is simply a way to avoid becoming poor. Single people worry about money. A 2017 study by the financial services company Northwestern Mutual found that 55 percent of single women and 49 percent of single men were unhappy with their financial situations. It also found that single people were nearly twice as likely as married people to feel financially insecure and that such worries increase with age.[15] As Boston psychotherapist Abby Rodman told MarketWatch, "Nothing spells financial anxiety more than the threat of growing old impoverished. So, if you don't have enough money, where will you get it? Marrying someone who has some wealth is one way to sidestep that potentially bleak future."

Financial concerns are also a common reason relationships end. In his book *The Marriage-Go-Round*, sociologist Andrew Cherlin recounts a conversation with a woman who had recently terminated a long-term relationship with her insolvent partner.

"Money means . . . stability," she told Cherlin. "I don't want to struggle; if I'm in a partnership, then there's no more struggling, and income-wise we were both still struggling." This woman wasn't looking to get rich, but she did expect her relationship to make her financially stable. In this view, she is far from alone. In fact, the number of people marrying due to financial anxiety may be increasing. A 2022 Match.com report revealed that 30 percent of singles state that due to inflation, they are now looking for a financially stable partner.[16] The same year, a survey by WalletHub found that, compared with the previous year, 37 percent more Americans said they wouldn't marry someone with bad credit.

The Fear of Marrying for Money

Mixing love and money is widespread, yet it remains taboo. In 2003, Fox tapped in to these financial anxieties with the dating show *Joe Millionaire*. The show featured a handsome construction worker and twenty beautiful women who, incorrectly, believed he was a millionaire. "Joe" dates the women and tries to figure out which have genuine feelings for him and which are only interested in his *non-existent* millions. Then, in the season finale, Joe's true financial status is revealed, and the remaining woman must decide if she's still interested. The final episode was watched by 34.6 million viewers. That year, only the Super Bowl had a larger TV audience.[17]

American men are inundated with warnings to protect their cash, and their hearts, from unscrupulous women. Rapper Kanye West's song "Gold Digger" is typical:

> *18 years, 18 years*
> *She got one of yo' kids, got you for 18 years*

Evan Marriott, "Joe Millionaire."

I know somebody payin' child support for one of his kids
His baby momma car and crib is bigger than his is
You will see him on TV any given Sunday
Win the Super Bowl and drive off in a Hyundai.

Men's pro sports leagues like the NFL and NBA further exacerbate such fears and even run seminars to educate rookies on the dangers of gold diggers.[18] At one of these seminars, former NFL pro Irving Fryar infamously cautioned a room of young players, "The C.I.A. has nothing on a woman with a plan." NBA star LeBron James similarly warned, "Watch your money, and watch out for women." In reflecting on these lessons, Giants lineman Jeff Hatch noted, "You'd think that women were an evil, evil species." In fact, many men do. As Canadian journalist Sabrina Maddeaux notes, "The mere mention of a gold digger is enough to prompt a litany of unsupported and borderline misogynist propaganda to spew from [men's] mouths."[19]

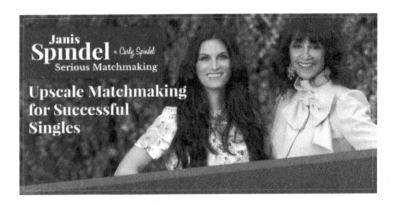

In recent years, businesses have sought to capitalize on gold-digging fears by offering to protect men from potentially mercenary women. One such company is the online dating site Millionairematch.com, which was created to match wealthy singles with other wealthy singles and weed out gold diggers through income verification. Upscale dating agencies offer similar services. The famous NYC matchmaker Janis Spindel, owner of Club J-Love, charges men between $50,000 and $250,000 to pre-screen for "riff raff and gold diggers." Similarly, Samantha Daniels, founder of the elite matchmaking service Samantha's Table, states that clients pay top dollar for her "gold digger radar" and boasts she "can smell women from a mile away who only care about money."[20]

Financial fears are one reason marrying for money is so widely condemned. A second, but equally pervasive concern, is the belief that money corrupts love.[21] In a 2005 article, *New York Times* columnist David Brooks expressed a version of this fear when he lamented the increasing use of separate checking accounts by married couples. According to Brooks, husbands and wives were forgetting the distinction "between the individualistic ethos of the market and the communal ethos of the home." He warned then that "a union based on love can easily turn into a merger based on self-interest, where the main criterion becomes: Am I getting a good return on my investment?"

In her book *Contested Commodities*, law professor Margaret Radin writes about this fear of mixing love and money and the long-standing belief that if the commodified version of a thing exists, then the non-commodified versions will cease to exist.[22] As the famous MasterCard ad once proclaimed, "There are some things money can't buy." Love is assumed to be one of these "things."

Men who fear gold diggers will often force a potential spouse to "prove" their love by disclaiming any financial interest in the marriage. A revealing study on the use of prenups in New York showed that these agreements are often used as a gold-digging litmus test. One attorney interviewed for the study recounted a particularly telling incident in which he was asked to draft a prenup with "egregious" terms. After receiving the document, the client insisted his fiancée sign it. She reluctantly agreed, but as soon as she acquiesced, the man capitulated and said it was no longer necessary. As the attorney explained, "Because she said she would do it, [the man knew] 'ok, you're not marrying me for my money.'"[23] She had passed his test.

Gold-digging tests are considered necessary because marital deception is rarely actionable. The law expects that romantic partners will lie and will protect spouses when they do. The 1943 decision in *Nereni v. Nereni* is illustrative. Here a young woman sought an annulment after discovering her new husband had concealed a serious medical condition, but the court refused her request. According to the court, "No draconian law could or should be formulated to stop a man or maid from pursuing during courtship the harmless deceptive arts to which both almost universally resort by wrapping themselves in an aura which is not strictly theirs to use."[24] The court claimed everyone lies when they're courting and held there is nothing wrong with tricking a potential spouse with "a bewitching glass eye or a set of pearly false teeth." Such lies, said the court, are to be expected. Concealing one's financial motives also does not render a marriage invalid.[25]

In her book *Intimate Lies*, law professor Jill Hasday notes that lying about money is common among romantic partners, yet "courts are reluctant to award remedies when financial deception occurs within marriage." This is true even when the financial motives are blatant. In the 2013 case *In re Estate of Smallman*, the Tennessee court acknowledged that a woman who married her husband two weeks before he died was a "bad person" and "gold digger," but held these facts were still not a proper basis for invalidating a marriage.[26] *Smallman* is not unique. In fact, courts rarely sympathize with a tricked partner. For example, in the stunning 1975 New York case *Avnery v. Avnery*, the gold-digging husband repeatedly lied about his affection for the moneyed wife, yet the court admonished the woman. In denying the wife's annulment claim, the court condescendingly noted, "The fraud required for an annulment must be 'of such a nature as to deceive an ordinary prudent person' not an ordinary woman in love." More recently, in the 2010 case *Flowers v. Flowers*, the court accepted the husband's claim that the wife was a gold digger who held no romantic feelings for him but found her financial motives irrelevant. It callously declared, "Later-in-life marriages are often entered into for reasons other than a sexual relationship."

Benefits of Marrying for Money

The widespread fear of gold digging obscures the fact that most marriages are, at least in part, economic arrangements. Legally, marriage is an agreement to pool resources, financial and otherwise, for the benefit of the couple. It is also an assur-

Shaniqua Tompkins.

ance that, should the marriage end, both spouses are entitled to a share of these jointly accumulated assets. These are important protections, yet they are almost impossible to secure outside of marriage.[27] Despite the rising rates of non-marital cohabitation, most states refuse to recognize the shared property interests of unmarried intimates.[28] Marriage is the only way most romantic partners can receive a portion of the property they helped accumulate. Shaniqua Tompkins, the longtime girlfriend of rapper Curtis Jackson, a.k.a. 50 Cent, learned this lesson the hard way.

Tompkins and Jackson were in a romantic relationship for twelve years, but never married. Then, when the relationship ended, Tompkins sought financial compensation from Jackson. According to Tompkins, she and Jackson agreed that she would provide the domestic and homemaking services, including the care of the couple's child, that allowed Jackson to devote himself to his music. In return, Tompkins would share in Jackson's future financial success. If the couple had married, such an agreement would have been unnecessary. Spouses have a legal right to a share of all property accumulated during the relationship. In addition, a spouse's homemaking services may also entitle them to alimony. However, because Tompkins was only a girlfriend, the court held that the work she provided, taking care of the home and the child (the same services she would be compensated for as a wife), was "of a nature which would ordinarily be exchanged without expectation of pay."[29] The court rejected her economic claim and dismissed her case as nothing more than an "unfortunate tale of a love relationship gone sour."

If women want to be compensated for their relationship efforts, they must marry, and they are expected to know this. In the 1994 Mississippi case *Davis v. Davis*, the court stated this rule explicitly. *Davis* involved an unmarried couple, Elvis and Travis Davis, who had lived together for thirteen years. On at least one occasion, and possibly several, Travis asked Elvis to marry him. Elvis declined, but her refusal did not end the relationship. For more than a decade, Elvis devoted herself to caring for Travis and their family. Elvis testified that she took care of the home and the children (both her child with Travis, as well as his children from a previous relationship) and did innumerable other household tasks including cooking, gardening, sewing, and painting. Due to these efforts, Travis was able to devote himself to his businesses — which grew significantly during the couple's relationship. When they met, Travis had a net worth of $850k. When the relationship ended, he had more than $7 million in assets. Elvis argued that she had a right to a share of this increase, but the Mississippi Supreme Court disagreed. According to the court, if Elvis had wanted compensation for her domestic services, she should have married. "When opportunity knocks, one must answer its call," wrote the court. Because Elvis "failed to do so," the court held, "her claim is all for naught."[30]

Theoretically, unmarried partners have the same right of contract as all other non-married parties, but in practice, they do not.[31] Cohabitants are held to higher standard of formality. As law professor Courtney Joslin writes, "The law authorizes courts to recognize joint business partnerships or ventures that exist in fact, even in the absence of formalities, express agreements, or even an understanding of the consequences of the parties' conduct. But courts refuse to apply these principles equally to recognize and give effect to the joint endeavor of starting and running a family. Instead, for this venture alone, formalities are required." When romantic partners seek compensation for "housewifely services," tasks such as cooking, cleaning, laundry, caring for children, paying bills, or the countless other things that keep a household running, their requests are rarely granted.[32] Legally, the dividing line for compensation is marriage. Whether this distinction is equitable is a different question.

A 2009 study by Professors Stanford Braver and Ira Mark Ellman suggests that most people find marriage-based distinctions far from fair. The study asked a random sample of adults to examine a series of heterosexual relationship vignettes and determine whether the man should pay the woman alimony after the relationship ended. Respondents, regardless of income, marital status, gender, or political affiliation, did not view marriage as the key factor in determining whether a romantic partner should be entitled to financial support. Instead, most awarded alimony based on perceived need and were willing to award support to an unmarried partner, even when such awards would not be permissible under the law. Braver and Ellman describe this rejection of the marriage-based distinction as "telling" and suggest "it is American law, not our respondents, that is peculiar."[33]

Marriage protects the non-moneyed party's economic interests in the relationship. However, both spouses can benefit when economic motivations are clear.[34] As sociologist Viviana A. Zelizer explains, "Economic activity and intimacy intersect all the time, and frequently create 'good matches.'" According to Zelizer, a "good match" doesn't mean that "you and I would approve of the bargain or that the match is equal and just. Instead, [it] mean[s] that the match is viable: It gets the economic work of the relationship done and sustains the relationship."[35] Consider the following ad placed in a 1985 issue of the *San Francisco Chronicle*. It reads:

> Attractive & successful young businessman, 32, would like to meet only a beautiful & classy lady 18-39 who is tired of working hard & wants to live well. I am only interested in a permanent living together relationship / marriage without children. Prefer someone with experience. Or interest in Real Estate to help me with my business.

The ad's author was offering money in exchange for a wife with looks, class, and "experience."[36] This was not altruism; he clearly expected to benefit from this exchange. More recent examples of such offers can be found on the dating website MillionaireMatch .com. The site was initially founded to connect wealthy singles to other wealthy singles (and explicitly exclude gold diggers), but many of the site's rich male clients were more interested in finding women with good looks rather than high incomes. Consequently, the site now includes many beautiful, non-moneyed women who are specifically looking for rich men. As one review notes, "These women are attractive enough to be extremely picky about only dating real millionaires. The 'Certified Millionaire' diamond on your profile will draw them in like moths to a flame."[37]

Although it is rarely acknowledged, marrying for money is often the only realistic opportunity most women have for

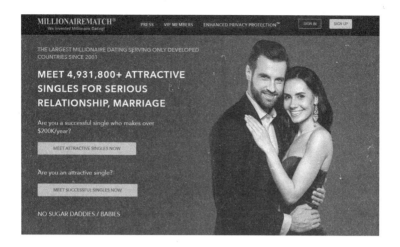

acquiring significant wealth.[38] The average American woman earns only 84 percent of what men earn, and this gender wage gap has remained stagnant for decades.[39] For the ultra-wealthy, this wealth difference is even more extreme. In 2022, only 13 percent of the world's billionaires were women. The percentage of female multimillionaires is nearly identical. In the United States, only 13.5 percent of millionaires are female, and the percentage who earned their wealth is even lower.[40] Not a single one of the top ten richest women on *Forbes*'s 2022 list earned her fortune. Forty percent received their wealth from their husbands while the remaining 60 percent inherited it from other family members.[41] As journalist Sabrina Maddeaux notes, "All the leaning in and hard work in the world won't change the fact that, even today, a self-made wealthy woman is a statistical unicorn." Thus, Maddeaux praises women who marry for money, describing them as the "front liners in the fight for class, economic and gender equality"[42]

Marrying for money also benefits women at the other end of the financial spectrum and may be preferable to the other financial arrangements women use to make ends meet. In 2015, more than a quarter million American women signed up to

become "sugar babies" on the website SeekingArrangement
.com.[43] The site connects young women with "sugar daddies"
who, in exchange for dates and other relationship perks, finance
their lifestyle. Some "sugar babies" are looking for fancy vaca-
tions or luxury goods, but many are primarily interested in
tuition payments. It is no coincidence that more than a third
of the eight million women on these sites are students. In fact,
SeekingArrangement.com explicitly targets college students and
gives free upgrades to those who register with an .edu address.
The site boasts, "When their biological dads can't pay for college,
Sugar Daddies are stepping up."[44]

Websites like SeekingArrangement tap in to the real financial
anxiety that many young women face after graduation. Studies
show that women take significantly longer to pay off their
student debts than men and that a whopping 53 percent of female
debtors (compared with 39 percent of men) are paying more in
student loan payments than they can reasonably afford. This
debt can then make it harder for women to change careers, start
their own businesses, or take lower-paying "dream" jobs.[45] It can
also make it hard to simply survive. According to the American
Association of University Women, "Student debt is making it
nearly impossible for many women to afford their basic living

expenses after graduating from college." Add children into the mix and the effects are even starker. The average single mother does not have enough funds to cover the costs of childcare. This financial insufficiency then makes further debt more likely and saving for things like retirement nearly impossible.[46]

Given the financial uncertainty facing many "sugar babies," it is not surprising that many will marry their "daddies" if given the opportunity. Brandon Wade, founder and CEO of SeekingArrangement.com, encourages such unions. "Women have married for economic reasons since the beginning of time. If you find a sugar daddy that is looking to settle down, then you're guaranteed a husband that will spoil and take care of you."[47] Notably, Wade is not alone in promoting marriage as a solution to female financial distress. As discussed in chapter 2, federal, state, and local governments have long encouraged poor women to marry for money. In 1992, Vice President Dan Quayle gave a speech declaring marriage "the best anti-poverty program there is." Since then, countless politicians have echoed these sentiments and backed them up with monetary incentives. In the 1990s, states like Wisconsin and New Jersey enacted bride-fare programs that provided recipients with increased monthly benefit payments, as well as the ability to exclude more income from the benefits eligibility calculation, if they agreed to marry. Then, in 1996, Congress passed the Personal Responsibility and Work Opportunity Act, which made marriage the centerpiece of welfare reforms.[48]

Opponents of government marital initiatives have tended to focus on the perceived harms of marital commodification. Hannah Rosenthal, executive director of the Wisconsin Women's Council, a research and advocacy group, called bride-fare programs "dressed-up marriage brokering for poor people." She noted, "It's dangling a paycheck in front of a girl and saying, 'We'll give you a bonus if you get married.'"[49] Sociologist Walter

Williams voiced similar concerns. "Marriage is much deeper than some government program," he said. "When you stand in front of the minister, you're supposed to be there because you love the person and are committed to them, not because you're going to get $80. That's a tainted marriage from the beginning. That trivializes marriage. If $80 will do it, that is bad news." Critics like Williams and Rosenthal condemn the commodification of marriage and assume love matches are preferable. That is debatable. Sometimes, the better marital option is getting paid.[50]

Jacqueline Kennedy, whose first marriage was famously plagued by infidelities, once stated, "The first time you marry for love, the second for money . . ."[51] Similarly, in the legendary gold-digger movie *How to Marry a Millionaire*, Schatze Page (played by Lauren Bacall) decides to marry for money only after her first marriage, a love match, leads to financial ruin. Early in the movie, Schatze informs her housemates she is divorced and Loco (Betty Grable) responds, "Oh then you must be loaded." Schatze replies:

> No. Mine was one of those divorces you *don't* read about. The wife finished second . . . I was absolutely nuts about that guy. You know what he did to me? First off, he gives me a phony name. Second, it turns out he was already married! Third, from the minute the preacher said amen, he never did another tap of work. The next thing I knew he'd stolen my television set and given it to a car hop. And when I asked him how about that, he hits me with a chicken!

As Schatze learned, love doesn't prevent financial exploitation; sometimes it facilitates it.[52]

The prenup "test" described earlier in this chapter highlights love's potential for financial abuse. Such tests are ostensibly used to ensure the non-moneyed party is marrying for love, but the moneyed party's intention to deny their future spouse a share of the marital property typically receives little scrutiny. The purpose of a prenup is to alter the default marital property rules and prevent the sharing of marital money upon divorce. When the less wealthy party is forced to "prove" their love with a prenup, they are also being forced to give up their financial rights. This financial manipulation is then exacerbated by the fact that parties are typically unrealistic about the prospect of divorce and thus the likelihood of their prenup ever coming into effect.[53]

When women assert their value and negotiate for it, they protect themselves from potential financial exploitation, yet the successful gold digger is rarely praised. In her best-selling book *Primates of Park Avenue*, author Wednesday Martin writes about the "trophy wives" of Manhattan's Upper East Side. The book is full of juicy tidbits about the extravagant lives of these ultra-rich women and includes the revelation that many receive end-of-year "wife bonuses." Martin writes:

> A wife bonus, I was told, might be hammered out in a pre-nup or post-nup, and distributed on the basis of not only how well her husband's fund had done but her own performance — how well she managed the home budget, whether the kids got into a "good" school — the same way their husbands were rewarded at investment banks. In turn these bonuses were a ticket to a modicum of financial independence and participation in a social sphere where you don't just go to lunch, you buy a $10,000 table at the benefit luncheon a friend is hosting.

More than any other revelation in the book, Martin's discussion of "wife bonuses" caused an uproar. In one review, *Chicago Tribune* writer Gina Barecca condescendingly described these payments as the reward women received "from their conspicuously powerful husbands for staying lithe, keeping the domestic staff in good order and rearing high-achieving children — think *Pretty Woman*, except Julia Roberts has a law degree she doesn't use." Barecca then quotes a friend who described these marriages as "tennis relationships," because "love means nothing."[54] Caitlin Moscatello, of *Glamour* magazine, was similarly appalled by Martin's "wife bonuses" but voiced different criticisms. She described such payments as "demeaning" and wrote, "At its worst, the payment structure magnifies patriarchal marriage to the point where it hurts the eyes . . . He's her husband, yes, but he also becomes *her boss*. She reports to him, spends her days trying to impress him, and he evaluates her. And as his earning potential presumably grows with the progression of his career, she in turn becomes increasingly dependent on him over time."[55]

What these criticisms fail to acknowledge is that the alternative to "demeaning" bonuses is simply not getting paid. It is commonly estimated that services provided by the average stay-at-home mom are worth almost $200,000 per year. Nevertheless, no court will force a husband to make such payments.[56] The law literally declares such services priceless, meaning they can't be paid for. Tellingly, anti-commodification arguments usually arise when it's women who wish to receive money for something not, as law professor Katharine Silbaugh notes, "when things typically associated with male personhood are being sold."[57] The California case of *Borelli v. Bruseau* exemplifies such treatment.

In *Borelli*, the husband suffered a debilitating stroke and subsequently required full-time care. He asked his wife to provide this care but also recognized this would be an extraordinary physical and emotional burden. Therefore, the husband promised to amend his will to compensate his wife for these services and, relying on this promise, the wife agreed to become her husband's full-time caregiver. Unfortunately, the husband did not keep his end of the bargain. Instead of amending his will to reflect his wife's sacrifices, he left nearly all his property to a daughter from a previous marriage. When the wife discovered the husband had reneged on their deal, she sued his estate to recover the property she had been promised. She lost. According to the *Borelli* court, spouses have a duty of care to each other, and the wife did nothing more than what a good and loving wife was already obligated to do. The court wrote, "Even if few things are left that cannot command a price, marital support remains one of them."

The idea that domestic services should be provided gratuitously is a remnant of the deeply gendered doctrine of coverture. Coverture meant that a wife's labor was owned by her husband, and thus he had no obligation to pay for the domestic services she provided.[58] Married women are no longer bound by the law of coverture, yet wives still cannot be paid for their contributions to a marriage. The only thing that has changed is the justification. Now courts claim caretaking services can't be compensated not because the husband owns this laboe, but because such compensation taints love and harms the institution of marriage.

When women marry for money, they reject the idea that domestic work should be provided for free. They also challenge the idea that marrying for love is always best. The modern love match is based on a very specific idea of love — one that is increasingly recognized as problematic. Sociologist Andrew Cherlin calls modern love "a very selfish form of love." He characterizes it as, "Marry as long as it is personally fulfilling and leave when it gets hard or less fun even if children are hurt."[59] Tellingly, Cherlin is not alone in holding this cynical view of contemporary marriage. In their article "The Suffocation of Marriage," Professors Finkel, Hui, Carsweel, and Larson argue that modern spouses are asking too much of marriage and suggest that the "emphasis on higher needs — has undermined spouses' marital quality and personal well-being." To illustrate their point, they cite the famous singleton Carrie Bradshaw, from the show *Sex and the City*. In the episode "American Girl in Paris Part Deux," Bradshaw proclaims, "Well maybe it is time to be clear about who I am. I am someone who is looking for love. Real love. Ridiculous, inconvenient, consuming, can't-live-witout-each-other love." According to Finkel and his colleagues, those who desire this type of demanding and ultimately unattainable love are headed for disappointment. As an alternative, they suggest a marriage based on more tangible needs, needs that are more easily met.[60] Marrying for money is one example.

The Problem with Marrying for Money

Forty years before Shaniqua Tompkins sued 50 Cent, Michelle Triola sought compensation from her former boyfriend, actor Lee Marvin. At Marvin's insistence, Triola gave up her own acting career and devoted herself full-time to caring for his needs. Then, when the relationship ended, she sought reimbursement for her sacrifices. The resulting *Marvin* litigation is famous because it is one of the few instances when a court granted compensation to an unmarried cohabitant. Nevertheless, rather than usher in a new appreciation of women's caretaking services, the decision had the opposite effect.

In 1979, *Saturday Night Live* parodied the Triola lawsuit. Original cast members Jane Curtin and Dan Aykroyd squared off in a "Point–Counterpoint" exchange satirizing Triola's request. The segment began with Curtin taking the pro-Triola position: "A woman in this modern-day relationship may well

Michelle Triola and Lee Marvin.

give up all her own personal pursuits . . . to give her full support to her man's career. Michelle is just asking that the courts recognize that reality . . . There is an old saying, behind every successful man there's a woman, a loving, giving, caring woman."

Aykroyd responds, "Jane, you ignorant slut," and proceeds to equate Triola with a prostitute. "Bagged out, dried up, slunk meat like you and Michelle Triola know the rules, if you want a contract sign on the dotted line . . . I guess what you and Michelle are saying is that when you're on your backs, the meter is running."[61]

Aykroyd ridiculed the idea of compensating women for their domestic labor. He was playing a boorish character in a satirical sketch and yet, the view he expressed is the one that endures. When women seek to enforce economic agreements made within the context of a relationship, they are treated as undeserving and contemptible. The Anna Nicole Smith inheritance battle is one of the most famous examples.

Smith was accustomed to being paid for her beauty. She began her career as an exotic dancer and model and in 1993, became *Playboy* magazine's Playmate of the Year. The following year, at age twenty-six, Smith married the eighty-nine-year-old billionaire oil tycoon J. Howard Marshall. Marshall was a cunning and sophisticated business player who understood that if he wished to enjoy Smith's youth and exceptional beauty, he would need to compensate her accordingly. Marshall promised to provide for Smith and she agreed to marry him, but when he died thirteen months later, Smith was left almost nothing. When Smith challenged her financial exclusion, she was labeled a "gold digging monster." The duplicitous Marshall was remembered as a naive, lovesick fool.[62]

Those who supported Smith's claim viewed the marriage as a reciprocal relationship that greatly benefited Marshall. As journalist Carol Sarler noted, the Smith-Marshall marriage was a "deal freely entered into by adults who understood each other. Perfectly."[63] Journalist Sarah Marshall also described it as a mutually beneficial exchange and suggested the backlash against Smith was because she was a woman who knew her own worth. Marshall wrote, "The only person more deserving of [public] humiliation than the cluelessly beautiful woman is the beautiful woman who, even more unforgivably, *knows* she is beautiful: the woman who knows she is worth something to the world, and leverages her value to escape a life she can no longer stand. The woman who looks back at a world that always wants something from her, and asks, *How bad do you want it? How much are you willing to pay?*"[64]

In 2007, the following post appeared on an online message board from a woman seeking a rich husband:

> What am I doing wrong? Okay I am tired of beating around the bush. I am a beautiful (spectacularly beautiful) 25-year-old girl. I am articulate and classy. I'm not from New York. I'm looking to get married to a guy who makes at least half a million a year. I know how [*sic*] that sounds like a lot, but keep in mind that a million a year is middle class in New York City, so I don't think I'm overreaching at all. Are there guys who make $500k or more on this board? Any wives? Could you send me tips? I dated a businessman who makes average around $200–250. But that's where I seem to hit a roadblock. $250,000 won't get me to central park west. I know a woman in my yoga class who was married to an investment banker and lives in Tribeca, and she's not as pretty as I am, nor is she a great genius. So what is she doing right? How do I get to her level? . . . How do you decide marriage vs. just girlfriend? I am looking for

MARRIAGE ONLY. Please hold your insults — I'm putting myself out there in an honest way. Most beautiful women are superficial; at least I'm being up front about it. I wouldn't be searching for these kinds of guys if I wasn't about to match them — in looks, culture, sophistication, and keeping a nice home and hearth.

The poster received the following answer:

I read your posting with great interest and have thought meaningfully about your dilemma. I offer the following analysis of your predicament. Firstly, I'm not wasting your time, I qualify as a guy who fits your bill; that is I make more than $500K per year. That said here's how I see it. Your offer from the prospective [*sic*] of a guy like me, is plain and simple a crappy business deal. Here's why. Cutting through all the B.S., what you suggest is a simple trade: you bring your looks to the party and I bring my money. Fine, simple. But here's the rub, your looks will fade and my money will likely continue into perpetuity . . . in fact, it is very likely that my income increases but it is an absolute certainty that you won't be getting any more beautiful!

So in economic terms you are a depreciating asset and I am an earning asset. Not only are you a depreciating asset, your depreciation accelerates! Let me explain, you're 25 now and will likely stay pretty hot for the next 5 years, but less so each year. Then the fade begins in earnest. By 35 stick a fork in you! So in Wall Street terms, we would call you a trading position, not a buy and hold . . . hence the rub . . .

marriage. It doesn't make good business sense to "buy you" (which is what you're asking) so I'd rather lease. In case you think I'm being cruel, I would say the following. If my money were to go away so would you, so when your beauty fades I need an out. It's as simple as that. So a deal that makes sense is dating not marriage . . . By the way, you could always find a way to make your own money and then we wouldn't need to have this difficult conversation. With all that said, I must say you're going about it the right way. Classic "pump and dump."

I hope this is helpful, and if you want to enter into some sort of lease, let me know.[65]

The above exchange may have been fabricated, but the issues it raises are genuine. As the responder points out, the two are only having this conversation because the poster hasn't found a way to make $500,000 per year herself. The responder implies that marrying for money is the lazy path to riches and suggests if the poster had just tried harder, she could have become rich through her own career accomplishments. This assumption is the problem.

When women marry for money, it is typically because they can't earn it themselves. For years, studies on mating preferences have demonstrated that men tend to focus on physical attractiveness while women are more interested in men's resource acquisition. One explanation for these results has been that they reveal innate evolutionary differences. Male choice reflects women's time-limited reproductive capabilities, while female choice represents a desire to find men who have the resources to help raise their children. More recent studies challenge this idea and show that when women's economic opportunities increase, their interest in marrying for money diminishes.[66]

In their paper "Stepping Out of the Caveman's Shadow: Nations' Gender Gap Predicts Degree of Sex Differentiation in Mate Preferences," UK researchers Marcel Zentner and Klaudia Mitura show that the supposed evolutionary biases in mate choice decline proportionally with nations' gender parity. In their study, 3,177 respondents completed an online mate preference survey. The respondents came from ten countries, ranging from Finland, where there was low gender disparity, to Turkey, where the gender gap was extremely high. They were then asked whether certain criteria — such as financial prospects and being a good cook — were important considerations when choosing a mate. They found that gender difference in mate preferences were "highest in gender-unequal societies, and smallest in the most gender-equal societies."[67] Such research suggests that as societies become more gender-equal, men and women increasingly seek the same qualities in a partner. Women also like attractive partners, but they will forgo sex appeal to achieve financial security.[68] The Smith-Marshall marriage follows this pattern.

Anna Nicole Smith did not marry J. Howard Marshall for his looks. She married him because her financial future was bleak, and he offered her a way out. In describing their relationship, Smith stated, "He took me out of a terrible place, took care of me. He was my savior. It wasn't a sexual 'baby, oh baby, I love your body' type love — it was a deep thank-you for taking me out of this hole."[69] Marriage drastically improved Smith's economic circumstances, but these improvements were temporary. As Smith discovered, marrying for money is a precarious solution to women's economic inequality and particularly to female poverty.

When the government tells low-income women to rely on men for support, it is abdicating its responsibility for solving the problems that contribute to female poverty in the first place. These problems are no secret. For the past fifty years, the inflation-adjusted hourly wage for the bottom 10 percent of female earners has remained stagnant. Worse, such low-wage jobs tend to involve fluctuating, insufficient hours and frequent layoffs.[70] Other glaring contributors to female poverty include workplace gender discrimination, lack of safe and affordable childcare, and the devaluing of women's caretaking labor. The government could promote policies to address these problems. Instead, as law professor Lucie White notes, the government has found it easier "to point a finger at poor women and accost them to escape poverty by catching a man."[71] Law professor Martha Fineman echoes such criticisms. In fact, she has urged the abolition of marriage as a legal category entirely, "precisely because it precludes consideration of other solutions to social problems."[72]

When marriage is the government's answer to female poverty, the sexism in the solution is undeniable.[73] Encouraging poor women to marry for money is also problematic because it doesn't work. Marriage can only provide women with financial stability if they marry good men with good economic prospects. One study on the effect of the government's pro-marriage welfare reforms found they didn't make poor women more likely to marry, but they did make them more likely to marry financially insolvent men.[74] Other research showed that when poor women were forced to rely on men for support, they often wound up entering into relationships with men they had no interest in marrying.

In 1997, the state of Wisconsin unintentionally demonstrated that poor women were turning to men as a financial last resort. That year, the state selected a random group of welfare recipients to receive the full extent of their child support payments with no corresponding reduction in their welfare benefits. These increased funds were not expected to change the women's living arrangements, but they did — drastically. By 2004, women who received the extra money were significantly less likely to have cohabitated with men other than the fathers of their children. The experiment revealed that low-income women had been reluctantly relying on men for financial assistance and that when they finally had enough income to support themselves independently, they avoided these problematic, and possibly abusive, relationships.[75]

One of the greatest problems with financial dependency is it creates the perfect conditions for domestic violence. Without sufficient assets of their own, victims of domestic abuse are often unable to leave an abuser while still providing for themselves or their children. When it is a choice between caring for their children or freeing themselves from abuse, many victims will stay with or return to an abuser. Fifteen to thirty percent of welfare recipients are victims of domestic violence, and many enter the welfare system specifically to escape from abusive relationships. Reducing government support and encouraging women to rely on men perpetuates this cycle of abuse.[76]

Two decades into the twenty-first century, women still earn significantly less than men, their caretaking services are treated as gratuitous, and they are expected to use men as their social safety net. Given these circumstances, marrying for money is a reasonable choice, but it is also an unfair one. Oscar Wilde once said, "Who being in love is poor?" But love doesn't pay the bills. Only when women have the same economic opportunities as men will they have an equal chance to marry for love. Of course, whether they will marry without the economic incentive is a different question. Wilde also wrote, "One should always be in love. That is the reason one should never marry."

Conclusion

Mae West famously quipped, "Marriage is a fine institution, but I'm not ready for an institution." Many Americans agree, and this is considered a problem. Although much has changed over the past two centuries, the unmarried continue to inspire alarm. In the 2023 book *The Two-Parent Privilege: How Americans Stopped Getting Married and Started Falling Behind*, economist Melissa Kearney blames the unmarried for a host of societal problems and then argues that the very future of our country depends on increasing marriage.[1] Other marriage advocates go even further. In 2022, the Institute of Family Studies released their report *Marriage Still Matters* (examining declining fertility rates across the globe) and suggested marriage may be the key to the continuation of the entire human race.[2]

Recently, Steven Crowder, a political commentator who prides himself on his "provocative" views, extolled the importance of marriage and publicly bemoaned the fact that his wife was "allowed" to divorce him without his consent. He wrote:

> I have been living through what has increasingly been a horrendous divorce. Let me say from the outset, to be clear, there was no infidelity or any kind of physical abuse on either side. And no, this was not my choice. My then-wife decided she didn't want to be married anymore. And in the State of Texas, that is completely permitted. It's been the most heartbreaking experience of my life, what I consider to be my deepest personal failure . . . Children need a mom and a dad, and divorce is horrible. But in today's legal

system, my beliefs don't matter. In Texas, divorce is permitted when one party wants it, period.[3]

Crowder's criticisms echo growing Republican proposals to bolster marriage by limiting the grounds for divorce. During the 2016 Republican National Convention, delegates considered adding language to their party's platform declaring, "Children are made to be loved by both natural parents united in marriage. Legal structures such as No-Fault Divorce, which divides families and empowers the state, should be replaced by a Fault-based Divorce." In the end, this proposal was not adopted, but similar language has been incorporated into state Republican party platforms.

In 2022, the Republican party of Texas added language to its platform calling for an end to no-fault divorce: "We urge the Legislature to rescind unilateral no-fault divorce laws, to support covenant marriage, and to pass legislation extending the period of time in which a divorce may occur to six months after the date of filing for divorce." In 2023, the Nebraska GOP party platform adopted similar language seeking to limit no-fault divorce "to situations in which the couple has no children." That same year, the Louisiana Republican party strongly considered endorsing a bill to eliminate the state's no-fault divorce provisions because such "laws have destroyed the institute of marriage."[4]

If marriage were the best solution to America's economic and social problems, such marriage promotion tactics might be justified, but history has repeatedly shown it is not. At best, marriage is a Band-Aid that Americans have used when society is too sexist, too racist, or just too lazy to implement better solutions. This use of marriage has sometimes (sort of) worked, at least in the short term, but ultimately, it has been more likely to exacerbate the problems it was intended to solve. Given this dubious success record, we should be looking for different fixes to America's problems, not doubling down on marriage.

Although marriage advocates are correct when they argue that marriage remains highly beneficial, this is only because America has made the deliberate choice to benefit the married. We could make a different choice, and eventually we may. Until then, we should stop acting shocked when marital incentives work. There is no such thing as marrying for the wrong reason. When people marry for benefits, they are doing exactly what American law and policy encourages them to do — they are getting married.

Notes

Introduction

1. Lindsay M. Keiter, "Connubial Adventurers: Playing the Matrimonial Lottery in British America," *Early American Studies: An Interdisciplinary Journal* 21, no. 1 (2023), 1. Published electronically Winter 2023, https://doi:10.1353/eam.2023.0000.
2. In America, there is a long history of comparing marriage to a lottery — both depended on luck. Moreover, marrying for love was not considered more likely to result in a happy marriage than marrying for many other reasons. As Keiter writes, in early America "chance was as good as choice in the pursuit of nuptial contentment." Keiter, "Connubial Adventurers," 10.
3. Keiter, "Connubial Adventurers," 31.
4. See, e.g., Margaret Radin and Madhavi Sunder, "Introduction: The Subject and Object of Commodification," in *Rethinking Commodification: Cases and Readings in Law and Culture*, ed. Martha Ertman and Joan C. Williams (New York: New York University Press, 2005), 10–11 (noting that everything exists "for a price, even if that price exists only implicitly in the 'shadows,' not subject to discussion in the light of day").
5. Margaret Radin, *Contested Commodities: The Trouble with Trade in Children, Body Parts, and Other Things* (Cambridge, MA: Harvard University Press, 2001).

Chapter 1

1. M. Champagne, "Eighth Dialogue of the Treatise of Love," in Marilyn Yalom, *The Amorous Heart: An Unconventional History of Love* (New York: Basic Books, 2018).
2. "By marriage, the husband and wife are one person in law; that is, the very being or legal existence of the woman is suspended during the marriage, or at least is incorporated and consolidated into that of the husband: under whose wing, protection, and *cover*, she performs everything; and is therefore called . . . a *feme covert*." William Blackstone, *Commentaries on the Laws of England* (Oxford, UK: Clarendon Press, 1765), 1:442, 443.
3. Nicolas L. Syrett, *American Child Bride: A History of Minors and Marriage in the United States* (Chapel Hill: University of North Carolina Press, 2016), 26 (emphasis added).
4. These penalties included a £500 fee and one year imprisonment for those who married without parental consent. North and South Carolina passed similar laws to deny a gold-digging husband access to the girl's estate. See Syrett, *American Child Bride*, 26–28.
5. As Rachel Frommer notes, "First-cousin marriage in the United States was commonplace, legal, and socially acceptable from the colonial period through the nineteenth century." She also notes that it was particularly widespread in the wealthier southern states. Rachel Frommer, "The Unconstitutionality of State Bans on Marriage Between First Cousins," *Cardozo Law Review de novo* (2021), 209.

6. Incest provisions are ancient and common throughout the world, but exceptions to these prohibitions, specifically cousin marriages, are more likely to occur in male-dominated societies that permit female inheritance. According to economics professor Duman Bahrami-Rad, "Studies show that when a woman inherits property, her male relatives are more likely to arrange her marital choices and pick that partner from within the family. This ensures the property remains within the family and the male family member's control." Duman Bahrami-Rad, "Keeping It in the Family: Female Inheritance, Inmarriage, and the Status of Women," *Journal of Development Economics* 153 (November 2021), https://doi.org/10.1016/j .jdeveco.2021.102714. See also Guenther Roth and Claus Wittich, eds., *Max Weber, Economy & Society* (Oakland: University of California Press, 1978), 365 (defining a kin group as "a group of expectant heirs").

7. Prizing and enforcing virginity was another problematic means of "preventing opportunistic or otherwise unsuitable men from seducing women in order to ben-efit from their dowries and property rights." Joanne Payton, *Honor and the Political Economy of Marriage: Violence Against Women in the Kurdistan Region of Iraq* (New Brunswick, NJ: Rutgers University Press, 2019).

8. Peter Koudijs and Laura Salisbury, "Marrying for Money: Evidence from the First Wave of Married Women's Property Laws in the US," October 2016, available at https://economics.yale.edu/sites/default/files/koudijssalisburymarriagemarkets_ march2018.pdf (quoting Elizabeth Warbasse, *The Changing Legal Rights of Married Women 1800–1861*, New York: Garland Publishing, 1987, 150, 170).

9. *Aberdeen Whig and North Mississippi Advocate*, March 16, 1839. Some say Hadley proposed the act at the urging of his wife, Piety. Piety Smith was the daughter of Andrew Jackson's wealthy friend David Smith, who had bequeathed his substan-tial assets to his daughters in trust. It is likely Hadley hoped to shelter his wife's assets from both his own creditors (Hadley was in substantial debt) and her own trustee. See Joseph A. Custer, "The Three Waves of Married Women's Property Acts in the Nineteenth Century with a Focus on Mississippi, New York, and Oregon," *Ohio Northern University Law Review* 40, no. 2 (2014), 402.

The legislation may have also been influenced by the Mississippi case *Fischer v. Allen*, 3 Miss. 611 (1829), which involved the interpretation and application of Chickasaw marital law. Under Chickasaw law, wives were permitted to own and control their separate property, and in *Fischer*, Elizabeth Allen, a Chickasaw Indian woman, objected to the confiscation of her premarital property, including an enslaved person, to settle her white husband's financial debts. She argued that, under Chickasaw law, the wife kept the property she owned before marriage separate from that of her husband, and the court agreed. Allen was therefore able to keep her property from her husband's creditors.

There is debate about the actual purpose of the act. The Panic of 1837 inspired attempts to limit the effect of such an economic crisis by protecting family assets. Many have argued that the real purpose of the act was more about protecting husbands' property from creditors through fraudulent conveyances to their wives. See Robert Gilmer, "Chickasaws, Tribal Laws, and the Mississippi Married Women's Property Act of 1839" (thesis, University of North Carolina–Asheville, 2003), available at http://toto.lib.unca.edu/sr_papers/history_sr/srhistory_2003/gilmer_robert.pdf.

10. Gilmer, "Chickasaws, Tribal Law."

11. There is some disagreement over which state was the first. The traditional view is that it was Mississippi. However, some scholars argue that Arkansas was actually first. See Michael B. Dougan, "The Arkansas Married Woman's Property Law,"

Arkansas Historical Quarterly 46, no. 1 (Spring 1987), 3 (stating that the Arkansas Territory passed the first Married Woman's Property Act in 1835).

12. Koudijis and Salisbury, "Marrying for Money."

13. Koudijis and Salisbury, "Marrying for Money," 176–77.

14. Similar bills were proposed in South Carolina in 1855 but failed to pass. According to Professor Suzanne Lebsock, "What seems to have made the difference in 1868 was not that the Radicals were more tender-hearted than their predecessors (although they may have been) but rather that in hard times, a married woman's-property act became a significant form of debt relief." Catherine Clinton, ed., *Half Sisters of History: Southern Women and the American Past* (Durham, NC: Duke University Press, 1994), 116.

15. See S.C. Const. art. XIV, § 8 (1868). See also Linda E. Speth, "The Married Women's Property Acts, 1839–1865: Reform, Reaction, or Revolution?," in J. Ralph Lindgren et al., *The Law of Sex Discrimination*, 4th ed. (Belmont, CA: Wadsworth, 2011), 12–15 (noting that when the 1868 South Carolina constitution was enacted, South Carolina joined the more than two dozen states already protecting married women's separate property).

16. Of course, from a women's rights perspective, these laws were a very small first step. The new rights did not give a wife the right to determine how her property was used. The benefit of the laws was that they restricted a husband's ability to borrow against his wife's property, and thus shielded a women's property from seizure by the husband's creditors and preserved the bulk of the wife's assets as inheritance for the couple's children. They also protected women from gold diggers. See Clinton, *Half Sisters of History*, 115 (noting that "the new married women's property provision did offer women some protection from fortune hunters and other varieties of unreliable manhood").

17. A fascinating 2002 study demonstrated that once married women gained control over their separate property, the incidence of men marrying wealthier women dropped precipitously. After married women's property acts were passed, men were much more likely to marry women with similar income. Rick Geddes and Dean Lueck, "The Gains from Self-Ownership and the Expansion of Women's Rights," *American Economic Review* 92, no. 4 (2002), 1079–92.

18. Historian Hendrik Hartog referred to her as "a kind of nineteenth century groupie." Hendrik Hartog, *Man and Wife in America* (Cambridge, MA: Harvard University Press, 2022), 176.

19. Cruger was not poor. The Crugers were a well-known merchant family that had engaged in lucrative trade between the United States and the Caribbean. His father also owned a substantial plantation in Charleston, South Carolina. Virginia Glenn Crane, "Two Women, White and Brown, in the South Carolina Court of Equity, 1842–1845," *South Carolina Historical Magazine* 96, no. 3 (1995), 198–220.

20. Cruger expressed his dismay at living "in so wild and remote spot." See Historic Buildings of Herkimer County: Jordanville and the Once Famous Castle, accessed June 9, 2023, https://herkimer.nygenweb.net/warren/gelstoncastle.html.

21. Hartog, *Man and Wife*, 176.

22. Hartog, *Man and Wife*, 185.

23. Cooper and Cruger met during Cooper's travels in Italy and became lifelong friends. The trip served as inspiration for the novel *The Bravo*, which Cruger favorably reviewed in a long, unsigned article written for the Charleston literary magazine. *Southern Review* 8 (February 1832), 382–99. Later, the Cruger-Douglas marriage served as the inspiration for *The Ways of the Hour*. In this tale, Fenimore

Cooper strongly sympathized with the husband (Cruger) and portrayed the wife (Douglas) as both evil and insane. For greater discussion of this story and its origins, see Barbara Ann Bardes and Suzanne Gossett, "Cooper and the 'Cup and Saucer' Law: A New Reading of *The Ways of the Hour*," *American Quarterly* 32, no. 5 (1980), 499–518, accessed March 25, 2021, https://doi:10.2307/2712410.

24. Hartog, *Man and Wife*, 186; Sylvia Graham Olejniczaka, *To the Ladies: Reinterpreting Boscobel* (Bloomington, IN: Xlibris, 2014).

25. Margaret Valentine Turano, "Jane Austen, Charlotte Bronte, and the Marital Property Law," *Harvard Women's Law Journal* 21 (1998), 195.

26. In the 1800s, the profession of governess was widely considered a dismal fate, and paintings from the period depict it as humiliating and even tragic, a kind of living death. Other paintings in this vein include Richard Redgrave's 1844 *The Governess* and Rebecca Solomon's 1851 *The Governess*. For a discussion of the low status of the governess, see Laura Miller, "Between Upstairs and Downstairs," *Slate*, March 13, 2016, accessed June 6, 2023, https://slate.com/culture/2016/03/jane-eyre-and-the-precarious-status-of-the-victorian-governess.html. See also Turano, "Jane Austen, Charlotte Bronte," 196.

27. The practice of wife selling largely ended around 1857, when divorce became permissible. For further discussion of this practice, see Martha M. Ertman, "Marriage as a Trade: Bridging the Private/Private Distinction," *Harvard Civil Rights–Civil Liberties Law Review* 36, no. 1 (2001), 13–14.

28. Jill Elaine Hasday, *Intimate Lies and the Law* (New York: Oxford University Press, 2019).

29. *Gring v. Lerch*, 112 Pa. 244, 249, 3 A. 841, 843 (Pa. 1886).

30. The extent to which courts would hold men to their promise of marriage can be seen in cases like *Van Houten v. Morse*, 62 Mass. 414 (Mass. 1894). In *Van Houten*, the Massachusetts court concluded that Van Houten's concealment of her black ancestry was not a justification for breaking an engagement. The court then granted her breach of promise claim and awarded her a sizable settlement. Ultimately, the verdict caused a public outcry, and on appeal the court held that race constituted valid grounds for a breach of promise.

31. Almost all common-law marriage cases involved women in need of financial support. Many involved a woman whose long-term domestic partner had died or deserted her and who sought judicial recognition of her relationship in order to inherit as a widow or to claim support as an abandoned wife. For further discussion of nineteenth-century common-law marriage claims, see Ariela R. Dubler, "Wifely Behavior: A Legal History of Acting Married," *Columbia Law Review* 100, no. 4 (2000), 968–69.

32. Nineteenth-century courts awarded wives alimony because they had no other option. Middle-class wives were entirely dependent on marriage for their economic support, and the courts recognized the disaster that would occur should they eliminate marital support upon divorce. Consequently, courts held that the duty of support continued after divorce. In the 1892 New York case *Romaine v. Chauncey*, 129 N.Y. 566, the court explained the justification for alimony, writing: "During the marriage the husband owes to the wife the duty of support and maintenance . . . The divorce, with its incidental allowance of alimony simply continues his duty beyond the decree, and compels him to perform it, but does not change its nature." *Romaine*, 129 N.Y., 570. For further discussion of the legal justification for alimony in the nineteenth century, see Mary E. O'Connell, "Alimony After

No-Fault: A Practice in Search of a Theory," *New England Law Review* 23, no. 2 (1988), 437–513.

33. Francesca Beauman, *Matrimony Inc.: From Personal Ads to Swiping Right, a Story of America Looking for Love* (New York: Simon & Schuster, 2020).

34. When I read this letter to my family law students, I always ask if they think the outcome would be any different today. They are always sure the answer is yes and are shocked when I inform them that they are wrong. The only difference between Pen Holder and the wives of today is the availability of divorce. Rights within marriage have barely increased. A married woman still has no right to access her husband's money. It is only upon divorce that a wife gains a legal right to a share of the money or property her husband earned or acquired during the marriage. For a discussion of women's unpaid labor both in the past and today, see Ann Crittenden, *The Price of Motherhood: Why the Most Important Job in the World Is Still the Least Valued* (New York: Henry Holt, 2001).

35. Albert Smith, "Speculations on Marriage and Young Ladies," *Bentley's Miscellany, 1837–1868* 11 (1842), 439–41, republished in *Spirit of the Times; A Chronicle of the Turf, Agriculture, Field Sports, Literature and the Stage*, May 21, 1842, 141, and *New World: A Weekly Family Journal of Popular Literature, Science, Art and News*, February 11, 1843, 181.

36. Beauman, *Matrimony Inc.*, 102. Other attacks were similar. An 1859 article on "Modern Marriages" published in the women's magazine *Godey's Lady's Book* described marrying for money as a "sordid and disgraceful bargain." "Modern Marriages," *Godey's Lady's Book*, December 1859, 505.

37. Elizabeth Abbott, *A History of Marriage: From Same Sex Unions to Private Vows and Common Law, the Surprising Diversity of a Tradition* (New York: Seven Stories Press, 2011), 93.

38. The wedding of Grimke and Weld was radical for many reasons. Not only did Weld disavow his rights under coverture, but he and Grimke also invited many African American guests, including two who had been formerly enslaved by the Grimke family. In addition, after the couple recited their vows, "a colored Presbyterian minister then prayed . . . followed by a white one." Accounts of the unconventional wedding quickly spread throughout the streets of Philadelphia and led to rumors that this had been an interracial wedding. This rumor then caused a riot that led to the destruction of the newly erected Philadelphia Hall. For a discussion of the Weld-Grimke wedding and its aftermath, see Gerda Lerner, *The Feminist Thought of Sarah Grimké* (New York: Oxford University Press, 1998), 170.

39. As historian Nancy Cott has noted, "Virtually every [free love] community . . . sprang from a critique of the conventional arrangement of work and marriage." Nancy F. Cott, *Public Vows: A History of Marriage and the Nation* (Cambridge, MA: Harvard University Press, 2000), 70.

40. Victoria Woodhall, *The Principles of Social Freedom* (New York: Woodhull, Claflin, 1871), https://www.loc.gov/resource/rbnawsa.n8216/?sp=1.

41. Other heart-balm actions included criminal conversation (adultery), alienation of affections (a suit for stealing away the love of a spouse), and seduction. I once had a student refer to these actions as "heart bombs," which I also think is entirely appropriate. See Michael Grossberg, *Governing the Hearth: Law and the Family in Nineteenth-Century America* (Chapel Hill: University of North Carolina Press, 1988), 36 (noting that by the early twentieth century, breach of promise actions had transformed to stress "the emotional aspects of the dashed nuptials").

42. Grossberg, *Governing the Hearth*, 52–53.

43. Grossberg, *Governing the Hearth*, 60.

44. "The Court's Mother-in-Law," *Sunbury American*, April 10, 1874, https://chronicl ingamerica.loc.gov/lccn/sn84026403/1874-04-10/ed-1/seq-4/.

45. Under the law at the time, the daughter could only seek to inherit if she was "legitimate," meaning the child of married parents. For a discussion of the reputation risks both Ashley and her daughter faced from this suit, see "Mother Was Once Lillian Ashley," *San Francisco Call* 107, no. 138, April 17, 1910, https://cdnc.ucr.edu/cgi-bin/cdnc?a=d&d=SFC19100417.2.35&e=-------en--20--1--txt-txIN--------1.

46. "Lucky Baldwin's Reply to Miss Ashley's $50,000 Suit," *Indianapolis Journal*, April 24, 1895, https://newspapers.library.in.gov/cgi-bin/indiana?a=d&d=IJ18950424.1.5&e=-------en-20--1--txt-txIN------.

47. Ashley's sister wasn't the first woman to shoot Baldwin. Fannie Verona Baldwin, Baldwin's second cousin, claimed she had been raped by Baldwin while she was teaching school at his ranch. After he refused to leave her alone, she shot him with a pistol inside his luxury hotel. Baldwin survived, but Verona commented, "I ought to have killed him. Yes, I ought to have killed him at the ranch." Three years later, she was acquitted due to Lucky's refusal to testify. "Verona Baldwin, Her Deposition Taken for Future Use," *Los Angeles Herald* 26, no. 160, March 31, 1887.
Surviving these two shootings is one explanation for how Baldwin acquired the moniker "Lucky," but there are other stories surrounding the name. One is that it refers to Baldwin's financial success, especially his luck regarding his ownership of shares in the Norcross silver mine. Baldwin had left instructions with his broker to sell his Norcross stock if it fell below $800. The stock then fell below the threshold sales price, but the broker had been unable to sell because Baldwin had taken the key to the safe holding the stock certificates. By the time Baldwin returned home from his travels, the stock price had rebounded exponentially and created a multimillion-dollar profit for him. Lucius Beebe and Charles Clegg, *Legends of the Comstock Lode* (Redwood City, CA: Stanford University Press, 1956).

48. *In re Baldwin's Estate*, 123 P. 267 (Cal. 1912) (en banc).

49. In describing his romantic entanglements, the court noted that Mr. Main was a man who "sought the graces of other women with a fervor not altogether Platonic." *Main v. Main*, 168 Iowa 353, 354 (1915).

50. Women's rights advocates feared that accepting any sex-based privileges would undermine their argument that women should have the same rights, privileges, and opportunity to participate in society as men did. As a result, they requested that many of the sex-based privileges of marriage be voided. For example, novelist Fanny Hurst claimed to want marriage liberated from the degrading rhetoric and ideas of economic exchange in which men provided money in exchange for women's reproductive and domestic labor. Hurst described alimony as "surely one of the most despicable forms of barter that can exchange human hands." Brian Donovan, *American Gold Digger: Marriage, Money, and the Law from Ziegfeld Follies to Anna Nicole Smith* (Chapel Hill: University of North Carolina Press, 2020), 47. Similarly, feminist journalist Dorothy Dunbar Bromley opined that "as long as women seek to profit materially from their relationship with men — both in and out of marriage — there will be no new era for the sex as a whole." Dorothy Dunbar Bromley, "Breach of Promise — Why?," *Woman Citizen* 12 (September 1927), 40.

51. Donovan, *American Gold Digger*, 74–76.

52. Harriet Spiller Daggett, "The Action for Breach of the Marriage Promise," in *Legal Essays on Family Law* (Baton Rouge: Louisiana State University Press, 1935), 47. See also Grossberg, *Governing the Hearth*, 55.

53. Donovan, *American Gold Digger*, 75.
54. Rebecca Tushnet, "Rules of Engagement," *Yale Law Journal* 107, no. 8 (1998), 2589.
55. Nicholson was a well-known social reformer and a fierce advocate for racial and gender equality. Although her anti-heart-balm work is now most often praised by misogynistic men's rights groups, her advocacy was firmly grounded in a quest for equality and social justice. See Larissa Marie Werhnyak, "'O, Perjured Lover, Atone, Atone!': A Legal and Cultural History of Breach of Promise to Marry, 1880–1940" (unpublished dissertation, University of Iowa, 2015, 198–200) (citing the transcript of a speech to the Indiana Assembly, undated, January 1935, Nicholson Collection, Indiana State Library, Indianapolis, 47).
56. Werhnyak, "O, Perjured Lover," 200. See also *Indiana History Blog*, "'A Hundred Years From Now — What?': Mary Garrett Hay Predicts Life in 2022," blog entry by Nicole Poletika, January 27, 2022, https://blog.history.in.gov/tag/roberta-west-nicholson/.
57. Hasday, *Intimate Lies*, 105.
58. Women who sought alimony were commonly referred to as gold diggers and parasites. A 1926 article titled *Wives Are Grafters* written by New York Supreme Court Justice Selah B. Strong was typical of such attacks. Strong described alimony recipients as "parasites, liars and cheats, money grabbers, and contributors to immorality on the wholesale scale." Donovan, *American Gold Digger*, 45. Other articles from this period echoed these attacks. In a 1927 article in the *Los Angeles Times*, the Reverend John Williams claimed, "Gold digging is growing more insidious everyday and deserves our immediate attention." That same year, journalist Dorothy Dunbar Bromley wrote an article for *Harper's Magazine* claiming that gold diggers were "by far the most numerous" of all the women seeking alimony. Donovan, *American Gold Digger*, 46. See also Bromley, "Breach of Promise," 8 (describing alimony recipients as "liv[ing] the life of parasites"); "Alimony Brides Make a Business of Collecting," *Lima News*, February 23, 1928 (reporting "that the familiar gold diggers far out-number all other alimony receivers").
59. During this period, breach of promise suits were increasingly attacked as tainting the purity of marriage, and the women who brought them were attacked as heartless, immoral, and mercenary. The 1927 statement of Nebraska state senator Chambers arguing in favor of anti-heart-balm legislation, banning breach of promise suits, was typical of such sentiments. Chambers declared, "We romantic men . . . believe love is something which should be the last of all things to sell at a price on the open market." "Sheiks and Breaches in Nebraska," *New York Times*, January 18, 1927, 24. Similarly, Indiana state representative Roberta Nicholson described breach of promise as perpetuating a "sordid and vulgar conception of marital affairs." Donovan, *American Gold Digger*, 78. Nicholson also claimed "999 out of 1,000 breach of promise and alienation of affection suits were nothing but shakedowns." Hasday, *Intimate Lies*, 105. See also "The Outlawry of Heart-Balm Suits," *Literary Digest*, April 13, 1935, 22 (proclaiming, "Love lost has no value, and . . . trafficking in love is a system of banditry").
60. For example, a 1923 Oregon law review article described common-law marriage suits as the province of "the harlot and the adventuress." See Errol Clarence Gilkey, "Validity of Common-Law Marriages in Oregon," *Oregon Law Review* 3, no. 1 (1923), 46: "In our opinion the doctrine of common-law marriages is contrary to public policy and public morals. It places a premium upon illicit cohabitation and offers encouragement to the harlot and the adventuress." Two years later, in

Huard v. McTeigh, the Oregon Supreme Court echoed these terms, writing, "The doctrine of common-law marriages is contrary to public policy and public morals. It places a premium upon illicit cohabitation and offers encouragement to the harlot and the adventuress." 113 Or. 279, 295 (1925). Similarly, when arguing in favor of a 1933 anti-common-law-marriage bill, New York judge Surrogate Foley wrote that the passage of such legislation would "stop blackmailing claims against estates and living persons." Letter from Surrogate James A. Foley to Governor Herbert H. Lehman, April 18, 1933, Chapter 606, 4, Bill Jacket Collection, New York State Library.

61. See Donovan, *American Gold Digger*, 57 (noting, "Heart balm suits had actually declined substantially from the end of the 19th century.").

62. These numbers are not unique to the *Tribune*. For example, between 1934 and 1935, the *New York Times* ran more than eighty stories on breach of promise and alienation of affection suits. Kyle Graham, "Why Torts Die," *Florida State University Law Review* 35, no. 2 (2008), 412.

63. David Bret, *Joan Crawford: Hollywood Martyr* (Cambridge, MA: Da Capo Press, 2006), 81–84.

64. In a 1935 Wisconsin law review article on heart-balm actions, Professor Nathan Feinsinger argued that the heart-balm panic was both unnecessary and harmful. According to Feinsinger, "Newspaper publicity has caused the public to ignore the private and public benefits of the actions discussed and have given to isolated cases of abuse the appearance of universality." N. P. Feinsinger, "Current Legislation Affecting Breach of Promise to Marry, Alienation of Affections, and Related Actions," *Wisconsin Law Review* 10, no. 4 (1935), 417.

65. See *In re Estate of Erlanger*, Brief of Proponents-Appellants, at 81 (1935). Professor Ariela Dubler has noted that under original common-law marriage jurisprudence, "acting like a wife essentially made one a wife." Ariela R. Dubler, "Wifely Behavior: A Legal History of Acting Married," *Columbia Law Review* 100, no. 4 (2000), 1009. Dubler notes the defense "persistently offered Fixel-Erlanger's spending and consumption patterns as evidence that she behaved in a wifely manner. The defense entered into evidence countless receipts, bills, and charge account records bearing Fixel-Erlanger's signature as Mrs. Abraham Erlanger. Moreover, as befit the proper spending propensities of a good wife, Fixel-Erlanger shopped for Abraham Erlanger. When the couple dined out, Fixel-Erlanger ordered their food. Fixel-Erlanger regularly chose Erlanger's clothes, food, and housewares. Dubler, "Wifely Behavior," 986.

66. Dubler, "Wifely Behavior," 992.

67. *In re Estate of Erlanger*, 145 Misc. 1, 229 (N.Y. Sur. Ct. 1932).

68. The court's 500-page opinion included specifics "of every encounter, every document, every conversation, every purchase, every dinner, every disagreement, and every excursion." Professor Ariela Dubler suggests the judge "felt the need to bolster his quite ordinary legal conclusion with such extraordinary evidentiary detail" because he recognized "his decision would be a controversial one." Dubler, "Wifely Behavior," 994.

69. In 1951, Morris Ploscowe, a New York judge and the author of the highly cited work *Sex and the Law*, made the connection between the *Erlanger* case and New York's subsequent anti-common-law-marriage legislation. Ploscowe noted that the *Erlanger* trial "was apparently too much for the New York Legislature, which abolished common-law marriage at the next Legislative Session after this decision." Dubler, "Wifely Behavior," 995.

70. During the Great Depression, films often portrayed the gold digger as a sympathetic character, making the most out of what she was given. In "The Gold Digger as Icon: Exposing Inequity in the Great Depression," *Studies in Popular Culture* 28, no. 3 (2006), 71–92, Clarence R. Stevens writes that the character of the gold digger exposed the "inequities between men and women in an economic situation that only allowed limited job access to women . . . exposing flaws in a system that forces her to circumvent acceptable avenues in order to survive." In these films, gold diggers were portrayed as a kind of modern-day Robin Hood — stealing from the rich and redistributing this wealth to the poor. Relatedly, as Brian Donovan writes in *American Gold Digger*, these films typically portrayed the gold digger's male counterparts "as foolish rich men who got what they deserved and, given the state of the national economy, perhaps did not deserve what they had to begin with." Donovan, *American Gold Digger*, 13.

71. Susan Zeiger, *Entangling Alliances: Foreign War Brides and American Soldiers in the Twentieth Century* (New York: New York University Press, 2010), 142.

72. Similarly, one reader of the military publication *Stars and Stripes* explained the soldiers' interest in foreign women, writing that American girls, unlike European women, "are hindrances instead of helpmates." Barbara G. Friedman, *From the Battlefront to the Bridal Suite: Media Coverage of British War Brides, 1942–1946*, vol. 1 (Columbia: University of Missouri Press, 2007), 1:81.

Chapter 2

1. "The Last of the Revolutionary War Widows," *New York Times*, June 18, 1905.

2. David Lamb, "96-Year-Old Is Last Widow of a Civil War Soldier," *Baltimore Sun*, February 7, 2003. The article described Alberta Martin as the last Civil War widow, but this was inaccurate. Maudie Hopkins and Helen Viola Jackson were both Civil War widows who died after Martin. Currently, Jackson is believed to have been the last surviving Civil War widow. Nevertheless, it is possible that there are others who died after her. See Meilan Solley, "The Last Surviving Widow of a Civil War Veteran Dies at 101," *Smithsonian Magazine*, January 7, 2021.

3. The couple never made their marriage public, and Jackson did not reveal the marriage until 2017. Jackson died in 2021 at age 101. See Solley, "The Last Surviving Widow."

4. Kristin A. Collins, "Administering Marriage: Marriage-Based Entitlements, Bureaucracy, and the Legal Construction of the Family," *Vanderbilt Law Review* 62, no. 4 (2009), 1115.

5. Unlike other potential forms of government support, pensions were not characterized as charity. However, this doesn't mean that receiving pensions was easy. In order to receive their pensions, widows were required to submit proof of their husband's service in the military and of the legality of their marriage. As Professor Kristin Collins writes:

> Many women had problems producing proof of either kind, but satisfying the pension clerks' standards for proof of marriage posed particular difficulties for widows. As was sensible at a time when marriage licensing and registration procedures were underutilized, statutory and administrative rules promulgated during the period required the Pension Office to recognize common law marriage and to take a generous view of what constituted a legal marriage.

Thus, under applicable statutes and regulations, pension clerks were supposed to evaluate claims to marital status using the same liberal standards as judges of the period. In practice, however, women who had not used municipal schemes to license and register their marriages faced significant, often insurmountable administrative resistance to the recognition of their marriages.

Collins, "Administering Marriage," 1130–31.

6. See, e.g., Cong. Globe, 27th Cong., 3d Sess. 388 (1843) (statement of Sen. Smith); Cong. Globe, 31st Cong., 1st Sess. 681 (1850) (statement of Rep. Venable).

7. As Professor Nancy Cott notes, "Legislators would not accept programs that appeared to negate marriage or lift the onus from men's shoulders." Nancy F. Cott, *Public Vows: A History of Marriage and the Nation* (Cambridge, MA: Harvard University Press, 2002), 171. Consequently, the appeal of widows' pension programs was that these laws helped reinforce the male duty of support. In addition, as law professor Angela Onwuachi-Willig has written, "Marriage allowed states to deflect their responsibility for supporting newly-emancipated Blacks to impoverished black men, who were forced to assume the financial caretaking role of their former slave owners in their private homes even though they had no resources or access to political and economic power." Angela Onwuachi-Willig, "The Return of the Ring: Welfare Reform's Marriage Cure as the Revival of Post-Bellum Control," *California Law Review* 93, no. 6 (2005), 1661.

8. As law professor Kristin Collins notes, "In these legislators' accounts, marriage to a soldier or veteran functioned as a proxy for women's services of various sorts, whether to country or to husband." Collins, "Administering Marriage," 1114.

9. The inability to divorce also reduced such fears. As law professor Kerry Abrams writes, "Since exiting a marriage was very difficult, the state did not need to worry that a person would marry only to obtain benefits because, sooner or later, the individual would feel the burdens as well." Kerry Abrams, "Marriage Fraud," *California Law Review* 100, no. 1 (2012), 44.

10. Act of June 8, 1866, ch. 106, § 14, 14 Stat. 56 (1866).

11. Act of March 3, 1873, ch. 234, § 11, 17 Stat. 566, 570 ("The widows of colored or Indian soldiers or sailors . . . shall be entitled to receive the pension . . . without other evidence of marriage than satisfactory proof that the parties were joined in marriage by some ceremony deemed by them obligatory, or habitually recognized each other as man and wife, and were so recognized by their neighbors, and lived together as such up to the date of enlistment.").

12. Cott, *Public Vows*, 103 (noting that by 1893 widows' pensions accounted for 40 percent of the federal budget).

13. Such women were left to rely on local poor laws, which typically required single women to work in state-funded manufacturing jobs or the poorhouse in order to qualify for relief. For a discussion of pre–Civil War poor laws and unmarried women's difficulties obtaining financial assistance, see Mimi Abramovitz, *Regulating the Lives of Women: Social Welfare Policy from Colonial Times to the Present* (Boston: South End Press, 1988).

14. In 1843, Oregon's provisional government authorized each male settler eighteen years of age and older to claim up to 640 acres of land — farmland and timberland, in one or more parcels. If they improved the land and lived on it for four consecutive years, they could receive clear title to it. Further amendments followed in December 1844 and July 1845. See Act of June 25, 1844, 1844 Or. Laws

77; Amendment to the Organic Law, art. III, 1843–1872. Then, in 1848, Congress declared all such local land laws null and void. This left Oregon temporarily without any land law at all. Congress remedied this with the 1850 Donation Land Act. See Ralph James Mooney, "Formalism and Fairness: Matthew Deady and Federal Public Land Law in the Early West," *Washington Law Review* 63, no. 2 (1988), 324.

15. During the Donation Land Act's five-year existence, eight thousand claimants acquired three million acres, most of it in the Willamette Valley.

16. Francesca Beauman, *Matrimony, Inc.: From Personal Ads to Swiping Right, a Story of America Looking for Love* (New York: Simon & Schuster, 2020), viii, 75.

17. Cong. Globe, 31st Cong., 1st Sess. 1080 (1850).

18. The Homestead Act of 1862 would later allow single women to claim their own plots of land. However, it did not give double portions to married couples. See 12 Stat. 392 § 1 (1855–1863), codified as 43 U.S.C. § 175 (repealed) ("Any person who is the head of a family, or who has arrived at the age of twenty-one years . . . shall, from and after the first January, eighteen hundred and sixty-three, be entitled to enter one quarter section or a less quantity of unappropriated public lands . . .").

19. The act took effect on September 27, 1850, granting 320 acres of federal land to white male citizens eighteen years of age or older who resided on property on or before December 1, 1850. If married before December 1, 1851, a couple received an additional 320 acres in the wife's name. Many marriages reportedly took place during this one year. As historian James M. Bergquist notes, "A by-product of the act and the ensuing land rush was the sudden rash of marriages in the territory, since a man could double his land claim by taking a wife." James M. Bergquist, "The Oregon Donation Act and the National Land Policy," *Oregon Historical Quarterly* 58, no. 1 (March 1957), 30.

20. Some men married Native women, but intermarriage was not popular with Oregon's male settlers. By 1860, there were only thirty-two recorded intermarriages in the six counties of southwestern Oregon and an additional thirty-four in the remaining fourteen counties. See Gray H. Whaley, "Oregon, Illahee, and the Empire Republic: A Case Study of American Colonialism, 1843–1858," *Western Historical Quarterly* 36, no. 2 (2005),157–78. The lack of intermarriage is particularly telling given the fact that such marriages did qualify for the double portion. See *Vandolf v. Otis*, 1 Or. 153, 156 (1854) (finding that such marriages qualified for the extra land because they had occurred while Oregon was still a territory but noting, "It is not to be supposed that Congress would, by law, sanction marriages between [the races]").

21. See Whaley, "Oregon, Illahee," 162. Nearly ten years after the Donation Land Act was passed, single women remained scarce in Oregon. On August 26, 1859, Charles Prosch, publisher of the *Puget Sound Herald*, ran an editorial encouraging single woman to immigrate. "Here is the market to bring your charms to, girls," he wrote. "Don't be backward, but come right along — all who want good husbands and comfortable homes in the most beautiful country and the finest climate in the world." Bauman, *Matrimony Inc.*, 145.

22. Teenage girls who migrated to the Oregon Territory with their families were often pressured to marry much older men whom they barely knew. In her article "'Why She Didn't Marry Him,'" Cynthia Culver Prescott describes a fourteen-year-old who married a man twice her age whom she had known only a week. She further notes that teen marriages were so common in those days (fifteen was the typical age for women to marry during the early years on the Willamette Valley frontier) that "men began wondering why a girl wasn't married if she was still single when

she was 16." Cynthia Culver Prescott, "'Why She Didn't Marry Him': Love, Power, and Marital Choice on the Far Western Frontier," *Western Historical Quarterly* 38, no. 1 (Spring 2007), 29.

23. Prescott, "'Why She Didn't Marry Him,'" 30.

24. David Peterson del Mar, *What Trouble I Have Seen: A History of Violence Against Wives* (Cambridge, MA: Harvard University Press, 1996), 15. See also Athanasios Michaels, *Oregon's History: People of the Northwest in the Land of Eden* (n.d.), 57, https://open oregon.pressbooks.pub/oregonhistory/ (noting that land claim marriages were often made "without women's input, and abuse was not uncommon").

25. Peterson del Mar, *What Trouble I Have Seen*, 15.

26. For further discussion of the *Wells* case, see Laura R. Prieto and Stephen R. Berry, eds., *Crossings and Encounters: Race, Gender, and Sexuality in the Atlantic World* (Columbia: University of South Carolina Press, 2020), 101–3.

27. For further analysis of the *Fish* case, see Bethany Ruth Berger, "After Pocahontas: Indian Women and the Law, 1830 to 1934," *American Indian Law Review* 21, no. 1 (1997), 22–23.

28. In both *Fish* and *Wells*, the marriages predated the treaties granting lands to the Indian wives' tribes. Consequently, neither husband could have specifically married for the treaty land. Nevertheless, these cases confirmed that marriage was a viable strategy for gaining such lands.

29. See Cherokee Code, art. 15, § 75 (effective Nov. 1, 1875). In the 1906 Cherokee Intermarriage Cases, 203 U.S. 76 (1906), the US Supreme Court upheld this provision but also ruled that any claims from intermarriages before the codification of the law were valid.

30. Notably, whites also received more "Indian land" from the act than did Indians. As Mathew Atkinson has written, the "brilliance" of the General Allotment Act was that it "seemed fair." Initially, a significant portion of land was reserved as "Indian land." However, as Atkinson notes, "the small number of living Indians meant that each could receive a small allotment without all the 'Indian Land' being distributed; America kept the change as a tip. This so-called 'surplus land' was turned over to white settlers who began their scramble a mere two days after the Dawes Act had passed; Whites received more 'Indian land' from the Act than the Indians did." Matthew Atkinson, "Red Tape: How American Laws Ensnare Native American Lands, Resources, and People," *Oklahoma City University Law Review* 23, no. 2 (1998), 383.

31. Initially, married Indian women were not entitled to their own allotments. This provision changed in 1891 after government officials eventually acknowledged that the act's failure to give married women their own allotments was a mistake. The government's concern was due to the problems that arose upon divorce rather than a recognition of the act's general unfairness to married women. See Allison M. Dussias, "Squaw Drudges, Farm Wives, and the Dann Sisters' Last Stand: American Indian Women's Resistance to Domestication and the Denial of Their Property Rights," *North Carolina Law Review* 77, no. 2 (1999), 685 (discussing the amendments to the Dawes Act to protect married women).

32. A later amendment to the Dawes Act provided that the children of a marriage between a white man and an Indian woman that was recognized by the mother's tribe would have the same rights and privileges to the property of the tribe as any other member. Dussias, "Squaw Drudges," 687–88.

33. As historian Nancy Cott notes, marriage was the only way white men could live on the reservation. "So-called squaw men — white men who came onto the

reservation 'in the character of husbands to Indian women'... were required to marry their Indian partners legally in order to stay on the reservation." Cott, *Public Vows*, 123.

34. For a discussion of varying attitudes toward Indian–white intermarriage at the time of the allotment program, see David D. Smits, "'Squaw Men,' 'Half-Breeds,' and Amalgamators: Late Nineteenth-Century Anglo-American Attitudes Toward Indian-White Race-Mixing," *American Indian Culture and Research Journal* 15, no. 3, (1991), 29–57, https://doi.org/10.17953/aicr.15.3.m3397023p4072641.

35. 1889 Report of Commissioner of Indian Affairs, H.R. Exec. Doc. No. 1, pt. 5, 51st Cong., 1st Sess. 295 (report of Thomas Priestley, Yakima Agency, August 16, 1889).

36. 1890 Report of Commissioner of Indian Affairs, H.R. Exec. Doc. No. 1, pt. 5, 51st Cong., 2d Sess. 219 (report of Hal J. Cole, Colville Agency, August 11, 1890).

37. 1890 Report of Commissioner of Indian Affairs, H.R. Exec. Doc. No. 1, pt. 5, 51st Cong., 2d Sess. 219, 233–34 (report of Webster L. Stabler, Yakima Agency, September 18, 1890).

38. In his thesis, "From Buffalo to Beeves: The Transformation of the Oglala Lakota Economy 1868–1889" (master's thesis, University of Montana, 2001), Jeffrey Means writes that marrying Lakota women gave white ranchers two distinct advantages over their competition. As the husbands of Lakota women, these men were able to obtain "the rights and advantages meant to provide Indians with an equal economic footing within the surrounding white communities," 35. This gave them an advantage over their white counterparts. In addition, they were able to use these advantages more effectively than their Lakota counterparts because, as Means notes, "they understood and could manipulate the market system of the whites more efficiently than the Oglala." As Means writes, "In Lakota culture if a man desired to accumulate personal wealth for its own sake it represented not only bad manners, it demonstrated character flaws, such as selfishness. Such flaws meant he would never hold a leadership position or gain the respect of his family or band because he placed his own needs over that of the tribe's. Such conflicting worldviews clearly placed the Oglala at an economic disadvantage when in direct competition with 'squaw men,'" 35–36. The second advantage these "squaw men" had over Oglala ranchers is that they "could make business decisions without asking permission from an Indian Agent. And within the capitalist system the ability to make timely and independent business decisions is not only beneficial it is necessary in order to compete," 36.

39. Means, "From Buffalo to Beeves," 36 (noting that in 1884, between seven and eight hundred thousand head of cattle illegally grazed on the Lakota reservation).

40. See Alexandra Harmon, "American Indians and Land Monopolies in the Gilded Age," *Journal of American History* 90, no. 1 (June 2003), 106–33, https:// doi.org/10 .2307/3659793.

41. Kevin Noble Maillard, "The Pocahontas Exception: The Exemption of American Indian Ancestry from Racial Purity Law," *Michigan Journal of Race and Law* 12, no. 2 (2007), 363.

42. Marriage was an effective way to obtain otherwise inaccessible Indian lands. Although white men could not purchase Indian trust lands, they could inherit them. If an Indian spouse died before their non-Indian spouse, then the non-Indian spouse would inherit the Indian spouse's interest, and the land is moved out of trust. Larry E. Scrivner, "Acquiring Land into Trust for Indian Tribes," *New England Law Review* 37, no. 3 (2003), 604 (discussing the use of intermarriage to acquire Indian lands).

43. See Keneisha M. Green, "Who's Who: Exploring the Discrepancy Between the Methods of Defining African Americans and Native Americans," *American Indian Law Review* 31, no. 1 (2007), 103 (discussing the headright system and how it was abused through intermarriage and intestate succession).

44. As David Grann writes in his book *Killers of the Flower Moon: The Osage Murders and the Birth of the FBI* (New York: Doubleday, 2017), 58, the Office of Indian Affairs (now the Bureau of Indian Affairs) maintained lists of "competent" and "incompetent" Osage Indians. Osage Indians with one or more white ancestors as mixed race were treated as competent, while those with no white ancestors were deemed incompetent and required to have a financial guardian.

45. These "guardians" quickly took control of their wards' finances, often requiring permission for all purchases including those as cheap and as necessary as toothpaste. One common scam was to purchase a car at market value and resell it to their ward at five times the purchase price. Grann, *Killers of the Flower Moon*, 154.

46. Grann, *Killers of the Flower Moon*, 154. "Incompetent" Osages also could marry white people who would then become their financial guardians. These so-called guardians had control over the revenue from the Osage headright interest, that unusual property right created by federal law and policy. And sometimes Osage life partners became their killers. Matthew L. M. Fletcher, "Failed Protectors: The Indian Trust and Killers of the Flower Moon," *Michigan Law Review* 117, no. 1253 (2019), 1260–61.

47. The headright system gave the holders of the right an interest in the mineral estate akin to a share in a corporation. Fletcher, "Failed Protectors," 1259.

48. Due to Grann's book and the subsequent film adaptation starring Leonardo DiCaprio, the Osage intermarriages are the best-known examples of white men marrying for Indian headrights. However, they were far from the only examples. See, e.g., "Marriage Plot Against Indian Boys and Girls Discovered," *Indian's Friend* 26, no 2 (November 1913), 8 (reporting on a plot to marry off the children of a Creek man to get ownership and oil rights to his valuable land).

49. Grann, *Killers of the Flower Moon*, 63, 162. In 1925, Congress restricted the inheritance of headrights by non-Indians where the decedent owning the headright was one-half or more Osage. This change may have been a recognition of the horrors caused by the headright system, yet whether it actually made a difference is debatable. Increasingly few members of the Osage tribe were one-half or more Osage, and although the 1925 amendment restricted the inheritance of headrights through intestate succession (thus possibly disincentivizing a quick spousal murder), Congress still permitted an Osage Indian to dispose of a headright by will.

50. *Shanks v. Dupont*, 28 U.S. 242, 243 (1830). For more discussion of the relationship between marriage and citizenship, see Linda K. Kerber, *No Constitutional Right to Be Ladies: Women and the Obligations of Citizenship* (New York: Hills and Wang, 1998), 34–38; Kerry Abrams, "Citizen Spouse," *California Law Review* 101, no. 2 (2013), 416.

51. The *Shanks* court's conclusion that "marriage did not divest a woman of her political allegiance was premised on the British common law principle of indelible nationality and the assumption that a national government had to act to result in a change of allegiance." Leti Volpp, "Divesting Citizenship: On Asian American History and the Loss of Citizenship Through Marriage," *UCLA Law Review* 53, no. 2 (2005), 418–19.

52. The statute read: "Any woman who might lawfully be naturalized under the existing laws, married, or who shall be married to a citizen of the United States,

shall be deemed and taken to be a citizen." Under this statute, foreign women could automatically gain citizenship upon marriage, but a citizen woman would only lose it if she left the US to live abroad with her foreign husband. The statute also affirmed the US citizenship of children born abroad to US citizen fathers, but not mothers. The citizenship of a wife and a child followed the male head of the household. Act of February 10, 1855, ch. 71, § 2, 10 Stat. 604. Years later, in 1907, Congress changed the law and established that "any American woman who marries a foreigner shall take the nationality of her husband." Expatriation Act of 1907, ch. 2534, 34 Stat. 1228, 1228–29 (1907), repealed by the Nationality Act of 1940, ch. 876, 54 Stat. 1137 (1940).

53. Cong. Globe, 33rd Cong., 1st. Sess. 169–71 (1854).

54. Act of July 14, 1870, ch. 254, § 7, 16 Stat. 254, 256. The 1898 case of *Broadis v. Broadis* recognized the US citizenship of Ellen Maria Broadis through her marriage to James Broadis. Ellen was "of African descent" and described by the court as "a Negro, having been at one time a slave." The court noted that it was unclear whether Ellen Broadis was born in Maine or Canada, but it was irrelevant because she was a citizen of the United States by virtue of the fact that she was married to one. As the court wrote, "The political status of her husband was impressed upon her." *Broadis v. Broadis*, 86 F. 951, 955 (C.C.N.D. Cal. 1898).

55. In the case of American Indian women, it is less clear that marital citizenship was a benefit. Arguably, the imposition of US citizenship was more of an assimilation tactic, especially given the fact that the women's non-Native husbands were barred from renouncing their allegiance to the US government and becoming tribal citizens instead. Act of August 9, 1888, ch. 818, § 2, 25 Stat. 392, 392. See also Nancy F. Cott, "Marriage and Women's Citizenship in the United States, 1830–1934," *American Historical Review* 103, no. 5 (December 1998), 1459 (noting, "Rather than being especially interested in making citizens of Indian women by means of this law, Congress hoped to keep American men who married Indian women from claiming exemption from U.S. jurisdiction.").

56. The first immigration restrictions were exclusively state law. These included restrictions that barred convicts, prostitutes, lunatics, idiots, and those likely to become public charges. The Supreme Court initially recognized state regulation of immigration, including requirements for ship passenger lists and bonds, as a valid exercise of state police power, noting in the 1837 case *New York v. Miln* 36 U.S. 102 (1837), 143, that such powers were necessary to guard "against the moral pestilence of paupers, vagabonds, and possibly convicts." See Alina Das, "Inclusive Immigrant Justice: Racial Animus and the Origins of Crime-Based Deportation," *University of California at Davis Law Review* 52, no. 1 (2018), 182.

57. The Chinese Exclusion Act was the first large-scale immigration restriction in the United States and the first entirely race-based restriction. For a comprehensive history of the exclusion act, see Volpp, "Divesting Citizenship."

58. Much of the difficulty was numbers. If Ah Moy had been permitted to enter based solely on her marriage to a permitted Chinese laborer, then under "this right, the number of [female] Chinese laborers who are entitled to come to the United States will be greatly extended beyond the number who can enter by virtue of their own individual rights." Case of the Chinese Wife, 21 F. 785, 786 (C.C.D. Cal. 1884).

59. *Tsoi v. U.S.*, 116 F. 920 (9th Circ. 1902). Brief of Appellant, 10, 11, 33.

60. The Gentlemen's Agreement recognized proxy marriages as fully valid while also barring Japanese men from reentry if they returned to Japan to marry. Consequently,

the women who married under this exception were known as picture brides because they arrived in the United States having only seen their spouse's picture. See Cott, *Public Vows*, 153.

61. Immigration Act of 1882, ch. 376, § 2, 22 Stat. 214.

62. Martha Gardner, *The Qualities of a Citizen: Women, Immigration and Citizenship, 1879–1965* (Princeton, NJ: Princeton University Press, 2005), 91.

63. See, e.g., Deirdre M. Moloney, *National Insecurities: Immigrants and U.S. Deportation Since 1882* (Chapel Hill: University of North Carolina Press, 2012) (noting that "women were disproportionately deemed public charges in the early twentieth century" and that this was especially true for certain ethnic groups such as Jewish women).

64. 40 Stat. 1772–73 (1918). See also Susan Zeiger, *Entangling Alliances: Foreign War Brides and American Soldiers in the Twentieth Century* (New York: New York University Press, 2010), 43–47 (discussing the military's portrayal of foreign women).

65. As war bride historian Susan Zeiger writes, "Frequently social welfare workers argued that many of the brides would not have been admissible to the country on their own standing — an insinuation that they were 'immoral.'" These critics "intimated, these alien marriages were likely to lead to sexual immorality, prostitution, crime, venereal disease and 'racial' degradation," and many believed it was their duty to "save" American soldiers from these women. One YMCA rescue worker named Miss Bain was said to have "rescued about 1,100 men from dangerous companions." Zeiger, *Entangling Alliances*, 25.

66. In describing the alleged motivations of the war brides, Cleveland stated, "Living in Europe is hard, America is rich . . . [and] the plum of free transportation is tempting even to those who are not unscrupulous." Zeiger, *Entangling Alliances*, 49. Others suspected that many of these women didn't even like the men they were marrying. According to Zeiger, "These critics maintained that the women have only pretended to care for the American soldier in order to attain the benefits of American life and citizenship, benefits to which they were not honestly entitled," 61.

67. Viola I. Paradise, "Three Per Cent: Some Human Factors in the Immigration Problem," *Harper's Magazine* 144 (1922), 511, https://babel.hathitrust.org/cgi/pt?id=hvd.32044092659788&view=1up&seq=552.

68. Under the 1921 act, unmarried children under eighteen and wives of US citizens were the only immigrants allowed to enter the country outside the quotas and without a lengthy wait for a visa. Corinne R. Field and Nicholas L. Syrett, eds., *Age in America: The Colonial Era to the Present* (New York: New York University Press, 2015), 171. In 1928 this right was extended to women to be able to send for their spouses if they had been married before May 1928. In 1930, Congress amended the 1924 act exempting Chinese wives with pre-1924 marriages. See Field and Syrett, *Age in America*, 171–72, 175.

69. Zeiger, *Entangling Alliances*, 53.

70. David Martin, "Why Auden Married," Letters to the Editor, *New York Review of Books* (April 24, 2014), http://www.nybooks.com/articles/2014/04/24/why-auden-married/.

71. War brides were given special immigration consideration. They received non-quota immigration status, expedited naturalization, room, board, and medical care under military auspices and free transportation under the US War Brides Act of December 28, 1945, Pub. L. No. 271, ch. 591, 59 Stat. 659 (1945). See also Zeiger, *Entangling Alliances*, 3.

72. Ilene Lelchuk, "War Brides Gather to Tell Tales and Keep Memories of Past Alive," *SFGATE*, August 1, 1999.

73. Lutwak "married" his already married aunt, Maria Knoll; Osborne "married" Lutwak's uncle, Munio Knoll (Maria's true husband); and Klemtner "married" Lutwak's uncle and Munio's brother. *U.S. v. Lutwak*, 195 F.2d 748, 751–52 (7th Cir. 1952).

74. Notably, when the parties were indicted, one of the veterans took up residence with her alien husband and she and her husband were then acquitted. As Professor Maria Isabel Medina notes, "Although she testified for the government at the trial, her spouse, one of the alien spouses, was acquitted by the jury. A fair construction of the acquittal is that the jury must have been convinced by the evidence presented that the marriage, regardless of the intent of the parties at the time they married, had become, by the time of the trial, a 'valid' marriage." Maria Isabel Medina, "The Criminalization of Immigration Law: Employer Sanctions and Marriage Fraud," *George Mason Law Review* 5, no. 4 (1997), 706.

75. *U.S. v. Tagalicud*, 84 F.3d 1180, 1185 (9th Circ. 1996).

76. Peter Berta, ed., *Arranged Marriages: The Politics of Tradition, Resistance, and Change* (New Brunswick, NJ: Rutgers University Press, 2022), 26.

77. Although there are exceptions to deportation in cases of abuse, domestic violence victims sometimes are unaware of their rights or doubt they will be enforced. For a discussion of immigrant women and domestic abuse, see Katerina Shaw, "Barriers to Freedom: Continued Failure of U.S. Immigration Laws to Offer Equal Protection to Immigrant Battered Women," *Cardozo Journal of Law and Gender* 15, no. 3 (2009), 668.

78. Colleen Long, "Requests to Bring in Child Brides OK'd; Legal Under US Laws," *AP News*, January 11, 2019. See also David Crary, "Efforts Intensify to Curtail Child Marriage in the U.S.," *Columbian*, February 19, 2016, https://www.colum bian.com/news/2016/feb/19/efforts-intensify-to-curtail-child-marriage-in-the -u-s/.

79. There had been some expansion of female federal benefits beginning even earlier, but this was more in line with nineteenth-century widows' pensions rather than an expansion of federal benefits in general. Specifically, in 1917, Congress passed the War Risk Insurance Act (WRIA). Like earlier pension acts, WRIA provided support for military widows, allotments or allowance for wives whose husbands were away fighting, and subsidized insurance for military wives. It also used an expanded definition of marriage that covered more women than earlier pension acts. Specifically, the WRIA recognized common-law marriage as a basis for *all* women's claims and for "colored or Indian soldiers and sailors," regardless of whether the marriage would satisfy state law. Kristin A. Collins, "Federalism, Marriage, and Heather Gerken's *Mad Genius*," *Boston University Law Review* 95, no. 2 (2015), 623.

80. Cott, *Public Vows*, 173. The goal of keeping married women out of the workforce was also encouraged in other ways. For example, § 213 of the Economy Act of 1932 specified that in any personnel reductions by the US government, a married person whose spouse was also employed by the government "shall be dismissed" before other employees. The act also stated that hiring "preference shall be given" to applicants whose spouse was not employed by the government. Three-quarters of the more than sixteen hundred workers fired following § 213 were women. The use of marital status as a basis for dismissals then quickly spread to state governments; by 1940, a majority of states had proposed or enacted legislation restricting married women's ability to hold state government jobs. See Patrice Ruane, "From

Pin Money Workers to Essential Workers: Lessons About Women's Employment and the COVID-19 Pandemic from the Great Depression and the Great Recession," *UCLA Journal of Gender and Law* 29, no. 2 (2022), 356.

81. As a result, more than 60 percent of female workers were left uncovered by the act. See Cott, *Public Vows*, 175–76.

82. In 1940, the year after derivative benefits were added to the Social Security Act, seven out of ten US families had the husband, but not the wife, in the labor force. Mary E. O'Connell, "On the Fringe: Rethinking the Link Between Wages and Benefits," *Tulane Law Review* 67, no. 5 (1993), 1529. This change transformed how women received government support. It also created a racial gap regarding which women received which kind of public assistance. As historian Eric Foner writes, the 1935 Social Security Act included public assistance programs, notably aid to dependent children and to the impoverished elderly. These were open to all Americans, regardless of race, who met a means test. But they set benefits at extremely low levels and authorized the states to determine eligibility standards. Because recipients did not pay Social Security taxes, they soon came to bear the humiliating stigma of dependency on government handouts. The gap between the two programs widened in 1939, when wives, elderly widows, and dependent survivors of covered male workers were moved from general public relief into the Social Security system, leaving single mothers and the non-white poor to dominate what would come to be called "welfare."

Eric Foner, "Expert Report of Eric Foner: *Gratz, et al. v. Bollinger, et al.*, no. 97-75321 (E.D. Mich.) *Grutter, et al. v. Bollinger, et al.*, No. 97-75928 (E.D. Mich.)," *Michigan Journal of Race and Law* 5, no. 1 (1999), 328.

83. In many ways, women's survivor benefits can also be viewed as benefits to the husband. As Professor Nancy Cott notes, survivors' benefits were not women's "own entitlements but entitlements for the male worker posthumously, honoring him by keeping his family from penury." This was even more true of retirement benefits, which were given to the wife but could be expected to support the husband's retirement as well. Cott, *Public Vows*, 176–77.

84. "Policy makers who crafted the amendments recognized that single men and all women contributors were being overtaxed, so to speak. They saw this as a useful incentive to men to marry and have families and to women to be stay-at-home wives and mothers rather than entering the labor force." Cott, *Public Vows*, 176. At sixty-five, "a married man who had worked right beside a single man for the same number of years . . . got 50% more out of the system." Cott, *Public Vows*, 177.

85. In 2021, median weekly earnings for wage and salary workers who usually worked full-time were $998. Median earnings for women were $912, or 83.1 percent of men's earnings. "The Economics Daily: Median Earnings for Women in 2021 Were 83.1 Percent of the Median for Men," Bureau of Labor Statistics, US Department of Labor, January 24, 2022, https://www.bls.gov/opub/ted/2022/median-earnings-for-women-in-2021-were-83-1-percent-of-the-median-for-men.htm. See also Key Findings from the personal finance advice site *The Ascent*, noting that the "median male salary in 2021 was $50,391, 27% higher than the median female salary of $36,726." Jack Caporal, "Are You Well-Paid? Compare Your Salary to the Average U.S. Income," *The Ascent*, updated June 13, 2023, https://www.fool.com/the-ascent/research/average-us-income/#key-findings.

86. As policy analysts have noted, "the potential for future poverty among never-married women with children remains quite high. More than one-third (34%) of these women's Social Security benefits will fail to put them above the poverty

line." See Melissa M. Favreault, Frank J. Sammartino, and C. Eugene Steuerle, "Social Security Benefits for Spouses and Survivors: Options for Change," in Melissa Favreault, Frank Sammartino, and Gene Steuerle, eds., *Social Security and the Family: Addressing Unmet Needs in an Underfunded System* (Washington, DC: Urban Institute Press, 2001), 177, 192–93. Unmarried women have much less money in old age than other groups. A 2012 Social Security report found that, for unmarried women — including widows — age sixty-five and older, Social Security makes up 50.4 percent of their total income. In contrast, Social Security benefits make up only 35.9 percent of unmarried elderly men's income and only 30.2 percent of elderly couples' income. See "Social Security Is Important to Women," Fact Sheet: Social Security, accessed June 19, 2023, https://www.ssa.gov/pressoffice/factsheets/women-alt.pdf.

87. Social Security Administration Publication no. 13-11785, Fast Facts and Figures About Social Security, 2020 (July 2020), https://www.ssa.gov/policy/docs/chartbooks/fast_facts/2020/fast_facts20.pdf. The biggest change is that a much larger percentage of women now receive benefits based on their own earnings and those of their husbands. The report notes that the number of women receiving benefits based entirely on their husband's earnings declined from 57 percent in 1960 to 19 percent in 2019, but the portion of dual entitlement increased from 5 percent in 1960 to 24 percent in 2019. See also Caroline Lewis Bruckner and Jonathan Barry Forman, *Women, Retirement, and the Growing Gig Economy Workforce*, 38 Ga. St. U. L. Rev. 259, 358 (2022) (examining the reasons why "women are generally more dependent on Social Security benefits than men").

88. Research, Statistics and Policy Analysis, Beneficiary Projection: Women and Dual Entitlement 2025–2095, Social Security Administration, available at https://www.ssa.gov/policy/docs/projections/populations/women-dual-2025.html.

89. Tying federal benefits to marriage is a problematic means of compensating care-givers for their work. As a result, some legal scholars have suggested that a better solution would be to award Social Security caretaking credits to mothers. This would eliminate the connection between support and marriage and base it entirely on caretaking work. Such proposals recognize that women's decreased earnings are often the result of childcare responsibilities and that unmarried mothers are those at the greatest risk for poverty in old age. The proposed caretaking benefit would be awarded based solely on the existence of children. Such a change would increase many single women's benefits and reduce married women's reliance on their hus-band's earnings. See, e.g., Nancy Staudt, April Yanyuan Wu, and Chao Wang, "Is Gender-Based Policymaking Relevant in the 21st Century?," *Georgetown Journal of Gender and the Law* 13, no. 1 (2012), 101 (discussing Social Security reforms includ-ing a caretaking credit). See also Nancy Staudt, "Taxing Housework," *Georgetown Law Journal* 84, no. 5 (1996), 1606–10 (suggesting that a tax system should impute wages to household work based on its economic value and then subject those wages to payroll and income taxation, thus treating women "who perform household labor as having earned their benefits in the same manner as waged laborers"); Katherine Silbaugh, "Turning Labor into Love: Housework and the Law," *Northwestern University Law Review* 91, no. 1 (1996), 1 (discussing other methods of valuing housework). See generally, Dorothy Brown, The Whiteness of Wealth: How the Tax System Impoverishes Black Americans — And How We Can Fix It.

90. It is important to note that the marriage tax benefit or penalty can also have racial implications. Minority couples are more likely to be similar earners, especially

African American couples; thus, the tax code is actually disincentivizing these groups from marrying. See Cott, *Public Vows*, 224 (discussing the racial implications of the marriage tax).

91. When the PRWORA was passed, congressional findings hinted that marriage might cure a number of problems, including low birth weights, low verbal cognitive attainment, child abuse and neglect, low educational aspirations, poor student performance, and the rising numbers of convicts in the juvenile justice system. In fact, according to these findings, marriage would even reduce the incidence of divorce and out-of-wedlock births among members of future generations. Onwuachi-Willig, "The Return of the Ring," 1675.

92. Congress noted that while "only 9 percent of married-couple families with children under 18 years of age have income below the national poverty level . . . 46 percent of female-headed households with children under 18 years of age are below the national poverty level." Personal Responsibility and Work Opportunity Reconciliation Act of 1996, H.R. 3734, 104th Cong. § 101 (1996). For further discussion of the PRWORA use of marriage as an anti-poverty measure, see Onwuachi-Willig, "The Return of the Ring," 1650 (discussing the PRWORA's pro-marriage objectives); Dorothy E. Roberts, "Welfare Reform and Economic Freedom: Low-Income Mothers' Decisions About Work at Home and in the Market," 44, no. (2004), 1052–53 (noting that debates surrounding the reauthorization of Temporary Assistance for Needy Families (TANF) have directed even more attention to "the state's role in encouraging marriage among welfare recipients and low-income parents"). For an example of state laws enacted in response to the PRWORA, see Okla. Admin. Code § 340:10-3-57 (2006) (setting up various special considerations for distribution of TANF funds, some of which give disparate consideration to unmarried couples and sometimes penalize them economically by withholding welfare funds).

93. Kaaryn Gustafson, "Breaking Vows: Marriage Promotion, the New Patriarchy, and the Retreat from Egalitarianism," *Stanford Journal of Civil Rights and Civil Liberties* 5, no. 2 (2009), 289–90; Andrew J. Cherlin, *The Marriage-Go-Round: The State of Marriage and the Family in America Today* (New York: Vintage Books, 2010), 27 (noting that "these government interventions on behalf of marriage have no counterpart in other Western nations, because nowhere else is the meaning and function of marriage such a contested issue").

94. On the coercive nature of these Healthy Marriage Initiatives under Temporary Assistance for Needy Families (TANF), see Teresa Kominos, "What Do Marriage and Welfare Reform Really Have in Common? A Look into TANF Marriage Promotion Programs," *St. John's Journal of Legal Commentary* 21, no. 3 (2007), 942 ("Marriage promotion programs attempt to coerce TANF recipients to make 'better' decisions in their personal relationships by threatening financial consequences . . ."); and Aly Parker, "Can't Buy Me Love: Funding Marriage Promotion Versus Listening to Real Needs in Breaking the Cycle of Poverty," *Southern California Review of Law and Social Justice* 18, no. 2 (2009), 507n ("Offering a family an additional third of the base monthly stipend is a form of government coercion to marry"). But see Wade F. Horn, "Wedding Bell Blues: Marriage and Welfare Reform," Brookings, June 1, 2001, https://www.brookings.edu/articles/wedding-bell-blues-marriage-and-welfare-reform/ (arguing that the current welfare system is flawed in that it does not successfully promote traditional marriage and proposing that alternative welfare incentives, including monetary incentives, for childbirths that take place within marriage).

95. See https://www.thenation.com/article/archive/hotgun-weddings/ (describing the $80-a-month incentive). See Katha Pollitt, "Shotgun Weddings," *Nation*, February 4, 2004 (describing the $80-a-month incentive in Wisconsin and the $100-a-month incentive in West Virginia).

96. In remarking on the Minnesota bridefare program, DHHS Secretary Wade Horn stated that the program "provide[s] dramatic new evidence that changes in welfare incentives can increase the likelihood that single parents will get married and that married parents will stay married." Wade Horn, "Welfare Incentives That Aid Marriage," *Washington Times*, November 28, 2000, E1.

97. Onwuachi-Willig, "The Return of the Ring," 1686.

98. Professors Cahn and Carbone also note that working-class men have more difficulty recovering from financial setbacks than women and that layoffs often exacerbate male substance abuse, violence, and other behavioral issues. Naomi Cahn and June Carbone, "Uncoupling," *Arizona State Law Journal* 53, no. 11 (2021), 39.

99. At twelve months, 90 percent of both groups were still married. After thirty months, the number for both groups was 81.5 percent. See Erika Lundquist et al., *A Family-Strengthening Program for Low-Income Families: Final Impacts from the Supporting Healthy Marriage Evaluation* (Washington, DC: OPRE Report 2014-09A). For further discussion of government marriage promotion programs, see Cahn and Carbone, "Uncoupling," 36; Gustafson, "Breaking Vows," 296.

100. Philip N. Cohen, *Enduring Bonds: Inequality, Marriage, Parenting, and Everything Else That Makes Families Great and Terrible* (Oakland: University of California Press, 2018), 68.

101. In addition, in a 2020 report titled "The Demise of the Happy Two-Parent Home," Senate Republicans proposed financial incentives to use an expanded child tax credit to encourage "family stability" and two-parent households. The report claimed, "By reducing the cost of single parenthood, more generous safety net programs may incentivize [single parenthood]." Social Capital Project Report, no. 3-20, July 2020, https://www.jec.senate.gov/public/_cache/files/84d5b05b-1a58-4b3f-8c8d-2f94cfe4bb59/3-20-the-demise-of-the-happy-two-parent-home.pdf.

102. Times have changed. As Professor Kerry Abrams notes, "When public benefits were initially allocated on the basis of marital status, marriage was becoming less permanent, but the vast majority of people who married stayed married until one of the spouses died ... There was cultural and legal consensus that sex and procreation were best left to married couples and so public benefits that encouraged or rewarded marriage were less controversial than they are today." Abrams, "Marriage Fraud," 56.

103. "If the purpose of marriage remains the desire to express one's love and commitment then creating other compelling reasons to marry makes it less likely that marriage will stay true to those ideals," writes Professor Kerry Abrams. She further suggests that "it may not be the spouses 'fraudulently' seeking benefits who are weakening marriage, but lawmakers who have asked marriage to do more than it can do." Abrams, "Marriage Fraud," 61.

Chapter 3

1. A Conversation with Helen Fielding, available at https://www.penguinrandom house.com/books/307372/bridget-joness-diary-by-helen-fielding/9780375419638/readers-guide/.

2. As historian Hendrik Hartog explains, in colonial America "dignity belonged to the married." He notes that during this period, wives enjoyed increased social status, and this was intentional. Colonial leaders had the "sustained and sustaining faith that the reproduction of generations should occur within marriages and that the way to produce that social good was by making it better to be married than to be not or never married, particularly when children were involved." Hendrik Hartog, "Coverture and Dignity: A Comment," *Law & Social Inquiry* 41, no. 4 (Fall 2016), 833, 837–38.

3. Elizabeth Abbott, *A History of Marriage: From Same Sex Unions to Private Vows and Common Law, the Surprising Diversity of a Tradition* (New York: Seven Stories Press, 2011), 251.

4. When asked whether she was sorry that she hadn't married while young, Dickinson vigorously defended herself — but in her journal she noted that she "felt the Pot on [her] head as she did it." As Marla Miller notes in her book *Rebecca Dickinson: Independence for a New England Woman*, "It's hard to know just what her metaphor meant, but it may be a reference to the cap she wore. Caps were deemed appropriate for mature women in eighteenth-century Massachusetts; brides tended to wear caps after their wedding or once they became mothers, to signal their adult status. By the late 1780s a woman Dickinson's age would typically have worn a cap . . . If that's what she was thinking of, then Dickinson's embarrassment at having donned the trappings of age without having reaped its usual rewards was acute." Marla Miller, *Rebecca Dickinson: Independence for a New England Woman* (New York: Rutledge, 2013).

5. In many colonies, solitary living was legally prohibited and the unmarried, both male and female, were required to live with relatives or become servants or apprentices in another household to ensure they remained closely supervised. Rachel F. Moran, "How Second-Wave Feminism Forgot the Single Woman," *Hofstra Law Review* 33 (2004), 223, 235 (discussing colonial treatment of single men and women). See also Mark E. Kann, *A Republic of Men: The American Founders, Gendered Language, and Patriarchal Politics* (New York: New York University Press, 1998), 52–78 (examining colonial views of unmarried men).

6. Letter from George Washington to George Steptoe Washington, March 23, 1789.

7. In the first issue of *Poor Richard's Almanac*, Franklin included a poem ridiculing an old bachelor who was still waiting for the perfect woman:

> Old Batchelor would have a wife that's wise
> Fair Rich and young, a maiden for his bed
> Not proud, not churlish but of faultless size;
> A country housewife in the City bred.
> He's a nice Fool, and long in vain hath staid;
> He should bespeak her, there's none ready made.

See Kann, *A Republic of Men*, 56–57.

8. The attack described by the Adamses is sometimes referred to as the Boston Coffee Party. See Kann, *A Republic of Men*, 57.

9. As historian Hendrik Hartog notes, as a caretaker of a family, a married man became the sovereign of a domain, "able to meet with other rulers and to participate with them in government." Hendrik Hartog, *Man and Wife in America* (Cambridge, MA: Harvard University Press, 2022), 101.

10. As historian Mark Kann writes, "This presumptive trust in married men's good behavior even persuaded skeptics such as Fisher Ames to support popular suffrage

and elections. Ames openly detested democracy for its 'loud clamors of passion, artifice, and faction.' Nevertheless, he was willing to put his faith in 'the calm review of public transactions which is made by the citizens who have families and children, the pledges of their fidelity.'" Mark E. Kann, "The Bachelor and Other Disorderly Men During the American Founding," *Journal of Men's Studies* 6, no. 1 (1997).

11. As Catherine Denial notes, "Such partnerships were standard practice in fur trade country and have been since the seventeenth century." Colonial fur traders were highly cognizant of the economic and political benefits of marrying Native women. Through marriage, white men gained access to their Native wives' kin group and their hunting territory. Catherine Denial, *Making Marriage: Husbands, Wives, and the American State in Dakota and Ojibwe Country* (St. Paul: Minnesota Historical Society Press, 2013), 78–80.

12. When Jean-Baptiste Faribault died in Faribault, Minnesota (a town named after his son), General Sibley wrote, "Among the pioneers of Minnesota there is none whose memory and whose name better deserves to be respected and perpetuated than JEAN BAPTISTE FARIBAULT." "The Sibley Historic Site," published by the Sibley House Association / MNDAR (1995), available at http://www. sibley-friends.org/Jfaribault.htm.

13. Notably, Pelagie's father, Joseph Ainse, had made a similar calculation regarding the benefits of intermarriage when he married Pelagie's mother, a member of the Mdewakanton band of the Dakota. Ainse was a French Canadian from Mackinac Island who became fluent in the Dakota language and worked with both the Ojibwe and Dakota as a fur trader and Indian agent. In 1783, their daughter Pelagie was born. Historical records also refer to her as Kinnie Hanse Ainse, Pelagie Hause, Elizabeth Pelagie Ainse Faribault, and Madame Faribault. See Margaret Vaughan, "How the Family of Pelagie Faribault Came to Own Pike Island Near Fort Snelling," *MINNPOST*, December 21, 2020.

14. Indian women had "their own reasons for promoting marriages with white men. Some Indian women valued the objects, such as metal kettles, that they gained through the fur trade and thus did what they could to ensure the trade continued. Others preferred life inside the forts, where food was more plentiful than was often the case in their villages. A few Indian women accumulated considerable influence through liaising between their tribal communities and the trading companies." Cynthia Enole, *Bananas, Beaches and Bases: Making Feminist Sense of International Politics*, 2nd ed. (Oakland: University of California Press, 2014), 179.

15. Denial, *Making Marriage*, 43.

16. Poinsett finalized negotiations on March 12, 1839, agreeing to buy the island for $12,000 (about $239,000 today). See Purchase of Island Confluence of The St. Peter's and Mississippi Rivers, Letter from the Secretary of War, 26th Cong., 1st Session, Doc. 82 (February 12, 1840), 5.

17. As historian Catherine Denial notes, the Dakota would have recognized that Jean-Baptiste's power was due to Pelagie and that it was appropriate for her to receive a gift in her name in acknowledgment of her work. However, under the laws of coverture, a wife's property became her husband's. Consequently, "within the cultural system Leavenworth best understood, the Dakota grant to Pelagie was in every sense a grant to her husband; Leavenworth likely expected the land to be governed and controlled by Jean Baptiste. Faribault's contemporaries, as well as subsequent historians, interpreted the transfer of Pike Island to Pelagie

Faribault in much the same way Leavenworth did: it was a gift to the husband, made through the body of his wife." Catherine Denial, "Pelagie Faribault's Island, Property, Kinship and the Meaning of Marriage in Dakota Country," *Minnesota History*, Summer 2010, available at https://storage.googleapis.com/mnhs-org-support/mn_history_articles/62/v62i02p048-059.pdf.

18. Adams believed that if American women were noble and virtuous, elected officials would reflect these traits. However, if American women were immodest or immoral, then according to Adams, "Our Governors, our Judges, our Senators or Representatives, and even our Ministers would be appointed by Harlots for Money, and their Judgements, Decrees and decisions be sold to repay themselves or perhaps to procure the smiles (and Embraces) of profligate Females." *The Works of John Adams*, vol. 3, June 2, 1778.

19. Letter from Abigail Adams to John Adams, March 31–April 5, 1776.

20. Alexis de Tocqueville, *Democracy in America* 262 (Francis Bowen ed. & Henry Reeve trans., 1862).

21. Daniel J. Sharfstein, "Crossing the Color Line: Racial Migration and the One-Drop Rule, 1600–1860," *Minnesota Law Review* 91 (2007), 613–14.

22. Sharfstein, "Crossing the Color Line," 592–93 (2007). A century later, the musical *Showboat* immortalized this idea in the scene that literalizes the one-drop rule. In the musical, one of the performers, Julie, is a mixed-race woman passing as white, who is married to a white man and performing on the stage with him. When the couple is cornered by the local sheriff, Julie's husband, Stephen, surreptitiously cuts her finger and drinks her blood, allowing him to claim he has more than a drop of black blood in him. The couple evades the law but are forced to leave the showboat since "local folks won't tolerate the races mixing on the stage."

23. Ta-Nehisi Coates, "Black Confederates Revealed," *Atlantic* (May 16, 2011).

24. On May 10, 1740, the South Carolina Assembly enacted the "Bull for the better ordering and governing of Negros and other slaves in this province," also known as the Negro Act of 1740. The law prohibited enslaved African people from growing their own food, learning to read, moving about freely, assembling in groups, or earning money. It also permitted white enslavers to whip and kill enslaved Africans deemed "rebellious." For a history of the Gibson family and their transition to whiteness, see Daniel Sharfstein, *The Invisible Line: A Secret History of Race in America* (London: Penguin Press, 2011).

25. Letter from Henry Laurens to William Drayton, February 15, 1783, in David Duncan Wallace, *The Life of Henry Laurens; With a Sketch of the Life of Lieutenant-Colonel John Laurens* (New York: G.P. Putnam's Sons, 1915).

26. A version of this argument was used in the 1855 racial status case of Abby Guy. Both Guy and her mother had been enslaved by the father of a man named William Daniel, and after his father's death, Daniel claimed he owned Guy. Guy disagreed. She argued that her mother, Polly, had been wrongly enslaved and that she was actually white and thus, Guy was also white (it is likely Guy and Daniel shared the same father). In attempting to refute Guy's claim, Daniel called on Thomas S. Thompson, a relatively wealthy farmer with six slaves, to testify that he had known Guy and her mother as slaves, although they were both "bright mulatto." Guy acknowledged that she had been held as a slave but — drawing on the legal acceptance of the idea that a white person cannot be a slave — she argued that she was white based on her social acceptance as white. Most of the testimony of Guy's witnesses focused on her social identity and how she had been living among whites "as an equal." Ultimately, this social acceptance was

then found to be enough to overcome the facts showing Guy had been a slave. See Ariela J. Gross, "Litigating Whiteness: Trials of Racial Determination in the Nineteenth-Century South," *Yale Law Journal* 108 (1998), 109, 148.

27. Cases like *Cantey* frequently turned on whether a person acted the way a white person was expected to act and whether they were accepted as white by white society. Writing on the *Cantey* case, law professor Ariela Gross notes, "Discussions of an individual's exercise of the social, political, and legal rights and privileges of a white person dominated courtroom testimony, sometimes serving as a counterweight to 'scientific' evidence, sometimes in conjunction with it." Gross, "Litigating Whiteness," 156–57. See also Sharfstein, "Crossing the Color Line," 592, 636 (noting that antebellum trials of racial determination highlight just how common it was for people of the "[free colored] class to assimilate to the white, and the desire of elevation").

28. Before the witnesses were sworn in, the trial judge had instructed the jury to decide their race as "a person of color" if:

> There be a clear visible admixture evidenced by the color of the
> skin, the hair, or features, the person is to be regarded as of the
> degraded class; but if these distinctive characteristics be wanting,
> and the person has been received and treated as white, although
> there may be proof of some admixture derived from a remote
> ancestor, yet such person is to be accounted white, and entitled to
> privileges as such.

The court further noted that the people in question were now "respectable . . . one of them is a militia officer, and their caste has never been questioned until now."

Racial designation was about more than color or ancestry. As the *Cantey* court explained, it was entirely possible that two persons with the same complexion and the same ancestry could occupy entirely different racial categories. The court noted, "It may be well and proper, that a man of worth, honesty, industry and respectability, should have the rank of a white man, while a vagabond of the same degree of blood should be confined to the inferior caste." Judge Harper further suggested that it would be unwise — in fact, he wrote, it would be — "very cruel and mischievous" to disturb the racial identity of one "whose caste has never been questioned until now." *State v. Cantey*, 20 S.C.L. 614, 615 (S.C. App. L. & Eq. 1835).

29. "It appeared that the father of the witnesses was a white man, and their mother a descendant in the third degree of a half breed who had a white wife; their mother's father was the issue of this marriage, and he also married a white woman; so that the witnesses had one-sixteenth part of African blood. The maternal grandfather of the witnesses, although of dark complexion, had been recognized as a white man, received into society, and exercised political privileges as such; their mother was uniformly treated as a white woman; their relations of the same admixture have married into respectable families, and one of them had been a candidate for the legislature." *State v. Cantey*, 20 S.C.L. 614, 616 (S.C. App. L. & Eq. 1835).

30. For example, William Emerson testified that Boullemet was "always considered a white boy at school . . . [and] was a kind of favorite at school." Similarly, Thomas Spear testified that Boullemet's children played with his children, even though he admitted that he had heard the rumor that Boullemet's mother was a colored woman. See Gross, "Litigating Whiteness," 109, 148. See also, Transcript of Trial, *Boullemet v. Phillips*, no. 4219 (La. New Orleans Parish Ct., Feb. 1840) (collection

of Earl K. Long. Special Collections & Archives, University of New Orleans, New Orleans, La., Supreme Court Records).

31. After the marriage the family was accepted into Santo Domingo's white society. Witnesses testified that "at Lafayette Balls and at Mr. Mackay's balls . . . Mr. Boullemet visited Mrs. Brennan, Mrs. Benvist, Mr. Baptiste, Mrs. Legalle, Mrs. Chapion, Mrs. Mouchon . . ." Gross, "Litigating Whiteness," 109, 148.

32. During the testimony, Boullemet even conceded his mother's ambiguous racial status, stating that if she wasn't white then she was "Indian." He just insisted that she was not "coloured." Claiming Indian ancestry was a common tactic of mixed-race families. In his 1880 novel *The Grandissimes*, George Washington Cable lampoons this tactic, noting that such narratives were frequently offered by "the most respectable" Creole families. Shirley E. Thompson, *Exiles at Home: The Struggle to Become American in Creole New Orleans* (Cambridge, MA: Harvard University Press, 2009), 297.

33. The petition also highlighted their help in catching runaway slaves, using this to demonstrate where their loyalties resided. Specifically, "that 'their partialities are decidedly for the whites.'" Petition of Sundry Inhabitants of the County of Stafford Praying That Wm. Horton and Others Free White Persons Who Have Acquired Title to Their Freedom Since 1806 May Be Permitted to Remain in This Commonwealth, Stafford County, no. 10243, January 14, 1833.

34. As historian Joshua Rothman writes, "The Whartons were white because they acted white: they carried out the civic activities that helped define whiteness, their chosen social associations and marriage partners were all from white families, and they performed specific acts showing they bore no allegiance to the enslaved community of which they had once been a part." Joshua Rothman, *Notorious in the Neighborhood: Sex and Families Across the Color Line in Virginia, 1787–1861* (Chapel Hill: University of North Carolina Press, 2003), 214. Interestingly, even after this ruling the racial status of the Whartons remained complicated. The 1840 census lists William, Barney, and Lewis Wharton not as whites but as the heads of "free colored" families. It also shows that William and Lewis owned seven slaves between them. A different brother, Lemuel Wharton, is listed as white and the owner of a single slave. In later censuses, the Whartons appear as white people. As Professor Daniel Sharfstein notes, "Whether the 1840 census taker knew who they were or how they were regarded, whether he simply eyeballed them, or whether he believed in the one-drop rule, the Whartons were not unambiguously white seven years after the legislature had essentially declared them so." Sharfstein, "Crossing the Color Line," 634–35.

35. The article claimed the women wanted such marriages because they sought the traditional division of labor. It claimed that marriage with a white man "exempts [women] from raising corn, a service they are obliged to render to an Indian husband." It thus encouraged such marriages as both aiding Indian women and hastening the "civilization" of Native nations. *Newburyport Herald*, June 2, 1821, 4. As historian Cynthia Enole notes, "Marriage to an Indian woman gave a white man a sense he was superior, that he was saving a woman from the deplorable condition of savagery." Enole, *Bananas, Beaches*, 179.

36. Even the designation as "Spaniard" could be problematic. In one instance, Arcadia became outraged when a comparison was drawn between African Americans and other "dark-skinned" races. In 1902 the General Federation of Women's Clubs in Los Angeles made the decision to officially exclude African American women

from their membership. Protesting this decision, clubwoman Caroline Severance remarked that she did not understand why white Americans associated socially with "Italians, Spaniards, and representatives of other dark-skinned races," but not with African Americans. Arcadia was so enraged at being labeled part of a "dark-skinned" race that she withdrew both her participation and contribution to the club's upcoming fundraiser. Many other prominent Mexican American women soon followed suit. See Eileen Wallis, *Earning Power: Women and Work in Los Angeles 1880–1930* (Reno: University of Nevada Press, 2010).

37. In 1835, a disgruntled, drunken sailor stabbed Stearns in the face and shoulders several times in a dispute over the price of a cask of brandy. Although he survived the attack, the wounds to his face left terrible, disfiguring scars. One of the deep cuts likely severed nerves, and for the rest of his life, he had a speech impediment. Behind his back he was called Cara de Caballo, or "horseface." Colleen Adair Fliedner, *Fascinating True Tales from Old California* (Lanham, MD: Rowman & Littlefield, 2023), 27.

38. As historian Nicholas Syrett writes, most of the "white" men in California claimed to be Spanish Mexicans but were actually of mixed-race heritage. Corinne R. Field and Nicholas L. Syrett, eds., *Age in America: The Colonial Era to the Present* (New York: New York University Press, 2015), 67. In contrast, Abel Stearns's ancestors hailed from England and had arrived in Massachusetts Bay Colony in the early seventeenth century. See Loren P. Meissner and Kim Jarrell Johnson, *A Brief History of Eastvale* (Charleston, SC: History Press, 2013), noting that "some sources state or imply that Abel Stearns's ancestry was Jewish, but further search to date seems to contradict this. Abel also greatly benefited from this marriage. In exchange for conferring his whiteness on Arcadia, he was able to unite himself with "one of the wealthiest landowning families in the territory" and increase his own status and landholdings. Field and Syrett, *Age in America*, 40–41.

39. In one instance, Johnson took Adaline to a Fourth of July barbecue at the home of a white neighbor who had invited him to give an Independence Day oration, but when the neighbor saw Johnson had brought Adaline, he insisted that she leave. Johnson's political critics were similarly offended by his efforts to have his daughters accepted into white society. However, Johnson was no abolitionist. In addition to never freeing Julia, after she died he began a relationship with another enslaved woman. Then, believing she had been unfaithful, he sold her and began a relationship with the woman's sister. Jon Meacham, *American Lion, Andrew Jackson in the White House* (New York: Random House, 2008), 88. See also Ronald Shafer, "He Became the Nation's Ninth Vice President. She Was His Enslaved Wife," *Washington Post*, February 7, 2021.

40. Interestingly, his district immediately reelected him to the House, but there is little question his relationship with Chinn hurt Johnson's political career. See Andrew Glass, "Senate Elects a Vice President," *Politico*, February 8, 2018.

41. The marriage garnered significant criticism. An article printed on November 29, 1832, in the *Lexington Observer & Reporter* covered the marriage of Thomas W. Scott to Adaline Johnson, writing, "This is the second time that the moral feelings of that portion of the people of Scott County who possess such feelings, have been shocked and outraged by the marriage of a mulatto daughter of Col. Johnson to a white man . . . How long will the people of Scott County — of Kentucky — permit such palpable violations of the laws of their state to be committed with impunity! How long will the moral and religious part of the community suffer

such indecent and shocking example." Nevertheless, the daughters' marriages served their purpose. From the 1840 federal census and onward, Imogene Johnson Pence and her descendants (Adaline died shortly after her marriage) were listed as white. Adele Logan Alexander, *Parallel Worlds: The Remarkable Gibbs-Hunts and the Enduring (In)Significance of Melanin* (Charlottesville: University of Virginia Press, 2012); Sheryll Cashin, *Loving: Interracial Intimacy in America and the Threat to White Supremacy* (Boston: Beacon Press, 2017), 71–72. In fact, the racial transformation was so complete that, until recently, Johnson and Julia's descendants did not even know they were descended from a black woman. As historian Amrita Chakrabarti Myers writes, "The reality of this was driven home to me when I met some of Julia's and Richard's relatives, none of whom knew, until they were older, that they were descended from a vice president. And this was no accident. At some point in the early twentieth century, perhaps because of heightened fears of racism during the Jim Crow era, members of Imogene Johnson Pence's line, already living as white people, chose to stop telling their children that they were descended from Richard Mentor Johnson . . . and his black wife. It wasn't until the late 20th century that younger Pences, by then already in their 40s, 50s, and 60s, began discovering the truth of their heritage." The Erasure and Resurrection of Julia Chinn, U.S. Vice President Richard M. Johnson's Black Wife, Association of Black Women Historians blog post, March 3, 2019, http://abwh.org/2019/03/03/the-erasure-and-resurrection-of-julia-chinn-u-s-vice-president-richard-m-johnsons-black-wife/. See also David Mills, "The Vice President and the Mulatto," *HuffPost*, May 25, 2011 (discussing the transformation of Chinn's descendants from black to white).

42. See the Militia Act of 1862, ch. 201, 12 Stat. 597 (1862). Marriage to a soldier freed women and their children from slavery. Later, these women could also claim back pay and property or "bounty" if they lost their soldier husbands. During the war, many of these newly emancipated women and children accompanied their soldier husbands to the Union camps. In November 1863 this led to a national scandal when a Kentucky general expelled these women and children from the camps, sending them off into a brutal winter where several froze to death. The order was quickly reversed and resulted "in a resolution reaffirming the emancipation of the wives and children of freed men who enlisted in the Union Army." James Oakes, *Freedom National: The Destruction of Slavery in the United States 1861–1865* (New York: W. W. Norton, 2013), 433.

43. White southerners were well aware of the civil rights manifest in marriage, and even after the Civil War many continued to refuse marriage to the formerly enslaved. "In these instances of resistance, white southerners were recognizing the civil rights manifest in marriage by refusing to grant them." Nancy F. Cott, *Public Vows: A History of Marriage and the Nation* (Cambridge, MA: Harvard University Press, 2002), 89–94. This connection was also made in contemporary abolitionist literature. The 1864 book *John Freeman and His Family*, which was published to "offer counsel to the colored people in their new circumstances," drew a clear connection between marriage and freedom. The book demonstrated Freeman's transition from bondage to freedom through three scenes of contract — social contract, labor contract, and marriage contract. Through these contracts, as a hired worker and as husband, Freeman "escaped "the clinging dust of slavery" and the "disability of race." Amy Dru Stanley, *From Bondage to Contract: Wage Labor, Marriage, and the Market in the Age of Slave Emancipation* (Cambridge, UK: Cambridge University Press, 1998), 38.

44. The other two were the right of father to his child — the parental relation; and the right of a man to the personal liberty with which he was endowed by nature and by God. Cott, *Public Vows*, 95.

45. For further discussion of freedmen marriages, see Cott, *Public Vows*, 79–91.

46. David Silkenat, *Moments of Despair: Suicide, Divorce, and Debt in Civil War Era North Carolina* (Chapel Hill: University of North Carolina Press, 2011), 98.

47. During this time the belief "that marriage civilized and controlled the brutish nature of all people encouraged the use of formal matrimony as a remedy for the widespread immorality that whites believed to prevail among blacks." Grossberg, *Governing the Hearth*, 133. See also Cott, *Public Vows*, 87 ("To give lie to believers in the natural promiscuity of blacks and to vindicate their own efforts, missionaries, officers in command of black troops and many ordinary agents expected ex-slaves to observe 'the sacred obligation of marriage' when given the chance").

48. Silkenat, *Moments of Despair*, 98. Sometimes, freedmen marriages were complicated by the legacy of slavery. Historian Nancy Cott relates the story of one man who wanted to return to his earlier partner after being legally married to someone else during the war. The man was arrested as a bigamist, but then the Arkansas agent who arrested him "brought the two women together and they agreed one would be the wife and the other give up in claim in return for a certificate and $100." Cott, *Public Vows*, 91.

49. Angela Onwuachi-Willig, "The Return of the Ring: Welfare Reform's Marriage Cure as the Revival of Post-Bellum Control," *California Law Review* 93 (2005), 1663 (noting that "it seems that even the 'colonized' themselves implemented the tool of marriage to 'civilize' each other . . . by actively encouraging all Blacks to abide by white society's standards for appropriate roles of husbands and wives").

50. Cott, *Public Vows*, 90.

51. Onwuachi-Willig, "The Return of the Ring," 1662 (noting that "a number of freed Blacks, many of whom desperately wanted to obtain the rights and freedoms of Whites, facilitated enforcement of marriage laws, and in a sense contributed to their own subjugation by revealing to authorities the identities of other newly freed Blacks who violated societal marital norms by having more than one partner").

52. By the turn of the twentieth century, 40 percent of urban-dwelling men under the age of thirty-five were unmarried. In Manhattan, between one-third and one-half of men over the age of fifteen were single. As these numbers grew, magazines began to encourage this type of wealthy bachelor living by portraying it as glamorous and exciting. For further discussion of bachelors at the turn of the past century, see Rebecca Traister, *All the Single Ladies: Unmarried Women and the Rise of an Independent Nation* (New York: Simon & Schuster, 2016), 87; Rachel F. Moran, "How Second-Wave Feminism Forgot the Single Woman," *Hofstra Law Review* 33 (2004), 223, 247.

53. As Professor Onwuachi-Willig explains, "Marriage among newly freed Blacks was necessary to minimize states' economic responsibility for them, especially for black children born during slavery. Because of the inability of Blacks to marry during the antebellum period, the children of Black slave couples were technically illegitimate and thus the government's responsibility." By encouraging marriage, and particularly by establishing economic roles within black families, the government was able to shift enormous financial responsibility from itself to "newly freed Black men, who were charged with providing for their households' economic needs." Onwuachi-Willig, "The Return of the Ring," 1658–59.

54. Fisk then added, "By industry and economy you can soon provide a real good home, and plenty of food and clothing for your family; and you should not rest until this is done." See Dorothy Sterling, ed., *We Are Your Sisters: Black Women in the Nineteenth Century* (New York: W. W. Norton, 1997), 320.

55. Those at the top, just like those at the bottom, had been relatively static. "A modern American sociologist attributed significance to the fact that it took families like the Astors and the Vanderbilts at least two generations, if not three, to attain a firm social footing. The rate of assimilation before the Civil War was much slower than in the period after." Maureen E. Montgomery, *Gilded Prostitution: Status, Money, and Transatlantic Marriages, 1870–1914* (New York: Routledge, 2013), 37.

56. Attendance was limited to "the 400," which was shorthand for the four hundred people who could fit in her ballroom. The list mostly included old Dutch names like Stuyvesant and Rhinelander. These were families who had lived in New York City for generations and made a substantial mark on Manhattan and its surrounding areas. Washington Irving referred to these people as the Knickerbockers (although they didn't like the name).

57. At the time, fancy dress balls were all the rage. Hostesses would give a ball and the guests would compete to have the most luxurious costumes — costumes that would enable the women to wear every jewel they owned.

58. According to historian Maureen Montgomery, it was the attempt by those like Caroline Astor "to create a more exclusive elite with a formalized structure in the 19th century [that] was an important catalyst for transatlantic marriages." Families unable to secure entry into Mrs. Astor's circle could bypass New York entirely and "establish a foothold in European society instead." Such marriages gave them almost automatic access to the upper circles of American society and allowed them to return to America "to reap the benefits of their social success in Europe." Montgomery, *Gilded Prostitution*, 44–49.

59. In the 1911 P. G. Wodehouse story "The Goalkeeper and the Plutocrat," an aristocrat remarks with wonder at the idea of employment: "I was lunching with a man at the Bachelor's only yesterday and who swore he knew a fellow who met a man whose cousin worked." For impoverished nobility with similar attitudes, marriage was often a preferable alternative. See also Montgomery, *Gilded Prostitution*, 84 (noting that marriage was "regarded as a shortcut to wealth . . . and certainly less drastic than selling land or going into business . . . The difficulty the aristocracy had in comprehending paid work points to what was, for them, a serious problem").

60. Montgomery, *Gilded Prostitution*, 146. Montgomery further notes that "the notion of American women buying their way into the best society, as opposed to being naturally taken up by members of that society, implied that, apart from their wealth, these women had little to recommend them." Montgomery, *Gilded Prostitution*, 144.

61. Montgomery, *Gilded Prostitution*, 138. Similarly, in 1905, British novelist Marie Corelli wrote in her chapter "American Women in England," "There is always a British title going a-begging — always some decayed or degenerate semi drunk peer whose fortunes are on the verge of black ruin, ready and willing to devour, monster like, the holocaust of an American virgin, provided bags of bouillon are flung with her into his capacious maw." Marie Corelli, *Free Opinions Freely Expressed on Certain Phases of Modern Social Life and Conduct* (London: Archibald Constable & Co., Ltd., 1905), Although criticisms of such marriages increased during this period, this is not to imply there were not criticisms earlier. For example, an 1861 article in *Sixpenny Magazine* criticized "Heiress Hunters," describing

them as men with "an old name and a young face" who "could ferret out dowries, scent a mile off a wealthy father-in-law, and fall at a dead set before a rich heiress." Montgomery, *Gilded Prostitution*, 113. English novelist Anthony Trollope offered similarly disparaging opinions of such men. For example, in his 1875 novel *The Way We Live Now*, he described marriage to a rich American as standard practice for financially strapped peers:

> In such families as his [Lord Nidderdale's] when such results have been achieved [meaning debts], it is generally understood that such matters should be put right by an heiress. It has become an institution, like primogeniture, and is almost as serviceable for maintaining the proper order of things. Rank squanders money; trade makes it; and then trade purchases rank by re-gilding its splendor.

62. In the summer of 1911, Representative Adolph J. Sabath of Illinois introduced a resolution directing "the Secretary of State to secure information concerning American ladies marrying titled foreigners . . ." He then went on to ask "to what extent our country is being benefitted by this trade and whether or not our earnest, soberminded and brave women are not frequently subjected to ridicule and to cheap European nobility wit by reasons of this craze on the part of these trust-made rich, who are suffering from chronic titleitis." Montgomery, *Gilded Prostitution*, 166.

63. Pat Jalland, *Women, Marriage, and Politics 1860–1914* (Oxford, UK: Oxford University Press, 1986), 253.

64. Nineteenth-century women's rights reformers like Susan B. Anthony and Sarah and Angelina Grimke recognized the problems of linking women's power and status to marriage and specifically sought rights for women as individuals rather than as wives. Their efforts eventually led to the passage of the Nineteenth Amendment. Beverly C. Tomek, "The Invisible Force of Expectation: Angelina Grimke and the Dilemma of Self-Determination in the Early Women's Movement." *Pennsylvania Magazine of History and Biography* 144, no. 3 (2020), 290–320, accessed July 20, 2021, www.jstor.org/stable/10.5215/pennmaghistbio.144.3.0290.

65. "Maternalists claimed their role as wives and mothers was the source of women's political personhood. Even before they had the vote, American women invoked a domestically rooted, maternal, moral, and religious authority to advocate successfully for temperance, against child labor and slavery, and then for women's and children's social welfare programs." Naomi Mezey and Cornelia T. L. Pillard, "Against the New Maternalism," *Michigan Journal of Gender & Law* 18, no. 2 (2012), 229, 233.

66. Maternalists claimed political rights and benefits on the basis of their roles as mothers. Their argument was that "mother-work" involved meeting children's needs and that to do so, mothers "must have access to the conditions that will allow them to flourish as persons: These included bodily integrity, moral autonomy, material security, relational integrity, and political efficacy." Maternalists therefore saw no contradiction between the traditional role of women at home and participation in public life. They viewed their actions in the public sphere as extensions of their role in the private sphere. See Lisa Brush, "Review: Love, Toil, and Trouble: Motherhood and Feminist Politics," *Signs* 21, no. 2 (1996), 431. See also Mezey and Pillard, "Against the New Maternalism," 229, 238–39 (noting that mothers' pensions, aimed at single mothers and adopted by the majority of American states between 1911 and 1920, were "America's first publicly funded social benefits other than military pensions and poor relief . . .").

67. Mezey and Pillard, "Against the New Maternalism," 229, 238–39.

68. Women would get their power from being wives and mothers, not from work. The result of this Hobbesian bargain was that women's political power became further linked to marriage, and this decision even affected the fight for women's suffrage. As historian Alice Kessler-Harris writes, "The mainstream American feminist movement placed the ballot for women ahead of the struggle for economic independence . . . ," and this choice was "buttressed by the development of an alternative conception of citizenship rights for women located within the family." Alison Kessler-Harris, *In Pursuit of Equity: Women, Men, and the Quest for Economic Citizenship in 20th-Century America* (Oxford, UK: Oxford University Press, 2003), 26.

69. During the 1920s, many feminists attempted to abandon the rhetoric of motherhood and female dependency and focus on equal rights and economic freedom. However, as Lisa Bush notes, their political efforts were often less successful than the maternalists at "translating basic demands into legislation, institutional reform, and mainstream political power." This focus, which might have appealed more directly to the interests of wage-earning mothers, was not as successful as sentimental maternalism in mobilizing a mass movement of women. Brush, "Review: Love, Toil, and Trouble," 434.

70. See Anna Diamond, "The History of Wives Replacing Their Dead Husbands in Congress," *Smithsonian Magazine*, February 3, 2020 (explaining that "the parties assumed that husband and wife shared the same values, so they could count on the wives to uphold their husband's politics in office").

71. Of the ninety-five women who served in Congress before 1976, thirty-five were congressional widows. These women ran as political replacements for their dead husbands. However, once elected, these women were no longer obligated to simply parrot their husband's agenda; nor did they have to accept the role of placeholder for a male politician. Many of these widows became successful politicians in their own right and often remained in politics well beyond their husband's term. See Diamond, "The History of Wives Replacing."

72. Diane Kincaid, "Over His Dead Body: A Positive Perspective on Widows in the U.S. Congress," *Western Political Quarterly* 31, no. 1 (1978), 96–104.

73. 110 Cong. Rec. 2577 (1964).

74. In explaining his decision to double the rate paid to married men, Ford stated, "The man does the work in the shop, but his wife does the work in the home. The shop must pay them both." Notably, men were deemed ineligible for the higher wages if their wives worked outside the home. See Naomi Cahn and June Carbone, "Uncoupling," *Arizona State Law Journal* 53 (2021), 1, 16. See also Leo E. Strine Jr., "A Job Is Not a Hobby: The Judicial Revival of Corporate Paternalism and Its Problematic Implications," Harvard John M. Olin Discussion Paper Series no. 804 (January 2015) (discussing the expectation that Ford employees get married).

75. A man's social status was largely based on his ability to earn a living and support a family. Similarly, women's status was based on being supported by a successful man. Before the family wage, middle-class status, based on male support and female dependence, was unavailable to most wage-earning families. After Ford implemented the family wage, middle-class status was suddenly an option for wage-earning men and their wives. Cahn and Carbone, "Uncoupling." See also Ileen A. DeVault, "Family Wages: The Roles of Wives and Mothers in U.S. Working-Class Survival Strategies, 1880–1930," *Labor History* 54, no. 1 (2013) 1–3

(describing how women traditionally helped supplement working-class men's wages).

76. Katharine F. Lenroot, "Child Welfare 1930–40," *Annals of the American Academy of Political and Social Science* 212, no. 1 (1940). Notably, support for the family wage wasn't just limited to programs affecting women and children; the family wage principle was an essential aspect of every significant New Deal program from the National Industrial Recovery Act of 1933 to the Social Security Amendments of 1939.

77. Mary Anderson, *Woman at Work: The Autobiography of Mary Anderson as Told to Mary N. Winslow* (Minneapolis: University of Minnesota Press, 1951), 156–57.

78. Marion Crain and Ken Matheny, "'Labor's Divided Ranks': Privilege and the United Front Ideology," *Cornell Law Review* 84, no. 1542 (1999), 1595–96 (FNdd1) (1999).

79. By glorifying women who could afford not to work, the family wage helped further condemn working-class women whose income was needed to support their families, and these working-class women were disproportionately women of color. See Catherine Albiston, "Institutional Inequality," *Wisconsin Law Review* 2009, no. 5 (2009), 1093, 1167. ("Family wage ideology exacerbated class and race distinctions. For example, the ideology of the self-sufficient, independent worker who earns a family wage constructed poverty as an individual failing rather than as social oppression, justifying and legitimizing class differences.") See also Martha May, "The Historical Problem of the Family Wage: The Ford Motor Company and the Five Dollar Day," in Naomi Gerstel and Harriet Engel Gross, eds., *Families and Work* (Philadelphia: Temple University Press, 1987), 111, 114–15 (discussing how the family wage solidified class distinctions based on female dependency and further condemned working-class families, who were mostly women of color).

80. Marcus Felson and David Knoke, "Social Status and the Married Woman," *Journal of Marriage and Family* 36, no. 3 (1974), 516–21 (finding that the wife's participation in the labor force had only a marginal importance for subjective class, although couples did consider the wife's income as part of the family wealth calculus).

81. The study found that men and women, on average, agree on how to weight the contributions of wife's and husband's income and occupation to subjectively identified class: "Wife's income and husband's income equally affect class identification but only husband's occupational prestige — not wife's — affects class identification." Professors Yamaguchi and Wang note that this suggests the persistence of traditional views of identifying the occupation of the husband with the family's class position in society. Kazuo Yamaguchi and Yangtao Wang, "Class Identification of Married Employed Women and Men in America," *American Journal of Sociology* 108, no. 2 (2002), 440–75.

82. In 2010, the Pew Research Center asked women how important it was that a "good husband or provider provide a good income." Sixty-seven percent of black women said it is very important, compared with 35 percent of white women. Similarly, when asked whether financial stability was an important criterion in a potential husband, 50 percent of black women answered yes, while only 25 percent of white women agreed. Stephanie M. McClure and Cherise A. Harris, eds., *Getting Real About Race: Hoodies, Mascots, Model Minorities, and Other Conversations* (Los Angeles: Sage Publications, 2017), 152.

83. Alison Byrne and Julian Barling, "When She Brings Home the Job Status: Wives' Job Status, Status Leakage, and Marital Instability," *Organization Science* 28, no. 2

(April 2017) (finding that lower-status husbands were resentful of their wives' success and less happy in their marriages). See also Fisman et al., "Gender Differences in Mate Selection: Evidence from a Speed Dating Experiment," *Quarterly Journal of Economics*, May 2006 (finding that men did not value women's intelligence or ambition when it exceeded their own); Julie Brines, "Economic Dependency, Gender, and the Division of Labor at Home," *American Journal of Sociology* 100, no. 3 (1994), 652–88 (finding that men's housework contributions do not increase when the husband is more economically dependent on his wife and suggesting that it is to avoid threatening the husband's sense of masculinity); Sarah Fenstermaker Berk, *The Gender Factory: The Apportionment of Work in American Households* (New York: Plenum Press, 1985), 7 (noting that "the total time spent by married women on household labor is substantial and remains so regardless of most household or biographical characteristics").

84. Glenn Payette, "Your Social Status Could be More Important in Your Marriage than You Think," CBCNews, May 12, 2018 (noting that "we are socialized to think that men are the higher breadwinners . . . But be realistic about the changing roles in society").

85. Letlow's appeal and success was closely tied to her status as a good and loyal wife. In a statement on Letlow's victory, Louisiana governor Edwards indicated that she would be a good congresswoman, because she was a loyal and loving wife. He wrote, "This is a proud day for Julia, her children, all of her supporters, and our state, but it is also a bittersweet day as she wins the seat opened by the passing of her late husband, Luke . . . just as she has continued to exemplify strength, determination, and tenacity in the wake of a terrible tragedy. I know that these same characteristics that got her through the last few months will make her an excellent advocate for Louisiana in Washington, D.C." Gov. Edwards Congratulates Congresswoman-elect Julia Letlow on Her Victory in Louisiana's Fifth Congressional District, Press Release, Office of the Governor, March 20, 2021.

86. Indeed, in Justice Anthony Kennedy's evocative description of "a lonely person" calling out "only to find no one there," modern readers will surely recall the popular story of London "singleton" Bridget Jones, who famously worried that she was destined to die alone, only to be "found three weeks later half-eaten by an Alsatian." Melissa Murray, "*Obergefell v. Hodges* and Nonmarriage Inequality," *California Law Review* 104 (2016), 1207, 1215. See also Melissa Murray, "One Is the Loneliest Number: The Complicated Legacy of *Obergefell v. Hodges*," *Hastings Law Journal* 70 (2019), 1263, 1268 (noting that Justice Kennedy's decision "promotes marriage (and only marriage) as the normative ideal for intimate life").

87. Cherlin, *The Marriage-Go-Round*, 25 (2009). Similarly, Hendrik Hartog has written that one of the most important markers of the modern world is that it has become possible to be an unmarried woman in the world today and live life with "almost as much dignity as possessed by a married woman." Hendrik Hartog, "Coverture and Dignity: A Comment," *Law & Social Inquiry* 41, no. 4 (Fall 2016), 833, 837.

88. Title VII prohibits gender discrimination, but gender discrimination and marital status — while potentially overlapping at times — are not the same.

89. The Fair Housing Act, Title VIII of the Civil Rights Act of 1968, which expressly prohibits discrimination in the sale and rental of housing, does not prohibit discrimination against unmarried couples. Federal law only protects unmarried couples from housing discrimination in two narrow areas. First, the Equal Credit Opportunity Act (15 U.S.C. §§ 1691–1691f [1988 & Supp. I 1989]) prohibits dis-

crimination against unmarried couples in credit transactions in housing. Second, the United States Housing Act of 1978 (42 U.S.C.A. §§ 1437–1437u [West 1978 & Supp. 1991]) prohibits discrimination against unmarried couples in public housing. As a result, couples may be preferred to singles, and adults without children are preferred to adults with children. Increasingly, state laws or city or county ordinances may prohibit discrimination based on marital status, but it is still the minority. For a list of states that do or do not have protections based on marital status in the areas of housing, employment, credit, and insurance, see http://www .unmarriedamerica.org/ms-statutes.htm.

90. Wendy L. Morris et al., "No Shelter for Singles: The Perceived Legitimacy of Marital Status Discrimination," *Group Processes & Intergroup Relations* 10, no. 4 (October 2007), 457–70, https://doi:10.1177/1368430207081535. (This study demonstrated the clear and unapologetic preference for married couples in housing rentals.) See also Nancy Leong, "Negative Identity," *Southern California Law Review* 88 (2015), 1357, 1406 (noting that "as the research I catalogued demonstrates, [marital status discrimination] concerns are more than hypothetical — those asked to play the role of landlord preferred both married and unmarried couples to single people and cohabiting friends").

91. Norman Holt and Donald Miller, "Explorations in Inmate-Family Relationships," California Department of Corrections, Research Report No. 46 (1972), available at https://www.prisonlegalnews.org/media/publications/holt_miller_prisoner_and_ family_relationship_recidivism_study_1972.pdf.

92. Candace Kruttschnitt, "Social Status and Sentences of Female Offenders," *Law and Society Review* 15, no. 2 (1980–1981), 247, 262. (Interestingly, this study did not find a sentencing difference for married male defendants.) See also Rita J. Simon and Jean Landis, *The Crimes Women Commit, The Punishments They Receive* (Lexington, MA: Lexington Books, 1991) (suggesting that women may receive less severe sanctions when they are "subject to more informal social control," meaning that of a husband); Anne M. Coughlin, "Excusing Women," *California Law Review* 82, no. 1 (1994), 46 (discussing "the criminal law's reliance on husbands as the primary source of control for women's misconduct").

93. Tracy Snell, Capital Punishment, 2005, Bureau of Justice Statistics Bulletin, December 2005 (last revised January 30, 2007), available at http://bjs.ojp.usdoj .gov/content/pub/pdf/cp05.pdf.

94. Joan DelFattore, "Death by Stereotype? Cancer Treatment in Unmarried Patients," *New England Journal of Medicine*, September 5, 2019.

95. Micahael Cobb describes marriage as the only way to "attain social legitimacy."

96. Thomas Roges, "In Defense of Single People," *Salon*, July 9, 2012.

97. The hundreds of responses fell roughly into three categories: money, children, and status. The first two categories are frequently mentioned as the downsides of divorce. The third is more surprising, but perhaps the most illuminating.

98. Other comments included statements like "failure at womanhood," "fear of being socially ostracized," "fear of judgement cannot be overstated," "divorce can shatter your whole social life," "shame," and "the status of being married."

99. Other online commentators also reveal the ongoing status importance of marriage. For example, blogger Lydia Kinne wrote a post titled "Craving the Social Status of Marriage" in which she noted, "There are so many reasons a girl craves to be married — but I think one of the most subtle is to gain the approval and acceptance of society (and the church). This is often fueled by a sense of pity for you until

you're able to find a man who will love you. It's as if you have to prove your worth by finding someone who finds you worthy of love. And sometimes it feels worth it to get married just so that people will stop pitying you." https://lydiakinne.com /2017/03/08/craving-the-social-status-of-marriage/ (last visited April 9, 2023).

Chapter 4

1. "Married in Court," *New York Times*, October 12, 1884.

2. Until the late twentieth century, the criminal law in most jurisdictions prohibited fornication — sex outside of marriage. Marriage was the only permissible locus for sexual activity. As Professor Ariela Dubler writes, through marriage, "lust was transformed into virtue." Ariela R. Dubler, "Immoral Purposes: Marriage and the Genus of Illicit Sex," *Yale Law Journal* 115 (2006), 763. Similarly, historian Nicolas Syrett notes that marriage made "illicit sex legal. Actions performed outside of marriage that were dangerous, debasing, or immoral were transformed into safe, respectable and moral within marriage." Nicolas L. Syrett, *American Child Bride: A History of Minors and Marriage in the United States* (Chapel Hill: University of North Carolina Press, 2016), 7. See also Melissa Murray, "Strange Bedfellows: Criminal Law, Family Law, and the Legal Construction of Intimate Life," *Iowa Law Review* 94 (2009), 1253, 1268–69 (discussing the long connection between criminal and intimate relations).

3. According to law professor Lea VanderVelde, prior to the Civil War there were 105 recorded seduction suits but only 10 occurred in the South. VanderVelde suggests this difference was partially due to the greater mobility of those in the North combined with the southern practice of addressing such actions extra-legally through personal violence such as duels. She also notes that many of these suits were brought by working-class families against their daughter's employer or the employer's son. Due to the significant class difference, such families did not have the option to physically punish their daughter's seducers through duels or other types of "gentlemanly" violence. Instead, they used seduction suits. Lea VanderVelde, "The Legal Ways of Seduction," *Stanford Law Review* 48 (1996), 817, 835–37.

4. As historian Michael Grossberg has explained, the conflation of the two causes of action was caused by the growing emphasis on romantic love, the rise of the privatized family, and a judicial desire to protect vulnerable women. See Michael Grossberg, *Governing the Hearth: Law and the Family in Nineteenth-Century America* (Chapel Hill: University of North Carolina Press, 1988), 34–38. A promise to marry became the critical element in striking the balance between consent and coercion. Courts hearing seduction cases recognized that the illicit connection between the defendant and the prosecutrix had occurred with her consent but were willing to find that that a woman's consent might be coerced by a promise to marry. As a Georgia court noted in an 1892 seduction case:

> The coyness, shyness, and modesty which actuate a virtuous woman on such an occasion naturally find expression in the manifestation of some degree of unwillingness, or of an endeavor, feeble though it may be, to shield herself from that to which she is averse, but to which she really consents only for the sake of the man she loves and trusts. It would be mere mawkishness to affect ignorance of these well-known traits of the female character.

Jones v. State, 90 Ga. 616, 16 S.E. 380, 383 (1892). See also Stephen Robertson, "Seduction, Sexual Violence, and Marriage in New York City, 1886–1955," *Law and History Review* 24 (2006), 331, 344–45 (describing the historical, cultural, and legal shifts that allowed these two actions became intertwined).

5. Nineteenth-century courts were perfectly amenable to helping women marry their rapists. Consequently, as Stephen Robertson writes, "Both the existence of the crime of seduction, and the ability the law gave women who made that charge to both punish their assailant and to marry him — however inappropriate we now find marriage as a response to sexual coercion — complicate the generally accepted argument that, until the 1970s, women had no access to the law when sexually assaulted by men they knew." Robertson, "Seduction, Sexual Violence." However, this judicial support for the marriage solution was a double-edged sword. Courts not only pressured unwilling men into marriage but also pressured female breach of promise plaintiffs to drop their suits and marry instead. For example, in 1889 a young New York woman named Bina Leblang brought a breach of promise suit against David Stern. When the case came before the judge, he suggested that marriage might be a better solution. Bina insisted she did not want to marry David, but the judge was adamant. "You let them alone and give them a chance to talk together." The couple obeyed the judge and, according to the *New York Times* article, within half an hour they returned smiling and "ready for the judge to tie the knot." One can't help but worry how this marriage turned out for Bina. "Married in Court," *New York Times*, October 2, 1889.

6. Prosecutors would not have regarded the force to which Polokoff subjected Martha as sufficient to constitute a rape. New York DAs believed that only if a woman had suffered observable injuries, demonstrating that she had resisted to the limit of her capacity, would a jury agree that she had been raped. Robertson, "Seduction, Sexual Violence," 331, 355. For further discussion of the long-standing belief that a "real" victim would fight back, see Diana E. H. Russell, *The Politics of Rape: The Rape Victim's Perspective* (New York: Stein and Day, 1975) (describing how one victim was told she "should have resisted more physically"); Susan Griffin, "Rape: The All-American Crime," Ramparts Magazine, Sept. 1971, 26-35 (recounting how a women raped by a man holding a ten-inch knife to her throat was asked by a police officer, "Are you sure your life was in danger and you had no other choice?").

7. Polokoff was indicted by the grand jury, but, for reasons that are unclear, the DA recommended he be discharged. The DA claimed, without explanation (possibly because she was no longer pregnant), that a jury would not convict him. In this case, criminal charges did not lead to marriage. However, Olatka's suit shows how rape victims sought to use seduction suits to hold their attackers accountable. Robertson, "Seduction, Sexual Violence," 331, 367.

8. According to Murray, "Forcing the defendant to perform all of the obligations and responsibilities of marriage and live within its disciplined structure . . . was a punishment. Melissa Murray, "Marriage as Punishment," *Columbia Law Review* 112, no. 1 (2012), 32.

9. As historian Peggy Pascoe notes, "White men could and did debauch Black women with little or no fear of prosecution, laws against interracial marriage merely helped them hide their abuse of Black women and escape from economic responsibility for the children they fathered." Peggy Pascoe, *What Comes Naturally: Miscegenation Law and the Making of Race in America* (Oxford, UK: Oxford University Press, 2009), 178. Notably, this treatment stands in stark contrast with

the treatment of the rape or potential rape of white women by black men, which was typically punished by death. See brief for Petitioner, *Ehrlich Anthony Coker, Petitioner, v. State of Georgia, Respondent*, 1976 WL 181481 (U.S.) (recounting the racist history of punishment for rape in the state of Georgia).

10. 19 Wend. 192, 194–96 (N.Y. Sup. Ct. 1838). Similarly, in the 1891 case *State v. Coella*, the Washington Supreme Court wrote that a woman "could not have ruthlessly destroyed that quality [chastity] upon which most other good qualities are dependent, and for which, above all others, a woman is reverenced and respected, and yet retain her credit for truthfulness unsmirched." *State v. Coella*, 3 Wash. 99, 104, 28 P. 28, 29 (1891). The assumption underlying these decisions was that promiscuity implies dishonesty. Courts believed a woman's lack of chastity was probative of untruthfulness. As law professor I. Bennett Capers explains, this was "not because an unchaste woman was more likely to lie to conceal her lack of chastity, but because lack of chastity was lower on the scale of depravity than untruthfulness." Moreover, courts believed that a woman who had consented to sex once was both "more likely to consent again" and "more likely to have consented with the defendant, notwithstanding her claim to the contrary." I. Bennett Capers, "Real Women, Real Rape," *UCLA Law Review* 60 (2013), 826, 882. See also John Henry Wigmore, *A Treatise on the Anglo-American System of Evidence in Trials at Common Law*, 3rd ed. (Boston: Little, Brown, 1940), §§ 924–924a, 459 (declaring there is "at least one situation in which chastity may have a direct connection with veracity, viz. when a woman or young girl testifies as a complainant against a man charged with a sexual crime").

11. As Professor Capers notes, this evidentiary rule narrowed "the law's protection to virginal and hence deserving women," while also allowing defendants to present themselves to "factfinders as good men, notwithstanding actual evidence to the contrary. While the complainant's sexual history was fodder for defense lawyers, the defendant's sexual history was generally off limits."

12. As historian Hendrik Hartog writes, "With time and distance, the void, bigamous marriage often became the true, the real, the unquestionable." In fact, a bigamous marriage was often given more legal recognition than divorce. While a bigamous marriage could be recognized as valid without a legal divorce, a legal divorce might not be recognized as valid without a remarriage. As Hartog notes, one often needed remarriage after a divorce to avoid the criminal penalties of adultery. Hendrik Hartog, *Man and Wife in America* (Cambridge, MA: Harvard University Press, 2022), 285.

13. States had different ways of discouraging divorce. For example, New York allowed divorce but only for adultery — a messy and expensive procedure — while South Carolina prohibited it outright through a constitutional provision. Given such restrictions, it became common for unhappy spouses to simply skip the divorce and "remarry." As long as these remarriages weren't blatant (this usually required at least one of the spouses moving a significant distance), judges would usually recognize them. See Lawrence M. Friedman, "Crimes of Mobility," *Stanford Law Review* 43 (1991), 637, 642–44. As historian Hendrik Hartog notes, American judges felt that "bigamous marriages were less threatening to the institution of marriage than either voluntary divorces or contractual separations." Hartog, *Man and Wife*, 91.

14. "Charged with Bigamy," *New York Times*, August 11, 1897, p. 2, col. 3.

15. Chris Enss, *Object: Matrimony: The Risky Business of Mail-Order Matchmaking on the Western Frontier* (Guilford, CT: TwoDot, 2013), 3.

16. American police reports confirm the paucity of bigamy prosecutions in the nineteenth and early twentieth centuries. In Philadelphia, for example, there were seven bigamy arrests in 1885 and twelve in 1897. In New York City, there were fifty-five arrests in 1905, sixty in 1913, and ninety-five in 1922. In Los Angeles, in 1924–1925, thirteen men and four women were arrested for bigamy. These were a tiny percentage of crimes for the period. For example, the twelve bigamists arrested in Philadelphia in 1897 were lost among 62,628 total arrests. See Friedman, "Crimes of Mobility," 637, 641.

17. It is hard to know exactly how common nineteenth-century bigamy was, but it appears to have been widespread. See, e.g., Max Rheinstein, *Marriage Stability, Divorce and the Law* (Chicago: University of Chicago Press, 1973), 35 (noting that "when registration of civil status was rudimentary in the United States . . . disappearance was an easy substitute for divorce"); Timothy J. Gilfoyle, "The Hearts of Nineteenth-Century Men: Bigamy and Working-Class Marriage in New York City, 1800–1890," *Prospects* 19 (1994), 135, 137 ("As 19th-Century Americans became increasingly mobile and urban, bigamy appears to have been a more viable solution to marital unhappiness"); Ariela R. Dubler, "Governing Through Contract: Common Law Marriage in the Nineteenth Century," *Yale Law Journal* 107, no. 6 (April 1998), 1885, 1896–97 ("With divorce largely unavailable, urban men (and, to a lesser extent, women) concocted their own remedies for unhappy marriages, in the form of self-executed dissolutions of failed relationships and then subsequent 'remarriages,' albeit informal ones").

18. See Beverly Schwartzberg, "Lots of Them Did That: Desertion, Bigamy, and Marital Fluidity in Late-Nineteenth-Century America," *Journal of Social History*, 37 (2004) at 587 (explaining that when Amelia heard her husband had "married Cordelia A. she supposed she had a right to marry too"). See also Hartog, *Man and Wife*, 283 (noting that many cohabiting women felt "[s]o long as she lived with him, she might as well say they were married. With time, the law might conclude that they were, or had become married because they resided together and said they were married").

19. The legal acceptance of her bigamous second marriage also protected her parental rights. Remarriage reduced the likelihood that Butler could accuse her of immorality and claim custody of her children. As Marion explained years later, she deliberately called herself a widow after her second, bigamous marriage ended "in order to prevent her children being taken away by William Butler." Schwartzberg, "Lots of Them Did That," 587–89.

20. The "marital coercion defense" is a female corollary to this criminal defense strategy. The defense is rooted in an English common law presumption that a wife who committed an offense (other than murder or treason) "in the presence of her husband must have been acting under his coercion and therefore she could not be held personally responsible for her actions. Furthermore, the requirement that the husband be present was defined figuratively, so that courts were willing to extend the benefit of the presumption of coercion to wives whose husbands were present only in spirit. As they would put it, the husband's 'constructive presence' would suffice." Anne M. Coughlin, "Excusing Women," *California Law Review* 82, no. 1 (1994), 31–32. In addition, courts were often highly unreceptive to this defense. See, e.g., *U. S. v. De Quilfeldt*, 5 F. 276, 278 (C.C.W.D. Tenn.1881) (noting that this defense was highly disfavored). Thus, although the marital coercion defense was a privilege of marriage, it does not appear to have been a reason women married.

Rather, it has been suggested that the doctrine was crafted not to exempt women from punishment but to make such punishment more equal.

Various commentators have claimed that the marital coercion doctrine was fashioned by judges during the mid-thirteenth century to protect women from harshly inequitable penalties arising from the fact that men, but not women, could claim benefit of clergy in felony cases. According to Rollin Perkins:

> If a man and his wife were convicted of a felony they had com-
> mitted together, and in which he had been perhaps the leading
> spirit, the husband (if able to read) would be punished with a mere
> brand upon the brawn of the thumb and imprisonment not to
> exceed a year, while nothing less than the sentence of death would
> be available for the wife.

Rollin M. Perkins, *Perkins on Criminal Law*, 2nd ed. (Mineloa, NY, Foundation Press, 1969), 912. It was to escape this "absurd result" that judges developed the marital coercion doctrine, thereby sparing the wife from conviction and execution. Perkins, *Criminal Law*, 912–13.

It is also likely that marital coercion defense did not provide a marital incentive because it did not just provide the wife with a defense but also shifted the blame to the husband. Thus, husbands had a strong incentive to ensure their wives did not commit crimes, and they had the physical power and legal right to typi-cally ensure wives complied with their wishes. For examples of husbands being punished for their wives' crimes, see *Commonwealth v. Barry*, 115 Mass. 146 (1874); *Commonwealth v. Wood*, 97 Mass. 225 (1867); *State v. Boyle*, 13 R.I. 537, 538–39 (1882).

21. Jeremy Bentham, *Rationale of Judicial Evidence*, 5 vols., 1827, 338.

22. Gilbert Abbott À Beckett, *The Comic Blackstone*, 1846, 121–22n. Interestingly, even when setting forth this rule, Blackstone is loath to defend it. Instead, he describes it as an antiquated practice that persisted primarily among the British lower classes:

> But, with us, in the politer reign of Charles the Second, this power
> of correction began to be doubted; and a wife may now have
> security of the peace against her husband; or, in return, a husband
> against his wife. Yet the lower rank of people, who were always
> fond of the old common law, still claim and exert their ancient
> privilege: and the courts of law will still permit a husband to
> restrain a wife of her liberty, in case of any gross misbehaviour.

William Blackstone, *Commentaries*, 444–45.

23. See Reva B. Siegel, "'The Rule of Love': Wife Beating as Prerogative and Privacy," *Yale Law Journal* 105 (1996), 2117, 2129 (noting that women's rights advocates argued that "these horrors, result inevitably from the subjection and disfranchise-ment of women, just as similar outrages used to result from the subjection and disfranchisement of negroes. Equal Rights and Impartial Suffrage are the only radical cure for these barbarities").

24. For example, in the North Carolina case *State v. Rhodes*, 61 N.C. 453, 457 (1868), the court outwardly repudiated the chastisement doctrine, stating it "is not, that the husband has the *right* to whip his wife much or little" but effectively upheld it under the new justification of marital harmony. In refusing to punish marital vio-lence, the court stated, "We will not inflict upon society the greater evil of raising the curtain upon domestic privacy, to punish the lesser evil of trifling violence." It then added:

However great are the evils of ill temper, quarrels, and even personal conflicts inflicting only temporary pain, they are not comparable with the evils which would result from raising the curtain,
and exposing to public curiosity and criticism, the nursery and the
bed chamber. Every household has and must have, a government
of its own, modeled to suit the temper, disposition and condition
of its inmates. Mere ebullitions of passion, impulsive violence, and
temporary pain, affection will soon forget and forgive . . .

As lawyer James Schouler wrote in his 1870 family law treatise, *A Treatise on the
Law of the Domestic Relations*, "The rule of love, had superseded the rule of force"
(Boston: Little, Brown, 1870), 59. For further explanation of this change, see Siegel,
"'The Rule of Love'" (explaining that "once marital status laws were reformed in
the Reconstruction Era they gained legitimacy. These laws were 'naturalized' as just
and reasonable, in significant part because each was now formally and substan-
tively distinguishable from its contested predecessor: Each could be justified in
terms of social values that were distinct from the orthodox, hierarchy-based norms
that characterized its predecessor").

25. Professor Reva Siegel has described this as "preservation-through-transformation."
Siegel explains that despite changes in its rules and rhetoric surrounding the marital status, the practical effect of these so-called changes was minimal. Marriage
continued to "distribute material and dignitary privileges ('social goods') in such a
way as to maintain the distinctions that comprise the regime (e.g., constitute 'race'
or 'gender') in relatively continuous terms." Siegel, "'The Rule of Love,'" 2117, 2118.

26. See Matthew Hale, *The History of the Pleas of the Crown*, ed. Robert H. Small, 1736
(1st American edition 1847), 629. Professor Hendrik Hartog has suggested that a
better explanation for the marital rape exception lies "inherent in the nature of
marriage. Sexual intercourse between a husband and wife was authorized by law,
thus, 'the element of unlawfulness' was lacking when a husband coerced his wife.
By contrast all other sexual intercourse was unlawful. And thus, unmarried sexual
intercourse when coerced became rape." Hartog, *Man & Wife*, 308.

27. As the US Supreme Court explained in *Tinker v. Colwell*, 193 U.S. 473, 474 (1904),
a husband's a right to exclusive sexual intercourse with his wife was "a right of
the highest kind . . . [on] which the whole social order rests." Further, historian
Hendrik Hartog explains that these rights included the right to punish other
men for interfering with the marital right, and although monetary damages were
permissible, "much of the critics' commentary of the tort of 'criminal conversation'
carried the intimation that a real man would have killed or at least thrashed the
seducer rather than taking him to court." Hartog, *Man & Wife*, 142.

28. According to Professors Hava Dayan and Emanuel Gross, this legal argument
relied on the 1617 Manning case, 83 Eng. Rep. 112 (K.B.), "which tied provocation
to adultery and specifically referred to the feeling of jealousy as a noble manly
emotion: 'When a man is taken in adultery with another man's wife, if the husband shall stab the adulterer, or knock out his brains, this is bare manslaughter:
for jealousy is the rage of the man, and adultery is the highest invasion of property
. . .'" "Uxoricide Under the Auspices of the Model Penal Code: A Legislative Proposal to Amend Section 210.3(b) of the Model Penal Code," *Georgetown Journal of
Gender and the Law* 15 (2014), 411, 417. Moreover, from the beginning, the doctrine
has been deeply gendered. As law professor Carolina Forrell writes, "It was created
for and has always been used far more often by men than women." She further

notes that the defense began as a common-law doctrine about men defending their honor but, over time, "the defense of provocation came to excuse 'heat of passion' rather than honor." According to Forrell, the defense was and continues to be "specially designed for men." Caroline Forrell, "Gender Equality, Social Values and Provocation Law in the United States, Canada and Australia," *American University Journal of Gender, Social Policy & the Law* 14 (2006), 27, 32.

29. During the murder trial, Abby testified that McFarland was "unspeakably cruel, that he would fly into fits of uncontrollable rage, hitting her with anything he could find that was breakable." She also testified that on multiple occasions, he threatened to strangle her. He would reach for her with his "hands extended . . . [and his] fingers bent like claws, as if he were about to clutch [her] throat," while crying out that he wanted her dead. Abby described her life with McFarland as living "under the protection of a drunken and brutal master." For further discussion of the McFarland murder trial, see Melissa J. Ganz, "Wicked Women and Veiled Ladies: Gendered Narratives of the McFarland-Richardson Tragedy," *Yale Journal of Law & Feminism* 9 (1997), 255, 256.

30. On November 30, 1869, the Reverends Henry Ward Beecher and Octavious Frothingham married Albert and Abby shortly before Albert died of his gunshot wound.

31. As historian Nancy Cott writes, "In commenting on McFarland's trial, many journalists endorsed husbands' property rights in their wives as firmly as the Republican Party had in its policy towards the freedmen — embracing husbandly superiority and lifelong fidelity as crucial to marriage. The *New York Herald* summed up common opinions after the Jury had spoken . . . The editorial said it was less the defendant than 'the principals, the morality and the social questions involved' that proved so riveting. 'The whole community' saw 'dangerous doctrines . . . which tend to undermine the social fabric and sacred ties of marriage' as being on trial." Nancy F. Cott, *Public Vows: A History of Marriage and the Nation* (Cambridge, MA: Harvard University Press, 2002), 108.

Moreover, although the McFarland trial was one of the most notorious cases involving the murder of a wife's lover, it was far from unique. As Hendrik Hartog notes, in all such trials, the arguments were the same: The lover deserved to die and in defending his home from an intruder, the husband was doing what any natural husband would do and what any member of the jury would do in the same situation. Hartog, *Man & Wife*, 224.

32. This change was due to the extraordinary efforts of social welfare reformers who worked tirelessly to enact legal protections for children. Other child welfare protections from this period included child labor laws, compulsory schooling requirements, child abuse protections, and the creation of juvenile courts. See Mary Odem, *Delinquent Daughters: Protecting and Policing Adolescent Female Sexuality in the United States, 1885–1920* (Chapel Hill: University of North Carolina Press, 2000), 14 (noting that Georgia was the one exception to the age of consent reforms, leaving it at fourteen). See also Jane E. Larson, "'Even A Worm Will Turn at Last': Rape Reform in Late Nineteenth-Century America," *Yale Journal of Law & the Humanities* 9 (1997), 1 (describing the nineteenth-century campaign to raise the age of sexual consent).

33. In fact, it appears he adopted the child specifically to gain legal control over her and, presumably, easier sexual access. Syrett, *American Child Bride*, 171.

34. Brian Donovan, *American Gold Digger: Money, Marriage and the Law from the Ziegfeld Follies to Anna Nicole Smith* (Chapel Hill: University of North Carolina Press,

2020), 37–38 (noting that the characterization of Peaches as a gold digger undercut her victimhood and redirected potential suspicion about child exploitation).

35. Francesca Beauman, *Matrimony, Inc.: From Personal Ads to Swiping Right, a Story of America Looking for Love* (New York: Simon & Schuster, 2020), 133.

36. Sterling herself told police that she had met Bitty on a London street where she was wandering one day. After chatting, Bitty offered her a job in his cigarette factory, which she accepted (although the job proved short-lived because London authorities seized the factory's goods). See Ariela R. Dubler, "Immoral Purposes: Marriage and the Genus of Illicit Sex," *Yale Law Journal* 115 (2006), 756, 771.

37. In *Bitty*, the court held that "the prostitute may, in the popular sense, be more degraded in character than the concubine, but in the latter none the less must be held to lead an immoral life, if any regard whatever be had to the views that are almost universally held in this country as to the relations which may rightfully, from the standpoint of morality, exist between man and woman in the matter of sexual intercourse." *U. S. v. Bitty*, 208 U.S. 393, 402, 28 S. Ct. 396, 399, 52 L. Ed. 543 (1908).

38. Similar attempts were made to round up "immoral women" based on appearance within the US, and these efforts were not nearly so short-lived or inconsequential. See Scott W. Stern, *The Trials of Nina McCall: Sex, Surveillance, and the Decades-Long Government Plan to Imprison "Promiscuous" Women* (Boston: Beacon Press, 2018) (detailing the government's efforts to round up and imprison promiscuous women in concentration camps and focusing on the case of Nina McCall, who had never had sex yet was imprisoned for carrying gonorrhea based on a police officer's belief that she "looked" like someone who might have such a disease).

39. US Immigration Commission, Importing Women for Immoral Purposes: A Partial Report from the Immigration Commission on the Importation and Harboring of Women for Immoral Purposes, S. Doc. No. 61-196, 349 (2nd sess. 1909).

40. George Kibbe Turner, "The Daughters of the Poor: A Plain Story of the Development of New York City as a Leading Centre of the White Slave Trade of the World, Under Tammany Hall," *McClure's Magazine* 34, no. 1 (November 1909), 45–61.

41. Cott, *Public Vows*, 149. See also Brian Donovan and Tori Barnes-Brus, "Narratives of Sexual Consent and Coercion: Forced Prostitution Trials in Progressive-Era New York City," *Law & Social Inquiry* 36 (2011), 597, 606 (noting that African Americans and members of others groups considered racially inferior were also specifically targeted for white slavery prosecutions).

42. Act of Feb. 10, 1855, ch. 71, § 1, 10 Stat. 604.

43. The report also included an interview with a prostitute named Mary who readily admitted she had married for citizenship. As she told the detective, "Of course you know, that if I married that fellow Roe, it was only to beat deportation and be safe forever as I am now an American citizen." Importing Women for Immoral Purposes, 45 app. IV-B (reproducing affidavits from a report of the New York commissioner of police). Notably, foreign prostitutes' strategic use of marriage to avoid legal repercussions did not necessarily begin after they arrived in the United States. For example, in Marseilles, married prostitutes working in hotels and cafés were not required to register with the authorities, unlike their unmarried counterparts. As a result, a form of marriage arose between working girls and pimps. As one Marseilles madam explained, "The only ones the [police] pick up are the girls who annoy people. Anyone could hustle in Marseilles for years and not get into

trouble as long as she don't go from man to man like some of those 5-franc girls do down the street." Mir Yarfitz, *Impure Migration: Jews and Sex Work in Golden Age Argentina* (New Brunswick, NJ: Rutgers University Press, 2019), 71.

44. Immigration Act of 1917, § 19, 39 Stat. 889 (repealed 1952).

45. Alexx Altman-Devilbiss, "NC Sheriff's Office Will Arrest Your Ex During 'Valentine's Day Special,'" WPDE.com, February 7, 2022.

46. Although this law was rendered unconstitutional after the Supreme Court's decision in *Lawrence v. Texas* (striking down Texas's anti-sodomy law), it has never been repealed. See N.C. Gen. Stat. Ann. § 14-184. See also *Hobbs v. Smith*, No. 05 CVS 267, 2006 WL 3103008 (N.C. Super. Aug. 25, 2006) (the only NC district finding it unconstitutional).

47. Bettie Fennell, "Cohabitation Quandary," *Star News* (Wilmington, NC), March 24, 2004, available at https://www.starnewsonline.com/story/news/2004/03/24/cohabitation-quandary/30544105007/. For other cases involving cohabitation and parole, see *U.S. ex rel. Randazzo v. Follette*, 282 F. Supp. 10, 12 (S.D.N.Y. 1968), *aff'd*, 418 F.2d 1319 (2d Cir. 1969). See also M. C. Schwartz and L. Zeisel, "Unmarried Cohabitation — A National Study of Parole Policy," *Crime and Delinquency* 22, no. 2 (April 1976), 137–48 (finding that cohabitation was generally prohibited by parole boards).

48. Shortly thereafter, the American Civil Liberties Union filed a lawsuit asking the court to overturn West Virginia's prohibition on cohabitation. Andrew Schneider, executive director of the ACLU of West Virginia, explained the lawsuit, stating, "Until this archaic law is struck down, probationers and parolees will continue to be denied living arrangements that are otherwise acceptable." ACLU Opposes State-Ordered Practice of Religion, Challenges West Virginia's Anti-Cohabitation Law, Press Release, September 18, 2006.

49. The parole condition was overturned on appeal. *U.S. v. Woods*, 547 F.3d 515 (5th Cir. 2008). However, Woods was not the only Texas probationer to receive such a condition. See also *U.S. v. Torres*, 281 Fed. Appx. 394 (5th Cir. 2008) (striking down the cohabitation restriction as "overbroad") and *U. S. v. Worthington*, no. 96-1597, 1998 WL 279379, at *18 (6th Cir., May 21, 1998) (unpublished) (vacating a special condition prohibiting the defendant from cohabitating with any female as overbroad and unrelated to the defendant's drug offense). Today, such restrictions are increasingly prohibited, but they were widely used in the past. See, e.g., *U.S. ex rel. Randazzo v. Follette* (prohibiting the petitioner from having "sex[ual] relations with any woman not his lawful wife").

50. Melissa Murray, "Rights and Regulation: The Evolution of Sexual Regulation," *Columbia Law Review* 116 (2016), 600 (noting that modern sexual harassment "regulation involves the interaction of civil laws, administrative rules, professional codes of conduct, and judicial standards of review and serves to regulate nonmarital sex and sexuality — even after *Lawrence*"). See also Gary M. Kramer, "Limited License to Fish Off the Company Pier: Toward Express Employer Policies on Supervisor-Subordinate Fraternization," *Western New England Law Review* 22, no. 1 (2000), 77, 147 (discussing different regulations and strategies employers and employees are using to protect against claims of sexual harassment).

51. Melissa Murray and Karen Tani, "Something Old, Something New: Reflections on the Sex Bureaucracy," *California Law Review Online* 7 (2016), 122, 151–52. It should also be noted that there are also cases where the punishment occurs specifically because the parties are married. See, e.g., *Coker v. Whittington*, 858 F.3d 304

(5th Cir. 2017) (involving the removal of two police officers moving in with each other's wives before divorcing current wives).

52. Kelly Main and Lauren Hansen, "Workplace Romance Statistics: Survey Shows Employees Regularly Engage in Office Relationships," *Forbes Advisor*, April 24, 2023 (noting that the second leading driving factor is a lack of time outside of work to meet people, with 61 percent of respondents citing this as a key reason for dating someone at work).

53. According to Professors Russell K. Robinson and David M. Frost, "The law generally permits people who identify as heterosexual to touch, grope, and harangue people of the same sex, and then invoke their heterosexual identification, their marriages, and their children to rebuff the claim that the harassment was based on desire." See "The Afterlife of Homophobia," *Arizona Law Review* 60 (2018), 213, 289. Heterosexual marriage is certainly no barrier to same-sex desire, yet it is often treated as such either due to a mistaken belief about attraction or simply because the heterosexual marriage creates additional ambiguity. As Professor Kenji Yoshino writes, "Courts may believe that where any ambiguity exists, it is better to let the guilty homosexual go free than to convict the innocent heterosexual." "The Epistemic Contract of Bisexual Erasure," *Stanford Law Review* 52 (2000), 353, 449. See also Jessica A. Clarke, "Inferring Desire," *Duke Law Journal* 63 (2013), 525, 530–31 (noting that courts have read desire into far less suggestive scenarios when the harasser self-identifies as non-heterosexual). See, generally, Jane Ward, *Not Gay: Sex Between Straight White Men* (New York: New York University Press, 2015) (examining the long history of straight men in same-sex relationships).

54. Heterosexual marriage is certainly no barrier to same-sex desire, yet courts repeatedly treat it as proof that the alleged harasser would not experience such desire. For more recent cases, see *Wade v. Automation Pers. Servs., Inc.*, No. 1:12-CV-375, 2014 WL 11515694, at *5 (E.D. Tenn. July 7, 2014), *aff'd*, 612 F. App'x 291 (6th Cir. 2015). Also see, e.g., *Lord v. High Voltage Software, Inc.*, 839 F.3d 556, 562 (7th Cir. 2016) (finding no hostile environment claim because there was no evidence that the alleged harasser was gay or motivated by sexual desire); *Wasek v. Arrow Energy Servs., Inc.*, 682 F.3d 463, 468 (6th Cir. 2012) (finding no hostile environment claim because there was no credible evidence that the alleged harasser was bisexual); *McCown v. St. John's Health Sys., Inc.*, 349 F.3d 540, 543 (8th Cir. 2003) (finding no hostile environment claim because there was no evidence that the supervisor was gay or was motivated by sexual desire). However, these cases are all prior to *Obergefell* and *Bostock*, and this reasoning may be waning. It is also possible that the marriage defense may change and that the wife's testimony wouldn't be relevant to the underlying allegations of sexual harassment, would be extremely embarrassing to her, and could destroy the supervisor's marriage. 26 No. 8 Pa. Emp. L. Letter 3 (May 2016)

See, e.g., *Burke v. Villa*, 2021 WL 5591711 (E.D.N.Y., Nov. 30, 2021) (finding that the defendants' response — that Villa could not have engaged in sexually motivated conduct toward Burke because he is in a heterosexual marriage and has children — is without merit). In addition, courts have also moved away from the idea that the harasser must be homosexual for a claim of same-sex sexual harassment. See *Goings v. Lopinto*, No. CV 22-2549, 2023 WL 2709826, at *4 (E.D. La. Mar. 30, 2023), citing *Nguyen v. Buchart-Horn, Inc.* This court held "that the Supreme Court did not foreclose the possibility of same-sex harassment where the harasser is not homosexual."

55. As Professor Jessica Clarke has written in her analysis of this case, "The Hy-Vee court seems to have drawn an implicit contrast between Lynch's nonserious workplace vulgarity and her serious marriage, which it noted was to the 'same man' for sixteen years, to underscore the stability of the monogamous relationship. It did not hold that a married woman could not experience same-sex desire, but its interpretation of the facts seems to have been shaded by its interest in protecting the stability of Lynch's heterosexual identity and marital status, as well as the interests of her husband and children." Clarke, "Inferring Desire," 525, 574–75.

56. As Professor Jessica Clarke writes, "The court refused to read Carrere's statement that he would like to 'f**k that piece of ass' literally." Instead, "because Carrere was leaving that day, the court reasoned, the incident must have been 'nothing more than a final parting shot directed at plaintiff' rather than 'a realistic sexual proposition of the type necessary to be actionable under Title VII.'" Clarke, "Inferring Desire," 525, 574–75. For more recent cases employing similar logic, see *Parker v. Consol. Pipe & Supply Co.*, no. 5:18-CV-1960-CLS, 2020 WL 1285842, at *5 (N.D. Ala. Mar. 18, 2020) (presenting testimony that an employee could not have engaged in same-sex sexual harassment because he "is not homosexual. Mr. Breeding has been married (with children) for as long as I can recall and I have never heard or seen anything to make me think there was even a remote possibility that he was homosexual or bisexual"); *Wade v. Automation Pers. Servs., Inc.* (finding no credible evidence that an employee sexually desired the plaintiff, "especially since Gross is the mother of two children and was married to a man for nearly twenty years"). Other more recent same-sex sexual harassment cases, while not relying on marriage specifically, imply that a heterosexual marriage might have further influenced the courts' determinations. See, e.g., *Lord v. High Voltage Software, Inc.* (finding no hostile environment claim because there was no evidence that the alleged harasser was gay or motivated by sexual desire); *Wasek v. Arrow Energy Servs., Inc.* (finding no hostile environment claim because there was no credible evidence that the alleged harasser was bisexual); *McCown v. St. John's Health Sys., Inc.* (finding no hostile environment claim because there was no evidence that the supervisor was gay or was motivated by sexual desire).

57. See, e.g., *Burke v. Villa* (finding that the defendants' response — that Villa could not have engaged in sexually motivated conduct toward Burke, because he is in a heterosexual marriage and has children — is without merit). See also *Goings v. Lopinto* (finding "that the Supreme Court did not foreclose the possibility of same-sex harassment where the harasser is not homosexual"). Such cases indicate that the marriage defense in same-sex sexual harassment cases may be wanning in effectiveness. On the other hand, it is possible that the marriage defense will simply change. After *Bostock*, courts may focus more on marital harmony and preserving marriage rather than finding that the alleged harasser's heterosexual marriage precludes same-sex desire.

58. On appeal, the state supreme court upheld the use of the privilege because the statute had no premarriage acts exception. Nevertheless, the court criticized this use of the marital privilege, writing, "While it is true that Rita Sipler and the defendant were married, there is little evidence to show that this marriage relationship ever existed except on paper. Aside from this, however, even if it could be shown that the defendant and his wife were happily married, we cannot look favorably upon a rule of law which permits the defendant to keep the State's chief and perhaps only witness from testifying against him. As Wigmore, in his treatise

on evidence, states: '[T]he peace of families does not essentially depend on this immunity from compulsory testimony, and, [even if it did], that result [should not be] allowed to stand in the way of doing justice to others.'" *State v. Williams*, 133 Ariz. 220, 234 (1982).

59. See Ariz. Rev. Stat. Ann. § 13-4062(1) (1989). Some state courts have also limited this right. See, e.g., *Vance v. Rice*, 524 F. Supp. 1297 (S.D. Iowa 1981) (holding that a pretrial detainee's right to marry his fiancée was outweighed by the prosecution's need for the fiancée's testimony); *U.S. v. Bowen*, 2015 WL 1893416 (W.D. Mo. 2015) (unpublished) (denying the defendant's motion to marry a government witness); *U. S.v. Heard*, no. 17-CR-0083-LRR, 2018 WL 9439686, at *2 (N.D. Iowa Feb. 20, 2018) (finding that the government has articulated a legitimate and non-punitive reason to delay the defendant's marriage to a government witness); *State v. Wilson*, 471 Md. 136 (2020) (finding that marrying a potential witness with the intent to prevent the witness from testifying at a criminal proceeding under the spousal testimonial privilege supports convictions for witness tampering and obstruction of justice).

60. 237 F. Supp. 3d 1361, 1368 (N.D. Ga. 2017), *aff 'd*, 742 F. App'x 435 (11th Cir. 2018). The Davis case is far from unique. Marrying a witness to prevent testimony remains widely permissible. For example, in the 2007 Indiana case *U.S. v. Norris*, a criminal defendant sought permission to marry (such permission was needed because he was in pretrial detention), but the prosecution objected, arguing that the possible application of the marital testimonial privilege could hinder the prosecution. The court conceded that the "marriage ceremony may very well make the government's case more difficult to prove" but held that this was not a legitimate reason for preventing the marriage. *U.S. v. Norris*, 2007 WL 4335459 (N.D. Ind. 2007). Similarly, in the 2010 case *U. S. v. Bailey*, the Tennessee district court dismissed the government's objection to a pretrial detainee's motion to marry a potential witness. Like the court in *Norris*, the *Bailey* court held that "the Government's concerns about spousal privilege are not legally sufficient to restrict Defendant's right to marry."

61. In federal criminal proceedings in which a defendant is charged with the abuse of his or her spouse or child, this privilege doesn't apply. See *Trammel v. U. S.*, 445 U.S. 40, 46 (1980) (noting that the exception "for cases in which one spouse commits a crime against the other . . . was a longstanding one at common law . . . and] has been expanded since then to include crimes against the spouse's property . . . and in recent years crimes against children of either spouse"). In state court, these exceptions depend on the state. Tom Lininger, "Bearing the Cross," *Fordham Law Review* 74 (2005), 1353, 1371 n1106 (noting "that by 2005, all states recognizing the spousal testimonial privilege had created an exception for cases such as domestic violence in which one spouse has committed a crime against the other").

62. See *U. S. v. Schambers*, no. 1:12-CR-14-TLS, 2013 WL 2243883, at *3 (N.D. Ind. May 20, 2013). Although the court doesn't mention it, presumably, Schambers's now-wife could still be forced to testify regarding the alleged domestic violence. Nevertheless, that does not appear to be the crux of the state's case against Schambers. Thus, marrying the witness likely proved an effective defense strategy; *U. S. v. Schambers*, no. 112CR00014HABSLC, 2020 WL 290001, at *1 (N.D. Ind. Jan. 21, 2020) (describing the various charges against Schambers, including domestic battery).

63. Steve Lash, "House Panel Weighs Bill to Strip Spousal Privilege from Post-Crime Weddings," *Daily Record* (Maryland), (February 2, 2022).

64. Deborah Epstein, "Effective Intervention in Domestic Violence Cases: Rethinking the Roles of Prosecutors, Judges, and the Court System," *Yale Journal of Law & Feminism* 11 (1999), 3, 43. See also Cheryl Hanna, "The Paradox of Hope: The Crime and Punishment of Domestic Violence," *William & Mary Law Review* 39 (1998), 1505, 1520–21, 1539 (stating that privacy concerns continue to shape decisions affecting prosecution, sentencing, and other issues in domestic violence cases); James Ptacek, *Battered Women in the Courtroom: The Power of Judicial Responses* (Boston: Northeastern University Press, 1999), 155 (quoting a Massachusetts judge in a domestic violence case who refused to evict the batterer from the home and stated, "I don't like to break up families"); Jane K. Stoever, "Enjoining Abuse: The Case for Indefinite Domestic Violence Protection Orders," *Vanderbilt Law Review* 67 (2014), 1015, 1019 (noting that many judges remain reluctant to intervene in family matters, and impose more lenient sentences on defendants convicted of domestic violence crimes than on defendants who attack strangers).

65. Alexandra Blake Flamme, "*Hernandez v. Ashcroft*: A Construction of 'Extreme Cruelty' Under the Violence Against Women Act and Its Potential Impact on Immigration and Domestic Violence Law," *New England Law Review* 40 (2006), 571, 614–15.

66. District of Columbia Courts, Final Report of the Task Force on Racial and Ethnic Bias and Task Force on Gender Bias in the Courts, 1992, 126 (noting that only 50 percent of respondents report the same problem in domestic violence prosecutions involving unmarried intimates).

67. Report of the Missouri Task Force on Gender and Justice, 58 Mo. L. Rev. 485, 516 (1993).

68. Groggel found "that unmarried petitioners (victims) living with the respondents (abusers) fare significantly better than their married counterpart." She also found that judges in the study were more likely to grant protection orders to unmarried rather than married victims. Anne Groggel, "The Role of Place and Sociodemographic Characteristics on the Issuance of Temporary Civil Protection Orders," *Law & Society Review* 55 (2021), 38, 43–44, 56.

69. According to the police-court file that was part of the study, offenders convicted of spousal violence were less likely than other convicted violent offenders to receive prison (19 percent versus 29 percent). When examining specific offenses, the difference in the probability of prison between spousal violence offenders and other violent offenders still exists but is smaller. For common assault, the most frequently occurring offense, 17 percent of convicted spouses received prison, compared with 21 percent of other violent offenders. The difference was similar for aggravated assault: 32 percent for family violence offenders and 36 percent for other violent offenders. M. Gannon and J. Brzozowski, "Sentencing in Cases of Family Violence," *JustResearch* (Research and Statistics Division, Department of Justice) 12 (2004): 42–51, available at https://www.justice.gc.ca/eng/rp-pr/jr/jr12/p5e.html. Similar disparities were also documented in a 2014 study from Australia. See Christine E. W. Bond and Samantha Jeffries, "Similar Punishment? Comparing Sentencing Outcomes in Domestic and Non-Domestic Violence Cases," *British Journal of Criminology* 54, no. 5 (September 2014), 849–72.

70. C. A. Taylor and S. B. Sorenson, "Community-Based Norms About Intimate Partner Violence: Putting Attributions of Fault and Responsibility into Context,"

Sex Roles: A Journal of Research 53, no. 7–8 (2005), 573–89. See also Michelle Anderson, "Marital Immunity, Intimate Relationships, and Improper References: A New Law on Sexual Offenses by Intimates," *Hastings Law Journal* 54 (2003), 1465, 1512 (noting that victims of marital rape often receive little support from family and friends).

71. In 1975, South Dakota became the first state to abolish the marital rape exception. However, it was not until 1993, when the exception was abolished in North Carolina, that all states recognized marital rape as a crime. See Kari Hong, "Rape by Malice," *Montana Law Review* 78 (2017), 187, 199 (discussing the history of the criminalization of rape in the United States).

72. *People v. Brown*, 632 P.2d 1025, 1027 (Colo. 1981). As law professor Emily Sack notes, "For far longer than it affirmatively condoned domestic violence, the law continued to justify non-intervention in marital rape cases in order to protect marital privacy and harmony." Emily J. Sack, "Is Domestic Violence A Crime?: Intimate Partner Rape As Allegory," *St. John's Journal of Legal Commentary* 24 (2010), 535, 552–53.

73. Specifically, the court found that despite being separated it was not manifestly clear that the wife intended to end the marriage, and thus the marital rape exception still applied. *Kizer v. Commonwealth*, 228 Va. 256, 261 (1984).

74. The force requirement is a holdover from the past when it was presumed a wife consented to all sex within that marriage. In states with this requirement, this presumption remains and can only be overcome by proving a level of force or resistance that generally is no longer a required element in stranger rape law. See, e.g., Okla. Stat. tit. 21 § 1111 (2009) ("Rape is an act of sexual intercourse accomplished with a male or female who is the spouse of the perpetrator if force or violence is used or threatened, accompanied by apparent power of execution to the victim or to another person"); see also Nev. Rev. Stat. Ann. § 200.373 (LexisNexis 2009) ("It is no defense to a charge of sexual assault that the perpetrator was, at the time of the assault, married to the victim, if the assault was committed by force or by the threat of force").

75. Md. Code Ann., Crim. Law § 3-318 (West 2009) repealed 2023 Maryland Laws Ch. 728 (H.B. 4).

76. In South Carolina, an offender can be sentenced for up to thirty years for non-marital rape, but only for up to ten years for marital rape. S.C. Code Ann. § 16-3-652 (2008) (first-degree sexual assault carries a sentence of up to thirty years); Id. § 16-3-615 (2008) (spousal rape carries a maximum sentence of ten years). In fact, in South Carolina, a perpetrator can get more time for attempted rape. SC Code § 16-3-656 ("Assault with intent to commit criminal sexual conduct . . . shall be punishable as if the criminal sexual conduct was committed").

77. Va. Code Ann. § 18.2-61 (2009).

78. For example, Rhode Island exempts spouses from first-degree sexual assault charges when they know or have reason to know that the victim is "mentally incapacitated, mentally disabled, or physically helpless." R.I. Gen. Laws § 11-37-2 (1) (2009). See also N.H. Rev. Stat. Ann. § 632-A:2 (excepting legally marital spouses when the victim is "mentally defective and the actor knows or has reason to know that the victim is mentally defective" or when victim is a minor over the age of thirteen). See also Okla. Stat. tit. 21, § 1111 (2009) (stating that in Oklahoma, a spouse is exempt where the victim "is incapable through mental illness or any other unsoundness of mind . . . of giving legal consent" unless force or violence is used or threatened).

79. As one prosecutor in a different spousal rape case noted, "Jurors are reluctant to convict because of their belief in the tenets of marriage" and "[their] desire to promote that institution." Marital rape is often treated as less damaging. Lisa R. Eskow, note, "The Ultimate Weapon?: Demythologizing Spousal Rape and Reconceptualizing Its Prosecution," *Stanford Law Review* 48 (1996), 677, 701 (citing a California prosecutor who believes that jurors typically view spousal rape as inherently less severe because "the relationship acts as mitigation").

Similarly, a National District Attorneys Association guide for prosecutors conducting voir dire in marital and date rape cases says: "This is a difficult and tricky area for prosecutors. Unfortunately, many jurors have difficulty with marital rape . . . too many of them do not see it as a crime. The best approach for this is to use hypothetical questions/scenarios, relating rape to other crimes so that the stigmas & myths are debunked." See Sack, "Is Domestic Violence A Crime?," 535, 566.

The irony of this lesser punishment for marital rape based on the belief it is less traumatic is that substantial research demonstrates that this is a misperception. As Professor Emily Sack notes, "The psychological injury from partner rape can be far greater because the woman feels betrayed by this act of violence from someone with whom she previously has been intimate. Moreover, the physical injuries resulting from intimate partner rape can be severe." Sack also notes that "victims of intimate partner rape are themselves affected by the myths surrounding non-stranger rape. They may experience greater trauma because they may be more likely to feel guilt and shame, to hide the rape, to blame themselves and be blamed by others, and to believe themselves less deserving of help." Sack, "Is Domestic Violence A Crime?," 535, 561.

80. Sheila Weller, "America's Most Sexist Judges," *Redbook*, February 1994, at 83, 85 (the judge did concede that the man had gone too far, stating, "To have slapped you might have been more normal").

81. Sheila Weller, "More of America's Most Sexist Judges," *Redbook*, December 1994, 88, 90–91.

82. The judge then likened the case to automobile manslaughter committed by drunk drivers. Lynn Hecht Schafran, "There's No Accounting for Judges," *Albany Law Review* 58, no. 4 (1995), 1063, 1066, citing the Reporter's Official Transcript of Proceedings (Sentencing) at 4–5, *State v. Peacock* (No. 94-CR-0943).

83. Marital status is often the determinative factor in ruling whether a defendant will be granted a voluntary manslaughter instruction. A provocation defense is frequently not applied when the alleged infidelity occurred between unmarried partners. For cases where courts have denied the defense to a non-spouse who committed murder in response to a partner's infidelity, see, e.g., *People v. Martinez*, 2002 WL 1482547 (Cal. App. 2d Dist. 2002); *Savage v. State*, 274 Ga. 692, 558 S.E.2d 701 (2002); *State v. Fleming*, 2001-Ohio-1497, 2001 WL 871397 (Ohio Ct. App. 2d Dist. Montgomery County 2001); *Somchith v. State*, 527 S.E.2d 546, 548 (Ga. 2000); *People v. McCarthy*, 547 N.E.2d 459, 463 (Ill. 1989); *People v. Eagen*, 357 N.W.2d 710, 711-12 (Mich. Ct. App. 1984). But see *Murray v. State*, 247 Ga. App. 139, 543 S.E.2d 428 (2000) (applying the defense to a girlfriend's infidelity); *Williams v. State*, 245 Ga. App. 670, 538 S.E.2d 544 (2000) (permitting the defense when the victim had been "fooling around" with the defendant's girlfriend). Professor Joshua Dressler has explained this difference, noting:

> [A]n unmarried individual who kills upon sight of unfaithfulness by one's lover or fiancé is [considered] a murderer. Only a highly

unrealistic belief about passion can explain this rule in terms of excusing conduct. It is implausible to believe that when an actor observes his or her loved one in an act of sexual disloyalty, that actor will suffer from less anger simply because the disloyal partner is not the actor's spouse. Instead, this rule is really a judgment by courts that adultery is a form of injustice perpetrated upon the killer which merits a violent response, whereas "mere" sexual unfaithfulness out of wedlock does not. Thus, it has been said that adultery is the "highest invasion of [a husband's] property," whereas in the unmarried situation the defendant "has no such control" over his faithless lover.

Joshua Dressler, "Rethinking Heat of Passion: A Defense in Search of a Rationale," *Journal of Criminal Law and Criminology* 73 (1982), 421, 429.

84. The appellant described his state of mind after the confrontation with Pham as "way too angry." During the police interrogation, the appellant was asked repeatedly if he knew "that it's wrong when you kill someone, that you are not supposed to do that." He answered, "When I angry, angry, uh, I, I, I don't know. I. I uh, e-everything. I don't know, I, I don't, I don't think go to jail, I don't think nothing. I, I just uh, know, kill him." *People v. Le*, 158 Cal. App. 4th 516, 529 (2007).

85. Wilcox and Wilson admit that "married men can and do abuse or assault their wives," but they argue that "married fathers are much less likely to resort to violence," as if the marriage itself was the reason. W. Bradford Wilcox and Robin Fretwell Wilson, "One Way to End Violence Against Women? Married Dads," *Washington Post*, June 10, 2014.

86. In her article "Marriage Will Not Save Women from Male Violence," *Slate*, June 10, 2014, journalist Amanda Marcotte writes, "It's hard to overstate the gross negligence of this piece (which, by the way, is pegged to Father's Day). One of the most confounding issues when it comes to domestic violence is that many victims believe that if they just love a little harder and put a little more work into the relationship, they can turn an abusive partner into a loving one."

87. Unlike other immigrant women, whose immigration status can make them much more vulnerable to abuse, mail-order brides have significant legal and immigration protections. See, generally, Marcia Zug, *Buying a Bride: An Engaging History of Mail-Order Matches* (New York: New York University Press, 2016). Nevertheless, criticisms of such marriages remain widespread. See, e.g., Kirsten M. Lindee, "Love, Honor, or Control: Domestic Violence, Trafficking, and the Question of How to Regulate the Mail-Order Bride Industry," *Columbia Journal of Gender & Law* 16 (2007), 551, 553–54 (noting that "in appealing to these conceptions of marriage and gender, IMBs [international marriage brokerages] create and foster an image of 'mail-order brides' as submissive, dependent, and deferential. At the same time, by advertising them online and in glossy catalogues, IMBs commodify these women, who can be purchased for less than the price of an economy car").

88. See e.g., *State v. Jadowski*, 680 N.W.2d 810, 821 n. 42 (2004) (discussing the colloquial phrase "sixteen will get you twenty!" as a common exclamation expressing the widespread awareness of statutory rape laws and the strict liability aspect of the offense).

89. "Several were deserted by their statutory rapists, left to raise a child — or in many cases children — on their own when they are themselves only teenagers, some at the age of thirteen. They 'are totally unprepared to care for themselves or

their children, having been deprived of an education.'" Kelly C. Connerton, "The Resurgence of the Marital Rape Exemption: The Victimization of Teens by Their Statutory Rapists," *Albany Law Review* 61 (1997), 237, 237–38.

90. Moni Basu, "Sherry Johnson Was Raped, Pregnant and Married by 11. Now She's Fighting to End Child Marriage in America," CNN, January 31, 2018.

91. Fla. Stat. Ann. § 741.04 (West) (allowing seventeen-year-olds to marry but only if "the older party to the marriage is not more than 2 years older than the younger party to the marriage"); Ariz. Rev. Stat. Ann. § 25-102 (permitting marriage under eighteen, but over sixteen, provided "the person's prospective spouse is not more than three years older than the person").

92. VA Stat § 20-48 ("The minimum age at which persons may marry shall be 18"); N.J. Stat. Ann. § 37:1-6 (West) (a marriage or civil union license shall not be issued to a minor under the age of 18 years). Similarly, in 2020, Maine repealed the provision permitting children under sixteen to marry if the judge considered marriage in their best interest. Now no one under age sixteen may marry. ME Legis 535 (2020), 2020 Me. Legis. Serv. Ch. 535 (S.P. 167) (L.D. 545) (West).

93. See, e.g., Melissa Murray, "Strange Bedfellows," 1253, 1266 n38 (noting that twenty-four states and the District of Columbia have abolished the defense). For an example of such a marriage see *In re Interest of Miller*, 448 A.2d 25, 26, 38 (Pa. Super. Ct. 1982) (upholding the validity of a marriage between a female juvenile and adult male even though the man's motive was to avoid criminal prosecution for his relationship with the girl).

94. Figures indicate that at least 7.5 million incidents of statutory rape occur every year. Sadly, there is no question that the desire for underage sexual relationships is widespread. Marriage just makes it permissible. For further discussion of the marriage exception to age of consent laws, see Erin K. Jackson, "Addressing the Inconsistency Between Statutory Rape Laws and Underage Marriage: Abolishing Early Marriage and Removing the Spousal Exemption to Statutory Rape," *UMKC Law Review* 85 (2017), 343, 364 (arguing that underage "marriages allow adults to offer their consent to a minor girl's ongoing statutory rape"); Amber Plumlee, "Don't Put a Ring on It: Abolishing the Marital Defense to Statutory Rape," *Women's Rights Law Reporter* 41 (2019), 95, 110 (writing, "Marriage provides easier, legal, and thus possibly more frequent access to a young person's body").

Chapter 5

1. "Romance of War Puzzles Officials," *New York Times*, January 31, 1920.

2. Lena Edlund and Evelyn Korn, "A Theory of Prostitution," *Journal of Political Economy* 110, no. 1 (February 1, 2020). See also Michael Grossberg, *Governing the Hearth: Law and the Family in Nineteenth-Century America* (Chapel Hill: University of North Carolina Press, 1988), 205 (noting that marriage was the simplest and most socially acceptable method of legitimizing children).

3. Under the common law, a man's legal relationship to his offspring was determined by his relationship to their mother. As Professor Mary Shanley writes, "If the woman was his wife, a child was 'his,' so much so that he exercised exclusive custodial authority," and he could even name someone other than the mother to be the child's guardian after his death. Mary L. Shanley, "Unwed Fathers' Rights, Adoption, and Sex Equality: Gender-Neutrality and the Perpetuation of Patriarchy," *Columbia Law Review* 95 (1995), 60, 68.

4. In explaining the differences between the rights and obligations of marital vs

non-marital fathers, Professor Shanley writes, "The child of his wife took his surname, the nonmarital child did not. The marital child had a right to financial support from him, the nonmarital child did not. The marital child had the right to inherit from him if he died without a will, the nonmarital child did not." Shanley, "Unwed Fathers' Rights, Adoption," 60, 67.

5. *Safford v. Houghton's Est.*, 48 Vt. 236, 238 (1876). According to historian Michael Grossberg, by the nineteenth century, there was a "strong aversion to the idea of creating children by act which law makers felt could enable men to avoid marriage. They worried the fathers of illegitimate offspring might adopt them rather than marrying to legitimate them." Grossberg, *Governing the Hearth*, 273.

6. Lawrence M. Friedman, *Private Lives: Families, Individuals and the Law* (Cambridge, MA: Harvard University Press, 2004), 10, noting that "unfettered reproduction was viewed as dangerous to society and thus, the state developed a keen interest in controlling marriage (or, rather, the birth of children)."

7. As Goethe wrote, "A man must take his children on trust." August Strindberg, *Strindberg Plays: One: The Father, Miss Julie, The Ghost Sonata*, trans. Michael Meyer (London: Bloomsbury, 2013), 54 (quoting Goethe in *The Father*). See also Shakespeare's *Merry Wives of Windsor*, act 2, sc. 2, 1073–99, "See the hell of having a false woman! . . . Fie, fie, fie! cuckold, cuckold, cuckold!"

8. See Lord Mansfield's exclusionary rule of 1777, which held that under the law of England, "the declarations of a father or mother [could not] be admitted to bastardize the issue born after marriage," *Goodright v. Moss*, 98 Eng. Rep. 1257 (1777). See also Eran Zelnik, "Yankees, Doodles, Fops and Cuckolds," *Early American Studies* 16, no. 3 (Summer 2018), 514–44 (noting that although the trope of the cuckold had been around for centuries, it acquired new meaning during the upheavals of the eighteenth century).

Interestingly, these growing cuckold fears appear to have been unfounded. Empirical studies show that men who believe themselves to be the fathers of children are, in fact, almost always the fathers. A study published in 2013 reconstructing large family genealogies back four centuries in Belgium found a cuckoldry rate of less than 1 percent. See M. H. D. Larmuseau et al., "Low Historical Rates of Cuckoldry in a Western European Human Population Traced by Y-Chromosome and Genealogical Data," *Proceedings of the Royal Society B: Biological Sciences* 280 (2013). Other studies have found comparable rates in Spain, Italy, Germany, and agricultural villages in Mali. Carl Zimmer, "Fathered by the Mailman? It's Mostly an Urban Legend," *New York Times*, April 9, 2016, A1. Similarly, the most comprehensive analysis of US data concluded that 98 percent of the men raising children they believe to be their biological children are correct. Kermyt G. Anderson, "How Well Does Paternity Confidence Match Actual Paternity? Results from Worldwide Nonpaternity Rates," *Current Anthropology* 47 (2006), 511, 516.

9. This presumption was almost impossible to rebut. Under the laws of coverture, the husband and wife were considered one legal person. As a result, neither the husband nor the wife could testify regarding the husband's "nonaccess" to his wife (the evidence required to "prove, beyond all reasonable doubt, that the husband could not have been the father"). Indeed, as Professor Douglas NeJaime writes, "Traditionally neither the husband nor wife were permitted to testify to the husband's 'nonaccess,' meaning that the couple themselves could not penetrate the presumption with inconsistent biological facts. A jury could not legally find against . . . legitimacy, except on facts which prove, beyond all reasonable doubt,

that the husband could not have been the father." Douglas NeJaime, "The Nature of Parenthood," *Yale Law Journal* 126 (2017), 2260, 2272 (internal citations omitted).

10. Unmarried mothers typically received custody of their children based on their role as the child's "natural" guardian rather than their status as a legal parent. This status changed in the second half of the nineteenth century when unmarried mothers gained a legally recognized relationship with their non-marital children. However, the rights of fathers remained based on marriage. See Grossberg, *Governing the Hearth*, 207.

11. Nineteenth-century historian George Bancroft described Graham as "the leading spirit among a crowd of turbulent and reckless men, himself as wild and unprincipled as the worst." See David Langum, "Expatriate Domestic Relations in Mexican California," *Pepperdine Law Review* 7 (1979), 1. After Graham started abusing Bennett, her mother advocated murdering him and suggested putting poison spiders in his dumplings, but Bennett declined. Skip Littlefield, "Isaac Graham: The Rifle-Toting Firebrand of the Zayante," *Santa Cruz Sentinel*, March 3, 1985.

12. Historian Hendrik Hartog suggests that "the point of this cause of action was to establish the illegitimacy of the children. As a result, Bennett would establish her sole legal right to custody." Hendrik Hartog, "Marital Exits and Marital Expectations in Nineteenth-Century America," *Georgetown Law Journal* 80 (1991), 95, 125. For a modern example of this custody strategy, see *Brooks v. Brooks* 532 N.E.2d 208 (Ohio Ct. App. 1988). (Here a mother argued that the husband who had raised her child for thirteen years was not the biological father and thus not entitled to custody. The court rejected her "legitimization" efforts.)

13. Doyce Nunis, *The Trials of Isaac Graham* (Los Angeles: Dawson's Book Shop, 1967), 64.

14. Technically the court did not declare the marriage valid as to the parent. Instead, the court held that the marriage was valid as to the children; thus the children were born legitimate, and Graham had all the custodial rights of a married father. According to the court:

> The ceremony which was instituted by the parents, although illegal and void as to them, is declared sufficient to protect their offspring against the stain of bastardy, and its accompanying conditions. The law declares they shall be legitimate. They are, therefore, in relation to their father, the inheritors of his name, his heirs-apparent, and entitled to look for, and demand from him, his care, maintenance and protection. On the other hand, he has the unquestioned right to their custody, control, and obedience, to the same extent as if they were the issue of a valid marriage.

Graham v. Bennett, 2 Cal. 503, 506–7 (1852).

As a legal opinion, the Graham case is nonsensical. Nevertheless, what is clear from the court's decisions is that, for whatever reason, the court wanted Graham to have custody of the children despite no legal basis for such a ruling. One possibility is that the court feared Graham and his son. Graham was known for having planned a coup against the Mexican governor of Northern California, and his son had recently murdered Bennett's brother. For a history the case against Graham's son, see Nunis, *The Trials of Isaac Graham*.

15. See, e.g., *U. S. v. Green*, 26 F. Cas. 30 (C.C.D.R.I. 1824); *Macready v. Wilcox*, 33 Conn. 321, 324 (Conn. 1866); *State ex rel. Lasserre v. Michel*, 105 La. 741, 745, 30 So. 122, 124 (1901).

16. For early cases not granting custody to the father, see, e.g., *Nickols v. Giles*, 1796 WL 496 (Conn. Super. Ct. 1796) (refusing to grant the father custody of his child because the child was "well taken care of, and not likely to be so by the father"); *Commonwealth v. Addicks*, 1813 WL 2204, at *2 (Pa. July 10, 1813) (acknowledging the mother's immoral character, the court recognized that children of "tender age" need the "kind of assistance which can be afforded by none so well as a mother"); *U.S. v. Bainbridge*, 24 F. Cas. 946, 949 (C.C.D. Mass. 1816) (noting that the father's custodial right "is not unlimited; for whenever it is abused by improper conduct on the part of the parent, courts of law will restrain him in its exercise, and even take the custody permanently from him").

17. Grossberg, *Governing the Hearth*, 241, citing the Report of the D'Hautville Case (Philadelphia, 1840), 292–93.

18. *Lindsey v. Lindsey*, 14 Ga. 657, 660 (1854). See Denise K. Mills and Gina B. Weitzenkorn, "Emerging Spousal Support and Parenting Issues," *Colorado Lawyer* (October 2012), 45, 47 (noting that "if a father desired to prove a mother was unfit, he alleged she had committed adultery or was immoral in other ways"). Notably, the courts did not have similar concerns about adulterous men. See, e.g., *Bell v. Bell*, 154 Ga. App. 290, 291–92, (1980) (stating, "The man may notoriously sin in this regard; and yet, sometimes, retain a position of respectability, or quasi respectability, by means of which his relations and those of his family, with decent people, are maintained; his children may associate with such persons, and be educated to become good and useful members of society").

19. During this period, adoption was viewed as an acceptable way for unmarried women to find an outlet for their maternal longings. As Progressive Era reformer Ellen Key wrote, "In those cases where a woman's destiny from one cause has rendered the realization of love impossible she ought . . . to enrich her life and partially satisfy her motherly feeling by choosing one among the destitute children, who are unfortunately still to be found in abundance, to provide for and love." Ellen Key, *Love and Marriage*, 1911, 189. See also Julie Berebitsky, *Like Our Very Own: Adoption and the Changing Culture of Motherhood, 1851–1950* (Lawrence: University Press of Kansas, 2000), 103–4 (noting, "Often the single adoptive mothers portrayed in fiction and profiled in magazines were ordinary women who had missed out on marriage and motherhood through the misfortunes of fate, not through a blatant disregard of traditional gender roles").

20. Grossberg, *Governing the Hearth*, 230.

21. A Uniform Illegitimacy Act, promulgated in 1922, was abandoned in 1960 after having been adopted by only seven states — Nevada, New Mexico, North Dakota, South Dakota, Iowa, New York, and Wyoming. See Fowler V. Harper, "Policy Bases of the Conflict of Laws: Reflections on Rereading Professor Lorenzen's Essays," *Yale Law Journal* 56 (1947), 1155, 1177.

22. Bradley Hull, cited in Standards of Legal Protection for Children Born Out of Wedlock (Children's Bureau, U.S. Department of Labor, 1921), 82–93; and Emma O. Lundberg, Children of Illegitimate Birth and Measures for their Protection (Children's Bureau, U.S. Department of Labor, 1926), 11.

23. Berebitsky, *Like Our Very Own*, 103 (2000).

24. Proceedings of the National Conference of Social Work, 1945, available at https://quod.lib.umich.edu/n/ncosw/ACH8650.1945.001?rgn=main;view=fulltext. See also Berebitsky, *Like Our Very Own*, 103 (noting that by the 1950s, virtually no single women adopted).

25. Brief for Respondent, 25–27 Stanley v. Illinois, 405 U.S. 645 (1972) (No. 70-5014). The state further argued that a married father typically lives with his wife and children and thus "creat[es] the basic family unit upon which our society is based," while an unmarried father usually "establishes no fixed family unit, but only a transient relationship." See also *Stanley v. Illinois*, 405 U.S. 645, 654, 92 S. Ct. 1208, 1214, 31 L. Ed. 2d 551 (1972) (writing, "It may be, as the State insists, that most unmarried fathers are unsuitable and neglectful parents").

26. One year after *Quilloin*, the court decided *Caban v. Mohammed*, 441 U.S. 380, 382 (1979) and reconfirmed the constitutionality of distinguishing between marital and non-marital fathers. Like *Quilloin*, *Caban* also involved an unmarried father. However, Caban had behaved like a "husband." He had lived with and supported his children. Therefore, the court held Caban, unlike Quilloin, could object to the adoption of his children by their new stepfather.

27. Stopes was eventually granted an annulment after proving that her first marriage, which lasted five years, was never consummated. See Angus McLaren, *Impotence: A Cultural History* (Chicago: University of Chicago Press, 2008), 168 (discussing Stopes's non-consummation claim).

28. Margaret Sanger, *Happiness in Marriage* (Maxwell Reprint Company, 1926), 207 (citing finances, happiness, and health concerns as reasons married couples need birth control).

29. "By the 1930s nationwide polls indicated that as many as 70% of Americans supported the dissemination of birth control information." Geoffrey R. Stone, *Sex and the Constitution: Sex, Religion, and Law from America's Origins to the Twenty-First Century* (New York: Liveright, 2017), 189, 208.

30. Susan Frelich Appleton, "The Forgotten Family Law of *Eisenstadt v. Baird*," *Yale Journal of Law & Feminism* 28 (2016), 1, 13 ("In fact, when a family law casebook features *Eisenstadt* in coverage of alternative or nontraditional families, it reinscribes marriage as the norm by presupposing a marital baseline against which all departures are measured").

31. Daniel Kreps, "Reports Question the Paternity of Michael Jackson's Children," *Rolling Stone*, June 30, 2009 (suggesting that Michael's former doctor and the boss of Jackson's onetime wife, Debbie Rowe, is the biological father of elder children Prince Michael Jr. and Paris).

32. As Justice Scalia bluntly noted, "To provide protection to an adulterous natural father is to deny protection to a marital father." Fathers were married men, and unmarried men — especially unmarried, adulterous men — forfeited their parental rights. *Michael H. v. Gerald D.*, 491 U.S. 110, 141 (1989).

33. "Until late in the twentieth century, only the spouses themselves had standing to challenge the husband's paternity, so even if everyone knew he was not the genetic father, spouses could preserve their family by agreeing to raise the child and exclude the genetic father. About a third of states still retain this strict rule." Gregg Strauss, "Parentage Agreements Are Not Contracts," *Fordham Law Review* 90 (2022), 2645, 2653. See also June Carbone and Naomi Cahn, "Marriage, Parentage, and Child Support," *Family Law Quarterly* 45 (2011), 219, 224n26 (noting that "two-thirds of states give genetic fathers standing to rebut the marital presumption" while the remaining third do not). Such challenges can also be discouraged through other methods. See, e.g., Guide to Assist Hospitals with Their Paternity Acknowledgment Program, South Carolina Parenting Opportunity Program, South Carolina Department of Social Services (updated January 2010) (noting

that if a women is married at any time during her pregnancy, she can only put her husband's name on the birth certificate or leave that space blank); Fla. Stat. Ann. § 382.013 (West) ("If the mother is married at the time of birth, the name of the husband shall be entered on the birth certificate as the father of the child, unless paternity has been determined otherwise by a court of competent jurisdiction").

34. For examples of courts refusing to allow a paternity challenge, see, e.g., *In re Jesusa V.*, 85 P.3d 2, 15 (Cal. 2004) (holding that another man's biological paternity does not necessarily rebut the husband's presumption of parentage and that considerations based upon policy and logic, such as the welfare of the child, factor into the determination of who should be deemed the legal father); *N.A.H. v. S.L.S.*, 9 P.3d 354, 357 (Colo. 2000) ("We hold that the best interests of the child must be of paramount concern throughout a paternity proceeding, and therefore, must be explicitly considered as a part of the policy and logic analysis that is used to resolve competing presumptions of fatherhood [between a genetic father and the husband of the child's mother]"); *Kelly v. Cataldo*, 488 N.W.2d 822, 827 (Minn. Ct. App. 1992) (stating that the child's best interests should be considered in determining whether the mother's husband or the genetic father should be deemed the child's legal father).

See also Jessica Feinberg, "Restructuring Rebuttal of the Marital Presumption for the Modern Era," *Minnesota Law Review* 104 (2019), 243, 270 (noting that some states allows courts to deny challenges to the presumption in situations where, "although the base requirement for rebuttal (currently the lack of genetic tie between the spouse and child) is satisfied, rebuttal would be contrary to the best interests of the child"); Leslie Joan Harris, "*Obergefell's* Ambiguous Impact on Legal Parentage," *Chicago-Kent Law Review* 92 (2017), 55, 73 ("If the presumption is challenged by the offer of genetic evidence, a number of states have held that a court can refuse to admit that evidence if contrary to the child's best interests"); Rhonda Wasserman, "DOMA and the Happy Family: A Lesson in Irony," *California Western International Law Journal* 41 (2010), 275, 283 ("Some states permit the presumption of parentage to be rebutted only if doing so would serve the child's best interests. In these states, when alleged biological fathers claim paternity of children born during an intact marriage, courts decline to order blood tests or DNA tests to determine paternity unless the determination would be in the child's best interests").

35. For an example of a successful paternity challenge by a paramour, see *Fisher v. Tucker*, 388 S.C. 388, 392 (2010) (issuing an order of paternity in favor of the paramour where the married mother had left her husband and moved in with her lover — along with two of her children — told the lover he was the father, and had his surname listed on the child's birth certificate).

36. This study involved Dutch participants, but it is likely an American study would produce comparable results. This is particularly true given the fact that the US attaches significantly more rights to marriage and provides fewer protections for cohabitants than the Netherlands. See Lena Edlund, "The Role of Paternity Presumption and Custodial Rights for Understanding Marriage Patterns," *Economica* 80 (2013), 656 (demonstrating, at least in the abstract, that for many Western men, marriage is an economic contract for custody of children).

37. Nicole Hiekel and Renske Keizer, "Risk-Avoidance or Utmost Commitment? Dutch Focus Group Research on Cohabitation and Marriage," *Demographic Research* 32 (2015), 311–40.

38. As Hiekel and Keizer note, "Lower education men evaluated such an approach as a devaluation of the institution of marriage." Hiekel and Keizer, "Risk-Avoidance or Utmost Commitment?," 331. This disapproval makes sense if, as sociologist Lena Edlund has argued, "marriage may be viewed as a contract on children in which custodial rights are transferred from the mother to the father." Lower-earning men are less able to "transfer resources to women in exchange for marriage" and will therefore have fewer marriage prospects under such a system. Edlund and Korn, "A Theory of Prostitution," 181–214, 185.

39. As family law professor Courtney Joslin notes, "One can still find many family law decisions in which courts not only expressly rely on notions of morality, but more importantly, appear to place significant weight on notions of morality." Courtney G. Joslin, "The Perils of Family Law Localism," *University of California at Davis Law Review* 48 (2014), 623, 643–44.

40. *Helms v. Helms*, 185 Mich. App. 680 (1990).

41. *Ulvund v. Ulvund*, No. 224566, 2000 WL 33407372, at *4 (Mich. Ct. App., Aug. 22, 2000). It is likely that the mother's sexual orientation played a role in the court's decision. Being gay — regardless of any physical demonstration — has often been considered a sufficient reason for a change in custody. Prior to *Obergefell*, this was a particular problem for LGBTQ parents who did not have the option to marry. This is one of the many reasons same-sex couples fought for the right to marry. Marriage would have helped protect the mother by "curing" their relationship through marriage. For cases changing custody due to a partner's sexual orientation, see, e.g., *L.A.M. v. B.M.* 906 So. 2d 942 (Ala. Civ. App. 2004) (regarding a lesbian mother's sexual activity in the home, although not in the child's direct presence); *Sirney v. Sirney*, No. 0754-07-4, 2007 WL 4525274 (Va. Ct. App. Dec. 27, 2007) (prohibiting a lesbian mother from living with any person other than a spouse while her children were visiting and effectively forcing the mother's same-sex partner out of the home); *A.O.V. v. J.R.V.*, Nos. 0219-06-4, 0220-06-4, 2007 WL 581871 (Va. Ct. App. Feb. 27, 2007) (prohibiting the father's partner from sleeping in the couple's shared home when the children were in the care of their father, who had joint custody with the mother).

42. It was a single occurrence because she left him immediately afterward.

43. *Masters v. Masters*, 52 So.3d 1279, 1290 (Miss. Ct. App. 2011) (noting that one extra-marital relationship was not enough to justify a change in custody but that three could be). See also *Bamburg v. Bamburg*, 2014 Ark. App. 269 (2014) (prohibiting either party from engaging in unmarried cohabitation, overnight visits, or travel with a paramour, and noting, "Arkansas law has historically prohibited, as a matter of public policy, children being exposed to a parent's unmarried cohabitation or a parent's promiscuous conduct or lifestyle").

44. *Holmes v. Holmes*, No. CA 90-80, 1990 WL 162102, at *3 (Ark. Ct. App. Oct. 24, 1990).

45. *Powell v. Marshall*, 88 Ark. App. 257, 267 (2004).

46. *Robertson v. Robertson*, 370 P.3d 569, 572 (2016) (rejecting the father's argument "that the trial court should not have determined that [the mother] had higher moral standards than he did based upon the fact that she and her husband were married while Robertson was cohabitating with his girlfriend").

47. The trial court actually encouraged the mother to evade the marriage laws of New Mexico, advising her to follow through on her plan to marry the uncle in Costa Rica and then relocate to California, where the liberal recognition laws

would treat the marriage as valid. In fact, the court permitted the mother to retain custody on the specific condition that she and the uncle enter such a valid (albeit incestuous) marriage. *Leszinske v. Poole*, 798 P.2d 1049, 1051 (1990).

48. In contrast with the mother's behavior, the father took significant steps to make sure the child never witnessed sexual activity. According to the court opinion, "The father lives in Decatur with his sexual partner, T.K., a man. He and T.K. reside in a two-bedroom, one-bath home. He and T.K. testified that, when the child visits, the child sleeps in her own room. They also both testified that they did not sleep in the same room when the child was visiting. According to the father, T.K. sleeps in T.K.'s own bedroom and the father sleeps on the couch when the child visits." It is likely that the father's sexuality was a factor in the court's decision, but the mother's marriage made it possible for the court to dismiss the differences in the parents' behavior. *K.T.W.P. v. D.R.W.*, 721 So. 2d 699 (Ala. Civ. App. 1998). See also Suzanne A. Kim, "The Neutered Parent," *Yale Journal of Law & Feminism* 24 (2012), 1, 34 (2012) (describing the sexually neutralizing effect of marriage on parental sexual activity).

49. Compare with *Vanderveer v. Vanderveer*, where a court divested a mother of custody of her son because the mother had relocated to Florida to live — unmarried — with "a man she had met in a bar." The court then determined that the "moral atmosphere for the child" was inconsistent with the child's best interests. No. 0122-04-02, 2004 WL 2157930, at *1 (Va. Ct. App. Sept. 28, 2004). See also *Carmichael v. Carmichael*, 265 So. 2d 668, 669 (La. Ct. App. 1972) (transferring custody from the mother to the father because the mother did not conceal her relationship with her "lover" from her children, "had no regret . . . and apparently feels it is perfectly proper . . . for her children to know of their illicit relationship because some day they intend to marry."

50. Studies demonstrate that fathers are benefited in custody disputes when they can show they will have the assistance of a female caretaker — often a new wife. See Jennifer E. Horne, note, "The Brady Bunch and Other Fictions: How Courts Decide Child Custody Disputes Involving Remarried Parents," *Stanford Law Review* 45 (1993), 2073, 2096–101 (analyzing appellate custody cases involving parental remarriage and finding that many "courts considered fathers favorably if they could point to a person — generally a woman — who was willing to help them care for their children" and that this person was typically the father's new wife or his mother).

Despite such court decisions, there is no reason to think that a child will be better off with a stepmother than a mother. As Professor Mary Becker notes, "Stepparent relationships are notoriously difficult." Becker further notes that "in assuming that the child is better off with a stepmother and the father, judges regard women as fungible — any woman can take the place of a mother." Mary Becker, "Maternal Feelings: Myth, Taboo, and Child Custody," *Southern California Review of Law and Women's Studies* 1 (1992), 133, 181. See also E. Mavis Hetherington, Martha Cox, and Roger Cox, "Effects of Divorce on Parents and Children," in *Nontraditional Families: Parenting and Child Development*, ed. Michael E. Lamb (New York: Erlbaum Associates, 1982), 233, 252, 282–83 (finding that seeking custody of children of an earlier marriage was a strategy new wives used to separate husbands from earlier wives).

51. With this statement, the court implied that it was marriage that created a family, and thus a child and a single mother were not a family. *Puzzuoli v. Puzzuoli*, No. CA 89-310, 1990 WL 32446, at *1 (Ark. Ct. App. Mar. 21, 1990).

52. On appeal, the change in custody decision was remanded back to the trial court to make specific findings that the two-parent household would be preferable. The appellate court noted, "A child custody determination cannot be based on an assumption, unsupported by scientific evidence, that a working mother cannot provide such care. Such an assumption unfairly forces divorcing spouses to choose between parenthood and livelihood; and it is likely to disproportionately deprive women of custody, since statistics indicate that divorced men are more likely to remarry a spouse who does not work outside the home." *West v. West*, 21 P.3d (Alaska 2001), 838, 842 (internal citations omitted).

53. 83 N.E.3d 1278 (Ind. Ct. App. 2017). See also *Baushke v. Miller*, 79 N.E.3d 1013 (Ind. Ct. App. 2017) (awarding primary custody to the father, noting, "Father has remarried, and the child has a strong positive relationship with his stepmother").

54. *Sylvester v. Cartee*, 279 So. 3d 596, 603 (Ala. Civ. App. 2018).

55. Hetherington, Cox, and Cox, "Effects of Divorce on Parents and Children," 235, 281–82.

56. For more information on the history of assisted reproduction, see Judith F. Daar, *Reproductive Technologies and the Law* (Newark: LexisNexis, 2006), 25–29.

57. Perhaps the husband thought a handsome young doctor was the next best thing — maybe even better — than his own DNA. Nevertheless, the fact that the mother was never told is disturbing. For a history of the insemination, see A. D. Hard, *Artificial Impregnation*, 27 Medical World 27 (1909), 163.

58. See Judith F. Daar, "Accessing Reproductive Technologies: Invisible Barriers, Indelible Harms," *Berkeley Journal of Gender, Law & Justice* 23 (2008), 18, 82 (2008) (noting that in the mid-1950s, "the technique gained recognition from the medical community as a treatment for infertility, due largely to published reports documenting pregnancies using stored frozen semen"). See also R. Bunge and J. Sherman, "Fertilizing Capacity of Frozen Human Spermatazoa," *Nature* 172 (1953), 767.

59. B. Fain Tucker, "Legal Problems of Artificial Insemination," *Women's Law Journal* 33 (1947), 57, 58. See also Kara W. Swanson, "Adultery by Doctor: Artificial Insemination, 1890–1945," *Chicago-Kent Law Review* 87 (2012), 591, 633 (explaining that as Americans learned that hundreds or perhaps thousands of babies had been conceived by this method in the past decade alone, doctors and lawyers realized that this new hope posed many "delicate questions" for the law).

60. *Orford v. Orford* [1921], 49 O.L.R. 15, 22. See also Swanson, "Adultery by Doctor," 591, 593 (noting that, as Mrs. Orford discovered, "courts were disinclined to believe tales of donor insemination when adultery seemed so much more likely").

61. Judicial concerns regarding artificial insemination stemmed from the fact that it sought.to separate biological and social paternity and went against the law's long-standing assumption that all marital children were also biological children. It also triggered long-standing fears that men might be deceived into claiming another man's child as their own. Consequently, courts refused to apply the marital presumption in AI cases. See, e.g., *Strnad v. Strnad*, 78 N.Y.S.2d 390 (N.Y. Sup. Ct. 1948) (holding that a child of AI was not legitimate); *Doornbos v. Doornbos*, no. 54S. 14981 (Superior Ct., Cook Co., Dec. 13, 1954), *aff'd.* 139 N.E.2d 844 (Ill. App. Ct. 1956) (holding that AI, with or without the consent of the husband, constitutes adultery by the mother, and declaring the child illegitimate).

Reproductive rights advocates pointed out the absurdity of equating AI with adultery. Alan Guttmacher described the legal analysis linking AI to adultery as "balderdash," noting that the two are "the antithesis of each other. One is done clandestinely to deceive and to enjoy carnal pleasure; the other decently and frankly to beget offspring without the emotional and physical enjoyment of coitus." Swanson, "Adultery by Doctor," 627–28.

62. Specifically, the Sorenson court held that AI is permissible when a man, "because of his inability to procreate, actively participates and consents to his wife's artificial insemination in the hope that a child will be produced whom they will treat as their own, [and when he] knows that such behavior carries with it the legal responsibilities of fatherhood and criminal responsibility for nonsupport." *People v. Sorenson*, 68 Cal. 2d 280, 285 (1968).

63. In 1985, twenty-five states had statutes dealing with artificial insemination, the majority of which "operate only to legitimize children conceived by a married woman inseminated with the sperm of a donor who is not her husband." "Reproductive Technology and the Procreation Rights of the Unmarried," *Harvard Law Review* 98 (1985), 669, 670–71.

64. The article suggested that "the unwillingness of many of the remaining ninety percent probably stems from personal philosophies or religious beliefs . . . induced or reinforced by state laws that lead them to believe artificial insemination is legal only when performed for married women." The article further criticized laws conditioning AI on marriage, writing, "These laws largely ignore the prospect that unmarried women will also seek access to the procedure, although at least 1500 such women are artificially inseminated annually. The meaning of these statutory omissions — whether they should be construed to prohibit or tacitly to allow unmarried women to be artificially inseminated — is currently far from clear, and the ambiguity undoubtedly discourages many physicians from performing the procedure." "Reproductive Technology and the Procreation Rights," 669, 670–71.

65. Responding doctors reported that they rejected one of five patients who requested AI, and the most common reason was that the woman was unmarried (52 percent). Vickie L. Henry, "A Tale of Three Women: A Survey of the Rights and Responsibilities of Unmarried Women Who Conceive by Alternative Insemination and a Model for Legislative Reform," *American Journal of Law & Medicine* 19 (1993), 285, 288–89.

66. For examples of state codes limiting AI to married couples, see Ala. Code § 26-17-704 (West); Ark. Code Ann. § 9-10-201 (2015); Idaho Code § 39-5405(3) (2015); Kan. Stat. Ann. § 23-2303 (West); Mo. Ann. Stat. § 210.824 (West); Mont. Code Ann. § 40-6-106 (West). See, generally, Daar, "Accessing Reproductive Technologies," 18, 45 (describing marital barriers to receiving AI).

67. Due to this preference, single women seeking AI are often forced to use a known donor, thereby opening themselves up to the risk that the donor will be able to assert parental rights and potentially subjecting the donor to parental obligations. See Richard F. Storrow, "Rescuing Children from the Marriage Movement: The Case Against Marital Status Discrimination in Adoption and Assisted Reproduction," *University of California at Davis Law Review* 39 (2006), 305, 312 ("When a single woman responds to this discrimination by electing to self-inseminate with the sperm of a known donor, she runs the risk that a court will . . . recognize the donor's paternity").

68. The only issue for the court was whether the marital status objection was a pretext for denying the treatment based on Benitez's sexual orientation. Sexual orientation discrimination was prohibited, but marital status discrimination was permissible.

Specifically, the court held that "if a jury were to find that Dr. Brody's and Dr. Fenton's refusal to perform IUI for Benitez was based solely on the fact she was unmarried without regard to her sexual orientation, Benitez's Unruh Act cause of action would be defeated." *N. Coast Women's Care Med. Grp., Inc. v. Superior Ct.*, 44 Cal. 4th 1145, 1151 (2008).

69. Joy Wright, "I Got Inseminated in a Burger King Bathroom Just Off I-57," *Huff-Post*, December 5, 2019.

70. After the man agreed to be Joy's donor, the two signed a contract in which the donor relinquished his parental rights. However, as a known donor, with insemination not through a medical facility, and no intended second parent, the validity of the contract was questionable.

71. See I. Glenn Cohen, "Beyond Best Interests," *Minnesota Law Review* 96 (2012), 1187, 1193 (noting that medical insurance coverage can include AI, as well as the much more expensive IVF, but this coverage is often limited to the married).

72. See, e.g., Jerry Brown, "IVF Loans: How to Finance IVF and Fertility Treatments," *Yahoo Finance*, June 20, 2023 ("17 states require insurers to either cover or offer coverage for infertility diagnosis and treatment"). See also supra note 68 (listing states limiting AI coverage to married couples).

73. Sheria Stein, "Hospital Chain Blocks Fertility Coverage for Its LGBTQ Employees," *Bloomberg Law*, July 18, 2022.

74. Gabriela Weigel, Usha Ranji, Michelle Long, and Alina Salganicoff, "Coverage and Use of Fertility Services in the U.S.," KFF.org, September 15, 2020 (noting that the VA covers fertility services, but the "couple seeking services must be legally married, and the egg and sperm must come from said couple").

75. This was started as a pilot program in 2019 but has been expanded through at least 2024. See Utah Code Ann. § 49-20-418 (West) (covering fertility treatments when "the patient or the patient's spouse has a demonstrated condition recognized by a physician as a cause of infertility").

76. Sarah Wildman, "Not Married? Your Insurance Might Not Cover Fertility Treatments," *Slate*, March 17, 2020. In 2021, Maryland eliminated their marital requirement. Md. Code Ann., Ins. § 15-810 (West).

77. See, e.g., Ariz. Rev. Stat. Ann. § 8-103 ("the marital status and the length and stability of the marital relationship of the prospective adoptive parents"); Utah Code Ann. § 78B-6-117(3) (2012) ("A child may not be adopted by a person who is cohabiting in a relationship that is not a legally valid and binding marriage under the laws of this state").

78. As law professor Marie-Amélie George has noted, "Adoption officials often express a preference for couples, and state laws may require them to place children with couples over single parents." "Expanding LGBT," *Florida Law Review* 73 (2021). See also Naomi R. Cahn, "Reframing Child Custody Decision-Making," *Ohio State Law Journal* 58 (1997), 1, 31 (noting the strong societal preference for married parents). See, generally, Berebitsky, *Like Our Very Own*, 3 (discussing how adoption practice developed into a manner of re-creating what many consider the "ideal and only legitimate family" — the biogenetic family consisting of a "heterosexual couple with 'planned for' children living in an 'emotionally' healthy home."

79. Eden Bubrig, "Do the Adoption Services of Catholic Charities Really Operate in the Best Interest of the Children Needing Adoption?," *Loyola Journal of Public Interest Law* 20 (2018), 85, 105.

80. In fact, courts have specifically recognized this marital motivation. See, e.g., *U. S. v. Fomichev*, 899 F.3d 766, 773 (9th Cir.) (9th Cir. 2018) ("We recognize that people

marry for many different religious, cultural, and social reasons. Marriages that are entered into for practical reasons may ripen into loving relationships, and happily unmarried couples may decide to marry for estate planning purposes, to secure health benefits, or to increase their chances of successfully adopting children"). See also *Piper v. Alaska Airlines, Inc.*, no. 93-35575, 1994 WL 424292 at *2–3 (9th Cir. Aug. 12, 1994) (involving a marriage to facilitate an adoption).

81. Why Did You Get Married? Wedding Wire, available at https://www.weddingwire.com/wedding-forums/why-did-you-get-married/faca174b86a3b14c.html.

82. "Marriage for Adoption Fraught with Peril," *Columbus Dispatch*, January 25, 2009.

83. Burundi, Chile, China, Dominican Republic, Egypt, Equatorial Guinea, Ethiopia, Hungary, Indonesia, Italy, Jordan, Madagascar, Malaysia, Nepal, Panama, Papua New Guinea, Sri Lanka, Syria, and Ukraine require international adoption by married couples only and, if specified, define marriage as between one man and one woman. See Jennifer B. Mertus, "Barriers, Hurdles, and Discrimination: The Current Status of LGBT Intercountry Adoption and Why Changes Must Be Made to Effectuate the Best Interests of the Child," *Capital University Law Review* 39 (2011), 271, 311.

84. See, e.g., The ABBA Fund, FAQ, https://abbafund.org/faq (offering loans of $6,000 to $8,000 for Christian families seeking to adopt); God's Grace Adoption Ministry, Application for Financial Aid, http://www.ggam.org/main.html (offering grants between $1,000 and $4,000 to married couples with incomes of $60,000 or less); JSC Foundation, https://www.jscfoundation.org/register/ (offering adoption grants to married Christian couples).

85. As law professor Susan Hazeldean explains, "In these states, the unmarried partner of a child's biological or adoptive parent cannot obtain parental rights through adoption unless the legal parent gives up his or her rights So if an unmarried couple want to form a family through adoption, only one parent can adopt their child. The other partner may function as a parent, but they will not have the security of a legally recognized parent-child relationship through adoption." "Illegitimate Parents," *University of California at Davis Law Review* 55 (2022), 1583, 1615. See also Jenna Casolo, Campbell Curry-Ledbetter, Meagan Edmonds, Gabrielle Field, Kathleen O'Neill, and Marisa Poncia, "Assisted Reproductive Technologies," *Georgetown Journal of Gender and the Law* 20, no. 2 (2019), 313, 355n243 (citing cases from Alabama, Kansas, Kentucky, Nebraska, North Carolina, Ohio, Utah, and Wisconsin, all preventing unmarried partners from adopting without terminating a biological parent's parental rights).

86. In a typical adoption, a prospective adoptive couple must undergo an initial home study, a waiting period, and a post-placement home study before a hearing is commenced and a final decree issued. However, such procedures are not needed to complete a stepparent adoption. As law professor Richard Storrow writes, in stepparent adoptions, pre- and post-placement home studies and "even waiting periods are routinely waived." See Richard F. Storrow, "Rescuing Children from the Marriage Movement: The Case Against Marital Status Discrimination in Adoption and Assisted Reproduction," *University of California at Davis Law Review* 39 (2006), 305, 338 (describing how stepparent adoptions differ from "stranger" adoptions). See also Rose Holden Vacanti Gilroy, "The Law of Assisted Reproductive Technologies: Imposing Heteronormative Family Structures onto Queer Families," *Tulane Journal of Law and Sexuality* 31 (2022), 27, 39–40, noting that "second parent adoptions can include home studies (which may include FBI

and criminal background checks), adoption hearings, and affidavits from a doctor or cryobank attesting to the facts of a child's conception."

87. Brian Sterling, "Couple's 'Accidental Precedent-Setting Case' for Same-Sex Marriage," WOOD TV, April 23, 2015 (quoting Rowse).

88. Katherine Franke, *Wedlocked: The Perils of Marriage Equality* (New York: New York University Press, 2017), 113. Law professor Nancy Polikoff has offered similar criticisms. Polikoff writes:

> While advocates for lesbian and gay parents once saw themselves as part of a larger movement to promote respect, nondiscrimination, and recognition of diverse family forms, some now appear to embrace a privileged position for marriage. They thus abandon a longstanding commitment to defining and evaluating families based on function rather than form, distancing themselves from single-parent and divorced families, extended families, and other stigmatized childrearing units.

Nancy D. Polikoff, "For the Sake of All Children: Opponents and Supporters of Same-Sex Marriage Both Miss the Mark," *New York Law Review* 8 (2005), 901, 918.

89. In her article "The Freedom to Choose to Marry," law professor Ruth Colker writes about the *Obergefell* decision and what the court does *not* say. Specifically, the fact that it does *not*, after praising the importance of marriage for parents, say that unmarried parents can be equally good parents. As a result, Coker argues that after *Obergefell*, "parents who have chosen not to marry will find it all the more difficult to justify their decision now that the court has recognized the 'harm' and 'humiliation' to the children of unmarried parents and suggested that the only way to cure that harm is for the parents to marry." Ruth Colker, "The Freedom to Choose to Marry," *Columbia Journal of Gender & Law* 30 (2016), 383, 418.

90. See Elizabeth Bartholet, "Adoption and the Parental Screening System," in *Families by Law: An Adoption Reader*, eds. Naomi R. Cahn and Joan Heifetz Hollinger (2004), 73.

91. As law professor David Meyer writes:

> The rise of assortative marriage, in which individuals with similar economic prospects are more likely to pair off with one another, would aggravate economic inequalities even if all were equally likely to marry. But, in fact, marriage is more common and more durable among those with more education and resources, and in retreat among those who might benefit most from a stable economic partnership.

David D. Meyer, "Family Law Equality at a Crossroads," *Michigan State Law Review* (2013), 1231, 1248.

92. See Dorothy Roberts, "The Social Context of Oncofertility," *DePaul Law Review* 61 (2012), 777, 795 (discussing "bias against patients of color, which leads physicians to devalue these patients' childbearing or the importance of giving them information about fertility preservation."). For further discussion of fertility bias against women of color, see Judith F. Daar, "Accessing Reproductive Technologies: Invisible Barriers, Indelible Harms," *Berkeley Journal of Gender, Law & Justice* 23 (2008), 18, 41 (noting that doctors often respond to the fertility issues facing women of color by "either subtly or explicitly suggesting that women of certain

racial and ethnic backgrounds do not 'need' to birth any more children"); Zakiya Luna and and Kristin Luker, "Reproductive Justice," *Annual Review of Law and Social Science* 9 (2013), 327, 340 (noting that "poorer women, non-native English speakers, and women of color often find many barriers to receiving an official diagnosis of infertility — let alone treatment").

93. According to Polikoff, recognizing "parental rights based upon the legal relationship between . . . two mothers, without simultaneously creating parentage for a partner who is not married to a birth mother . . . revives the discredited distinction between 'legitimate' and 'illegitimate' children." She describes this as the "new illegitimacy," noting that the rights and welfare of children, at least the children of same-sex couples, remain dependent on the marital status of their parents. Nancy D. Polikoff, "The New 'Illegitimacy': Winning Backward in the Protection of the Children of Lesbian Couples," *American University Journal of Gender, Social Policy & the Law* 20, no. 3 (2012), 721, 722–23. See also Joanna L. Grossman, "The New Illegitimacy: Tying Parentage to Marital Status for Lesbian Co-Parents," *American University Journal of Gender, Social Policy & the Law* 20, no. 3 (2012), 672 (describing the "new illegitimacy" as "a regime in which the rights and welfare of the children of lesbians are dependent on the marital status of their parents, reminiscent of an almost forgotten era in which the same was widely true of all children").

Chapter 6

1. Kate Bennett, "New Melania Trump Book Says She Renegotiated Her Prenuptial Agreement," CNN, June 12, 2020.
2. "Does Money Make Your More Attractive?" *Forbes*, February 14, 2006 (asking, "Is this latest Mrs. Trump in it for the money? Will the Next Mrs. Trump be in it for the money? Yes and yes").
3. Jennifer Savin, "Donald and Melania Trump's $2.5 Million Wedding Was So OTT," *Cosmopolitan*, January 25, 2021. See also Katie Stow, "Just All the Rich People Bullsh*t That Went Down at Donald and Melania Trump's $2.5m Wedding," Mamamia.com, February 1, 2021, describing the cake and writing, "The only downside (jokes, there are no normal-people-upsides to a $50K cake), was that on account of the cake being ginormous and very, very tall, it required a f**ktonne of rigging to keep it erect. So, no one could actually eat it. Instead, when it was demolished after the wedding, the staff were able to nab a bit of sponge."
4. Richard Johnson, "Melania Trump's 'Revenge' on Designers Who Won't Dress Her," Page Six, May 29, 2017 (describing the hustle and bustle in Trump Tower, writing, "Most days, the lobby is brimming with wardrobe boxes delivered for Melania"). See also Leah Simpson, "Inside Melania Trumps $100,000 Shoe Collection," *South China Morning Post*, June 11, 2022; Alyssa Hardy, "Melania Trumps White House Portrait Draws Backlash for Diamond Ring," *Teen Vogue*, April 4, 2017.
5. Surveys like The Virginia Slims' American Women's Poll, conducted in 1979, 1980, and 1985, consistently showed that a substantial percentage of men and women cited economic reasons as among the most important reasons for marrying. In 1979, 17 percent of women and 7 percent of men chose economic security as a reason for marriage. Similarly in 1985, economic security was chosen by 8 percent of men and 14 percent of women, and "because you can share responsibilities, income, etc., and have an easier, more comfortable life" was chosen by 23 percent of men

and 25 percent of women. See Rebecca Tushnet, "Rules of Engagement," *Yale Law Journal* 107 (1998), 2583, 2618.

6. By "money," they meant $1.5 million or greater. See "More Americans Say They Would Marry for Money Even If It Doesn't Buy Love," *Sun Journal*, August 2, 2009.

7. 75% of Women Would Not Marry Someone in This Circumstances. Would You? Available at https://www.yourtango.com/love/percent-women-would-not-marry-someone-unemployed, last visited June 21, 2023.

8. The survey also showed that this sentiment is held in nearly equal measure by both men and women (54 percent and 57 percent). Quentin Fottrell, "Do Americans Marry for Love or Money? Finally, an Answer," Marketwatch.com, February 14, 2019.

9. See Fottrell, "Do Americans Marry for Love or Money?" According to "a recent survey of more than 5,500 singletons aged 18 and over by dating site Match.com iPhone owners are 21 times more likely to judge others negatively for having a less expensive Android, while those who have an Android are only 15 times more likely to judge others negatively for having an iPhone."

10. Anouare Abdou, Love & Debt Survey: Men Will Go into Debt to Woo a Love Interest, but Won't Date Someone in Debt, Credello.com, February 14, 2022, available at https://www.credello.com/financial-resources/trending/love-and-debt-survey-2022/.

11. Says Mr. Prince: "For these women, it's just another step on their journey to the good life. They want to be paid what they think they're worth and then move on." Why We Marry for Money, wevorce.com, January 9, 2017, available at https://www.wevorce.com/blog/why-we-marry-for-money/, last visited June 23, 2023.

12. Municipalities with a surplus of men also have more unmarried women. This suggests it is not the availability of men that keeps female marriage rates down; rather, the limiting factor seems to be the low average income of the available men. Lena Edlund, "Sex and the City," *Scandinavian Journal of Economics* 107, no. 1 (2005), 35–36.

13. Yi Ming Li, Jian Li, Darius K.-S. Chan, and Bo Zhang, "When Love Meets Money: Priming the Possession of Money Influences Mating Strategies," *Frontiers in Psychology* 7 (2016), 387.

14. Specifically, when led to believe women were scarce, the savings rates for men decreased by 42 percent. Men were also willing to borrow 84 percent more money each month. Vladas Griskevicius, Joshua M. Tybur, Joshua M. Ackerman, Andrew W. Delton, Theresa E. Robertson, and Andrew E. White, "The Financial Consequences of Too Many Men: Sex Ratio Effects on Saving, Borrowing, and Spending," *Journal of Personality and Social Psychology* 102, no. 1 (2012), 69–80.

15. "Single People Worry More About Finances than Married People Do," Forbes.com, February 1, 2017, available at https://www.forbes.com/sites/northwestern mutual/2017/02/01/single-people-worry-more-about-finances-than-married-couples-do/?sh=7bd8630fcfb5, last visited June 21, 2023.

16. See Cady Lang, "It's Now 40% More Expensive to Be Single and Dating than It Was a Decade Ago," *Time Magazine*, November 16, 2022.

17. "'Joe Millionaire' Two-Hour Finale Averages Over 33 Million Viewers, Record Ratings," realitytvworld.com, February 18, 2003. On *Joe Millionaire*, the final contestant picked love over money. However, had she done the opposite, one can imagine that the condemnation would have been fast and vicious. In May 2010,

Ms. Ma, a twenty-two-year-old model from Beijing, became one of the most notorious women in China when she rejected a potential suitor on a popular Chinese dating show, stating, "I'd rather cry in a BMW car than laugh on the backseat of a bicycle." The government quickly responded with a new set of harsh rules governing China's dating shows. The government restricted the broadcasting of "incorrect social and love values such as money worship" and cautioned the contestants against "mouthing venturous remarks." Valerie L. Chang, "No Gold Diggers: China's Protection of Individual Property Rights in the New Marital Property Regime," *George Washington International Law Review* 45 (2013), 149.

18. NBA Rookies Get Schooled in the Ways of Certain Women, ThePostGame.com, August 28, 2012, available at http://www.thepostgame.com/blog/dish/201208/nba -rookies-get-schooled-ways-women.

19. Sabrina Maddeaux, "In Defense of the Gold Digger and the Fight for Class, Economic and Gender Equality," *National Post*, July 21, 2017, https://nationalpost .com/life/relationships/in-defence-of-the-gold-digger-and-the-fight-for-class -economic-and-gender-equality; Stephan Dubner, "Life Is a Contact Sport," *New York Times*, August 18, 2002.

20. Millionaire Match verifies income through clients' W2s. See Millionaire Match Reviews, VidaSelect.com, last accessed June 22, 2023, https://www.vidaselect.com/ millionaire-match-reviews-legit-or-scam/. Janis Spindel gauges seriousness by charging exorbitant prices for the men and by charging the women $250 just to be considered. Maddeaux, supra note 20. Samantha Daniels in contrast simply relies on her instinct and experience. Samantha Daniels, "I've Spent 20 Years as an Elite Matchmaker for the Ultra-Wealthy. Here's What Playing Cupid to Millionaires Is Really Like," *Business Insider*, February 14, 2020, available at https://www.business insider.com/millionaire-matchmaker-what-life-is-really-like-2020-2.

21. Notably, such condemnation is not limited to America. In May 2010, Ms. Ma, a twenty-two-year-old model from Beijing, instantly became one of the most widely talked about women in China when she rejected a suitor stating, "I'd rather cry in a BMW car than laugh on the backseat of a bicycle." Many Chinese were out-raged by Ms. Ma's comment and condemned her "money worshipping" attitude. In response, government quickly imposed a harsh new set of rules governing China's dating shows. The government restricted the broadcasting of "incorrect social and love values such as money worship" and cautioned the contestants against "mouth-ing venturous remarks." Chang, "No Gold Diggers," 149.

22. See Margaret Jane Radin, *Contested Commodities: The Trouble with Trade in Sex, Children, Body Parts, and Other Things* (Cambridge, MA: Harvard University Press, 2001), 95–104. See also Viviana A. Zelizer, "Money, Power, and Sex," *Yale Journal of Law & Feminism* 18 (2006), 303, 306 (explaining that this fear is based on the belief that we can't have both, "the existence of some commodified sexual interactions will contaminate or infiltrate everyone's sexuality so that all sexual relationships will become commodified").

23. Sharon Thompson, *Prenuptial Agreements and the Presumption of Free Choice: Issues of Power in Theory and Practice* (Oxford and Portland, OR: Hart Publishing, 2015), 196.

24. In *Nereni*, the husband had serious health issues and withheld this information from his wife prior to marriage. When the wife learned about his condition she sought an annulment, but the court refused her request. *Nerini v. Nerini*, 11 Conn. Supp. 361, 365 (Super. Ct. 1943).

25. See, e.g., *In re Marriage of Meagher & Maleki*, 131 Cal. App. 4th 1 (2005). Here a wife sought an annulment after discovering that her husband "had married her just for her money." Nevertheless, the court denied the annulment because it did not go to the essence of marriage (such cases seem to imply that marrying for money is fine or maybe victim should know better?). Courts have also refused annulments for other types of deception. See, e.g., *Coulter v. Hendricks*, 918 S.W. 2d 424, 425, 427 (Tenn. Ct. App. 1995) (observing that Tennessee will not annul marriages "entered into in jest"); *Adler v. Adler*, 805 So. 2d 952 (Fla. Dist. Ct. App. 2001) (disallowing annulment where the wife had lied about her previous marriages and the husband would not have entered into the marriage had he known); *Verhage v. Verhage*, no. 12-04-00309-CV, 2006 WL 1791565 *1 (Tex. App. 2006) (adjudicating a divorce, rather than an annulment, where the husband alleged that his "pen-pal wife" hnd married him for a green card).

26. *In re Est. of Smallman*, 398 S.W.3d 134 (Tenn. 2013).

27. Despite judicial statements that love is the purpose of marriage, courts universally recognize the economic rights of both parties in a marriage and, barring a relevant prenuptial agreement, will typically require an equitable allocation of assets upon divorce and will consider both the monetary and non-monetary contributions of both parties to the total marital wealth. Consequently, the law by and large protects and even encourages marrying for money. For example, in *Degnan v. Degnan*, 877 N.W. 2d 38, 46 (2016), the court of appeals admonished the lower court for punishing Barbara Degnan for considering future financial security as part of her decision to marry. The lower court had inappropriately awarded her less property and less alimony because of her marital motivations. In her concurrence, Judge Kaspner wrote, "Jane Austen would be astounded. Perhaps at twenty-five one enters marriage considering only love; one would be foolish to do so at fifty."

28. Nevertheless, some states do recognize such rights. For example, in Washington State, courts are authorized to distribute property that was acquired by unmarried partners as a result of their joint efforts. Washington State law recognizes the unfairness caused by a refusal to divide the property that was acquired as a result of those joint efforts in furtherance of the common venture. Similarly, in Oregon, courts may distribute the assets accumulated by the joint family venture if the parties either expressly or, importantly, *impliedly* "intended to pool their resources for their common benefit during the time they lived together." *Beal v. Beal*, 282 Or. 115, 577 P.2d 507 (1978). See also *Hay v. Hay*, 678 P.2d 672, 673 (Nev. 1984) (also permitting the distribution of assets accumulated through a joint venture). The above states have concluded that distributing property at the conclusion of a nonmarital relationship promotes marriage by not letting parties benefit financially from avoiding it. Other states have reached the opposite conclusion. Louisiana, Mississippi, Georgia, and Illinois all refuse to recognize rights between unmarried couples based on an expressed motivation to preserve the legal status of marriage. See Albertina Antognini, "The Law of Nonmarriage," *Boston College Law Review* 58 (2017), 1, 55 (discussing the rights of the unmarried).

29. The court held that "providing loving care and assistance to her boyfriend and the father of their son ... does not transform her relationship to one founded upon contract." *Tompkins v. Jackson*, 880 N.Y.S.2d 876 (Sup. Ct. 2009). Tompkins's plight is shockingly surprisingly similar to that of Eliza Ann Cropsey, a woman who preceded her by nearly two centuries. Cropsey entered into a marital-like relationship with James Ridgeway, but they were barred from marriage due to his

previous divorce for adultery. Because they never married, she could not inherit. Consequently, after he died, she went to court seeking compensation for services rendered as her husband's employee. Due to her help, his estate had grown from less than $1,000 when they met to $150,000 at his death, and she asked for an award of $40,000 out of his estate. The New York Supreme Court rejected her, finding that she was not a servant but had performed such services out of love. The court held that her story of long and faithful love for Ridgeway prevented her from claiming pay as a servant. The court then claimed to be rejecting her request out of respect. The judges held that her services were performed "from higher and holier motives," and thus she was entitled to nothing. Hendrik Hartog, *Man and Wife in America* (Cambridge, MA: Harvard University Press, 2022), 257.

30. *Davis v. Davis*, 643 So. 2d 931, 936 (Miss. 1994). See also *Malone v. Odom*, 657 So. 2d 1112, 1117 (Miss. 1995) (rejecting the plaintiff's claim for equitable division because she had had the opportunity to marry and "she chose not to").

31. As the California Supreme Court noted in the famous 1976 *Marvin v. Marvin* decision, "adults who voluntarily live together and engage in sexual relations *are nonetheless as competent as any other persons* to contract respecting their earnings and property rights." 18 Cal. 3d 660, 674 (1976). Or, as the Tennessee Supreme Court explained in the 2000 case *Martin v. Coleman*, despite the parties' personal relationship "ordinary laws pertaining to partnership, not the laws of domestic relations, apply." *Martin v. Coleman*, 19 S.W.3d 757, 761 (Tenn. 2000).

32. As law professor Courtney Joslin notes, "Although the law authorizes recognition of informal business partnerships, the same is not true of informal family partnerships. Courts will not recognize and give effect to the mutual decision." Instead, courts invoke the familial nature of these service to deny women the benefit of well-established market doctrines that would otherwise entitle them to compensation. See Courtney G. Joslin, "Nonmarriage: The Double Bind," *George Washington Law Review* 90 (2022), 571, 574.

33. Sanford L. Braver and Ira Mark Ellman, "Lay Intuitions About Family Obligations: The Case of Alimony," *Theoretical Inquiries in Law* 13, no. 1 (2012), 209–40.

34. Moreover, when a potential spouse's financial intentions are clear, the risk of deception is low. Law professor Ruth Lee has made this argument in the context of romantic gifts, stating that explicit gold digging is far less serious a problem than subtle gold digging. According to Lee, the donor who makes gifts to the explicit gold digger knows precisely what he (or she) is doing. Consequently, "the more obvious a woman is about being a 'gold digger,' the less morally reprehensible it is if she actually is one." Ruth Sarah Lee, "A Legal Analysis of Romantic Gifts," *Miami Law Review* 67 (2013), 595, 633.

35. Zelizer, "Money, Power, and Sex," 303, 307.

36. Francesca Beauman, *Matrimony, Inc.: From Personal Ads to Swiping Right, a Story of America Looking for Love* (New York: Simon & Schuster, 2020), 180 (noting that modern matrimonial ads "tend to have a robust attitude to the economics of marriage").

37. Millionaire Match, VidaSelect supra note 21.

38. According to the World Bank, women control only 1 percent of the world's wealth, and the World Economic Forum predicts it will take at least 170 years to put women and men on an even economic playing field. See Sudeep Reddy, "New Facts on the Gender Gap from the World Bank," *Wall Street Journal*, September 18, 2011.

39. Carolina Aragao, Gender Pay Gap in the United States Hasn't Changed Much in Two Decades, Pew Research Center, March 1, 2023, available at https://www.pewresearch.org/fact-tank/2021/05/25/gender-pay-gap-facts/.

40. See Gabriela Lopez Gomes, "The World's Richest Women Billionaires 2023," *Forbes*, April 4, 2023. See also Millionaire Statistics, balancingeverthing.com, May 20, 2023, available at https://balancingeverything.com/millionaire-statistics/.

41. Gigi Zamora, "The 10 Richest Self-Made Women in the World," *Forbes*, April 5, 2022.

42. Maddeaux, supra note 20.

43. See Maddeaux, supra note 20 (noting that the number "has been increasing about 30 per cent year-over-year since 2013").

44. Genevieve Shaw Brown, "'Sugar Daddy' Company Uses Billboards to Attract New 'Babies,'" ABC News, June 12, 2014.

45. Maddeaux, supra note 20.

46. AAUW, Deeper in Debt: Women & Student Loans (2021), available at https://www.aauw.org/resources/research/deeper-in-debt/. Notably, debt is not distributed equally among women. Black women owe an average of 13 percent more than they borrowed after twelve years in repayment. In that same time span, the average white woman's student debt shrinks by 28 percent. See Victoria Jackson and Brittani Williams, How Black Women Experience Student Debt, Education Trust (April 2022).

47. Dara Addeyo, "Say What?! Sugar Babies . . . Are Actually Marrying . . . Their Sugar Daddies," *Cosmopolitan*, June 14, 2013.

48. Under the Wisconsin program, welfare recipients who married received an increase of $80 per month. A similar program in West Virginia offered $100. See Katha Pollitt, "Shotgun Weddings," *The Nation*, January 17, 2002. Similarly, New Jersey's Wedfare program lifted potential barriers to the formation of stepfamilies by allowing some welfare mothers to marry without losing benefits. Specifically, if the parent remarries, the income of the stepparent will not be included when calculating AFDC eligibility unless the family's income exceeds 150 percent of the poverty line N.J. Stat. Ann. § 44:10-3.4(b).

49. Deborah Darden, who pulled herself up from welfare to job counseling, criticized the program as the wrong approach to solving poverty. "If the Governor improves the quality of life for them," she said, "people will naturally get married." Isabel Wilkerson, "Wisconsin Welfare Plan to Reward the Married," *New York Times*, February 12, 1991.

50. As law professor Martha Ertman argues in her book *Rethinking Commodification*, it is "better for women to think they are selling sex [or love or marriage] than to think they are sharing when it is being taken from them." Martha M. Ertman and Joan C. Williams, eds., *Rethinking Commodification: Cases and Readings in Law and Culture* (New York: New York University Press, 2005), 87.

51. She added that the third time was for companionship.

52. In *Tompkins v. Jackson*, Shaniqua testified that she loved Curtis: "I was going to be with him whether he was 50 Cent, with a hundred million dollars, or Curtis Jackson, working for sanitation." Unfortunately, the court found that such statements "demonstrate loving devotion and loyalty" and are precisely the ones that "undermine" both Shaniqua's claims. *Tompkins v. Jackson*, 22 Misc. 3d 1128(A), 880 N.Y.S.2d 876 (Sup. Ct. 2009).

53. As Professor Sharon Thompson writes in her paper "In Defence of the Gold-Digger," "testing the love of the non-moneyed party in this way, the wealthy party

implicitly does not trust them, or perhaps needs to convince third parties, such as affluent parents. Yet this is obscured by the gold-digging stereotype, which causes the intentions of the *non-moneyed* (not the moneyed) party to be interrogated." In addition, as Thompson notes, focusing "only on the motivations of the non-moneyed spouse not only leads to a false impression of the prevalence of gold-diggers but also has a detrimental impact on financial outcomes on divorce." Sharon Thompson, "In Defence of the 'Gold-Digger,'" *Oñati Socio-Legal Series* 6, no. 6 (2016), 1225–48.

54. Gina Barreca, "The $150,000 Purse and Other 'Wife Bonuses,'" *Chicago Tribune*, May 29, 2015.

55. Cailin Moscatello, "The Wife Bonus or What Happens When Your Husband Becomes Your Boss," *Glamour*, May 18, 2015. However, not all articles were critical of such bonuses. For example, journalist Shane Ferro writes that in a "traditional household" where one parent is working and the other is doing the traditional unpaid upkeep of the house and kids, "a wife bonus makes good sense. The wife is doing a significant amount of work to keep the family running, and she deserves her equal share of the family income. And then something extra at the end of the year." Shane Ferro, "Why a Wife Bonus Makes Complete Sense," *Business Insider*, May 29, 2015.

56. Salary.com, "How Much Is a Mother Really Worth?" (estimating that the annual value of a mother's work in in 2019 is $178,201).

57. According to Professor Silbaugh, "Only women's mixed motives relating to feminine activities are highlighted and offered as justification for leaving women without cash." Katharine Silbaugh, "Commodification and Women's Household Labor," *Yale Journal of Law & Feminism* 9 (1997), 81, 105.

58. See, e.g., *In re Callister's Estate*, 153 N.Y. 294 (1897) (holding that "a man cannot be entitled to the services of his wife for nothing, by virtue of a uniform and unchangeable marriage contract, and at the same time be under obligation to pay her for these services . . . She cannot be his wife and his hired servant at the same time . . . That would be inconsistent with the marriage relation, and disturb the reciprocal duties of the parties").

59. Andrew J. Cherlin, *The Marriage-Go-Round: The State of Marriage and the Family in America Today* (New York: Vintage Books, 2010), 193.

60. They note that the modern definition of love is now focused on the "mutual exploration of infinitely rich, complex, exciting selves." Finkel et al., "The Suffocation of Marriage: Climbing Mount Maslow Without Enough Oxygen," *Psychological Inquiry* 25 (2014), 1–41. See also Arash Emazadeh, "How Marriage Became Suffocation," *Psychology Today*, August 25, 2022 (explaining that people are both expecting more out of marriage and investing less in marriage than in the past).

61. *Saturday Night Live* transcript, season 4, episode 15, March 17, 1979.

62. Marshall had made his fortune through legally dubious practices such as labeling his wives and girlfriends "consultants" and artificially suppressing the value of his holdings to lower his income tax. However, what is most telling is the fact that by the time of his marriage to Smith, Marshall had managed to recoup nearly all the assets he had left his previous partner, Lady Walker, another exotic dancer who was also decades his junior. Not only was Marshall well acquainted with the practice of financially rewarding his romantic partners, he also knew how to trick them into getting it back. Specifically, after Lady Walker died, Marshall took legal action against her heirs, thus freezing their assets and making them unable

to pay their property taxes. Then, under threat of foreclosure, he pressured them to settle the case. In the end Walker's heirs kept two houses and her jewelry while Marshall recovered most of the money and cars. Marshall was no lovesick dupe. Brian Donovan, *American Gold Digger: Money, Marriage and the Law from the Ziegfeld Follies to Anna Nicole Smith* (Chapel Hill: University of North Carolina Press, 2020), 166, 191. See also Sarah Marshall, "How Anna Nicole Smith Became America's Punchline," *Buzzfeed*, February 7, 2017 (noting Anna's testimony that she had initially refused Marshall's proposals of marriage "so nobody could call me a gold digger, but I guess that backfired, didn't it?").

63. Carol Sarler, "His N' Hers Big Assets Make a Perfect Union," *The People* 23 (July 1994) (criticizing the "tut-tutting around the world's press that she is a 'gold digger'"). See also Donovan, *American Gold Digger*, 191 (noting that those who argued she deserved the money "made their claim in terms of the reciprocal relationship she had with J. Howard. In this account, she traded fourteen months of pleasure for his wealth").

64. Marshall, "How Anna Nicole Smith Became America's Punchline."

65. See Barbara Mikkelson and David Mikkelson, Craigslist Gold Digger, Snopes .com, October 10, 2007, available at https://www.snopes.com/fact-check/fools -gold-digger/ (concluding that the ad was likely real).

66. Evolutionary psychologists claim this difference arises from the different parental roles. Male choice reflects women's time-limited reproductive capacity and the desire to pick women whose attributes reflect such capacity, while women desire men with resources to help raise children. See, e.g., David M. Buss and Douglas T. Kenrick, "Evolutionary Social Psychology," in Daniel T. Gilbert, ed., *The Handbook of Social Psychology*, 4th ed., vol. 2 (Boston: Wiley, 1999), 982–1026.

67. M. Zentner and K. Mitura, "Stepping Out of the Caveman's Shadow: Nations' Gender Gap Predicts Degree of Sex Differentiation in Mate Preferences," *Psychological Science* 23, no. 10 (October 1, 2012), 1176–85.

68. See S. W. Gangestad, "Sexual Selection and Physical Attractiveness: Implications of Mating Dynamics," *Human Nature* 4 (1993), 205–36 (finding that as women possess increasing economic independence, they begin to focus more on sex appeal than they do on practicality when choosing a sexual partner).

69. Marshall, "How Anna Nicole Smith Became America's Punchline."

70. It was $8.24 in 1973, and it reached $10.52 just before the pandemic hit. At that rate, someone who works thirty-five hours a week, the national average, earns just over $19,000 a year. Katheryn Edwards, The Marriage Plot, *RANDblog*, April 4, 2022, available at https://www.rand.org/blog/2022/04/the-marriage-plot.html.

71. "It could raise the minimum wage, require quality on-site childcare and family leave. More could also be done to protect women from the physical, psychological, and sexual hazards that drive poor women to quit their jobs. We might use the numbers about poverty among single mothers to show that the need for such policies is beyond debate, and then put our heads and our purses together to cover their substantial costs." Lucie E. White, "No Exit: Rethinking 'Welfare Dependency' from a Different Ground," *Georgetown Law Journal* 81 (1993), 1961, 1986–87.

72. According to Fineman, the focus on the marriage solution has prevented us from recognizing and reorganizing around other caretaking units such as parents and children, which is a true dependency relationship. "Marriage is expected to do a lot of work in our society. Children must be cared for and nurtured, dependency must be addressed, and individual happiness is of general concern. The first question we

should be asking is whether the existence of a marriage is, in and of itself, essential to accomplishing any of the societal goals or objectives we assign to it." Martha Albertson Fineman, "Why Marriage?," *Virginia Journal of Social Policy and the Law* 9 (2001), 239, 244–45.

73. See Susan Frelich Appleton, "Standards for Constitutional Review of Privacy-Invading Welfare Reforms: Distinguishing the Abortion-Funding Cases and Redeeming the Undue-Burden Test," *Vanderbilt Law Review* 49 (1996), 1, 34–35 (asking how could "a scheme of financial incentives to encourage welfare recipients to marry, possibly escape charges of sex discrimination once this scheme acquires the nickname 'bridefare' and even government experts write about finding a husband as one of the most promising 'exits' from the rolls for welfare mothers?").

74. In their 2008 paper "Marriage Patterns Among Unwed Mothers: Before and After PRWORA," Deborah Roempke Graefe and Daniel T. Lichter looked at 1995 and 2002 data from the National Survey of Family Growth and found that even the most disadvantaged women were no more likely to marry after welfare reform than before — but that the men they married "tended to be a lower economic status after welfare reform than before." Deborah Roempke Graefe and Daniel T. Lichter, "Marriage Patterns Among Unwed Mothers: Before and After PRWORA," *Journal of Policy Analysis and Management* 27, no. 3 (2008), 479–97.

75. In 1997, Wisconsin received a federal waiver of the welfare cost recovery rules. This allowed the state to pass through all child support payments directly to the families while simultaneously disregarding the income from counting toward welfare eligibility. This allowed single mothers to "avoid live-in relationships with men who might have helped them financially in the short term but were not good candidates for marriage." However, they were just as likely to marry. Cherlin, *Marriage-Go-Round*, 198.

76. See, e.g., Rachel Batterson, "'States' Rights' and Self-Sufficiency or Federally-Imposed Draconia? The Personal Responsibility and Work Opportunity Reconciliation Act's Impact on Vermont's Welfare Policy," *Georgetown Journal on Poverty Law & Policy* 7 (2000), 21, 51 (citing studies demonstrating that "between 14% and 32% of welfare recipients are current victims of domestic violence and that between 33% and 65% were victims of domestic violence at some time in their lives"). See also Shelia Ards and Samuel Meyers, Final Report: The Effects of Welfare on Domestic Violence, Department of Justice, February 23, 2003, available at https://www.ojp.gov/pdffiles1/nij/grants/204008.pdf (demonstrating that welfare recipiency helps women leave abusive relationships).

Conclusion

1. Kearney writes that marriage, "for all its challenges and faults," remains our "best path to a more equitable future." Melissa Kearney, *The Two-Parent Privilege: How Americans Stopped Getting Married and Started Falling Behind* (Chicago: University of Chicago Press, 2023). See also Frank Newport and Joy Wilke, "Economy Would Benefit if Marriage Rates Increased," Gallup, October 28, 2013 (a Gallup poll suggesting that unmarried people were hurting the economy, and that more marriage was needed to help the country's bottom line).

2. Lyman Stone and Spencer James, Marriage Still Matters: Demonstrating the Link Between Marriage and Fertility in the 21st Century, Institute for Family Studies, October 2022, available at https://ifstudies.org/ifs-admin/resources/

reports/marriagestillmatters-final.pdf (suggesting that declining global fertility rates are closely linked to declining marriage rates).

3. Since then, video has emerged of Crowder verbally berating his then extremely pregnant wife. There have also been allegations that he exposed his genitals at work. Both are reasons why his wife might want to divorce him, yet neither would be grounds under a typical fault-only regime. See Joanna Grossman and Natalie Nanasi, "Unhappy Wife, Unhappy Life: The Misguided Attack by Conservatives on No Fault Divorce," *Verdict*, May 9, 2023.

4. Tessa Stuart, "The New Front in the GOP's War on Women: No Fault Divorce," *Rolling Stone* (May 2, 2023).